Time and Project Management Strategies for Librarians

Edited by Carol Smallwood, Jason Kuhl, and Lisa Fraser

Foreword by Robert P. Holley

THE SCARECROW PRESS, INC.
Lanham • Toronto • Plymouth, UK
2013

Published by Scarecrow Press, Inc.
A wholly owned subsidiary of The Rowman & Littlefield Publishing Group, Inc.
4501 Forbes Boulevard, Suite 200, Lanham, Maryland 20706
http://www.scarecrowpress.com

Estover Road, Plymouth PL6 7PY, United Kingdom

British Library Cataloguing in Publication Information Available

Library of Congress Cataloging-in-Publication Data

Time and project management strategies for librarians / edited by Carol Smallwood, Jason Kuhl, Lisa Fraser.
pages cm
Includes bibliographical references and index.
ISBN 978-0-8108-9052-7 (pbk. : alk. paper) -- ISBN 978-0-8108-9053-4 (ebook) 1. Librarians--Time management. 2. Library administration. 3. Library personnel management. I. Smallwood, Carol, 1939– editor of compilation. II. Kuhl, Jason, 1975– editior of compilation. III. Fraser, Lisa, 1963– editor of compilation.
Z682.35.T55T46 2013
025.1--dc23
2012046129

Printed in the United States of America

Contents

Acknowledgments   vii

Foreword   ix

Introduction   xi

I: Management Strategies   1

1   Consult Your Stakeholders and Prioritize with Six Sigma Tools   3
Elizabeth Nelson

2   Daily Operations   9
Pamela O'Sullivan

3   Feudal Society of the Stacks   13
Eric Owen

4   Necessary Sacrifices   23
LeEtta Schmidt

5   Productive to the Core: Core Competencies and the Productive Librarian   33
Jenny Dale and Lynda M. Kellam

6   Rural Librarians, Farm Out Your Work   41
Michelle A. McIntyre

II: Working with Staff   51

7   Circulation Staffing   53
Kimberly Wells

8   Going, Going, Gone: Management Strategies for Time and Staff When There Is Little of Either   61
Amber Lannon and Sara Holder

9   Staff-Level Management of Library Reference Services: Not Just Personnel Economy, an Enhanced Service System   71
Threasa Wesley

III: Students, Volunteers, and Interns   81

10   Interns and Volunteers: Finding and Deploying Free Labor   83
Portia Kapraun and Beth M. Sheppard

Contents

11 Making the Best of a Reduced Staff: Utilizing Student
Workers to Reach Library Goals   89
Emy Nelson Decker

12 Student Workers on the Job: Maximizing Output   97
Portia Kapraun and Beth M. Sheppard

IV: Monitoring Time and Projects   **103**

13 Developing and Implementing a Project Chart   105
Jessica Shomberg and Daardi Sizemore

14 How Many Hours in My Day? How Many Slices in My Pie?
Personal Productivity for the Busy Librarian   115
John C. Gottfried

15 A Librarian's Time Management Toolkit   125
Ellie Dworak

16 Nimble Project Management for the Time and Budget
Challenged   135
Erin White

17 A Novel Approach to Project Management: Seven Lessons
from NaNoWriMo   141
Karen Munro

18 Time Management for Busy Academic Librarians:
Strategies for Success   149
William H. Weare Jr.

V: Getting Organized   **159**

19 Avoiding Information Overload   161
Meredith Selfon

20 For Every Librarian a To-Do List   167
Sarah Troy

21 Optimize Small Library Efficiency with Daily Routines and
Organizational Strategies   177
Stephanie Sweeney

22 The Power of Lists   187
Meredith Selfon

23 Tame Your E-mail   191
Erin White

VI: Using Technology   **197**

24 Let's Not Meet: Making the Most of Time with
Asynchronous Collaboration   199
Jolanda-Pieta van Arnhem and Jerry M. Spiller

25 Making Memory Portable 209
Sanjeet Mann

26 Social Media as Time Drain: The Myth of Efficiency 215
Jennifer Nardine

VII: Work–Life Balance **225**

27 Managing Professional and Family Commitments 227
Libby Gorman

28 Time Management, Reducing Stress, and Getting
Organized 235
Linda Burkey Wade

29 Working from Home, or How to Get It All Done without
Going Crazy 245
Elizabeth Nelson

30 What Personal Life? 251
Pamela O'Sullivan

VIII: Professional Development **255**

31 Getting Things Done in the Library 257
Sanjeet Mann

32 The High Road or Easy Street? Saving Time by Picking
Your Battles 263
Kelli Hines and Deborah Farber

33 When Do I Have Time to Be Professionally Active? 271
Robin Fay

Index 279

About the Coeditors and Foreword Author 287

About the Contributors 289

Acknowledgments

Carol Luers Eyman, outreach and community services coordinator, Nashua Public Library, Nashua, New Hampshire

Jeffrey A. Franks, associate professor and head of reference at Bierce Library, University of Akron, Ohio

Larry Grieco, library director, Gilpin County Public Library, Black Hawk, Colorado

Elizabeth J. Hylen, contributor, *Bringing Visual, Literary, and Performing Arts into the Library* (ALA Editions, 2013)

Rita Marsales, cataloger, Menil Foundation Library, Houston, Texas; *American Libraries* contributor

Jack Montgomery, professor/librarian, Western Kentucky University

Heather Payne, corporate liaison to the libraries, City College, Fort Lauderdale, Florida

Geoffrey P. Timms, electronic resources and web services librarian, Mercer University, Macon, Georgia

Foreword

Time and Project Management Strategies for Librarians focuses on solutions to the key challenge for the twenty-first-century librarian: doing more with less. The thirty-three essays provide valuable tips, from the macro-level of management strategies for the entire library to the microlevel of the librarian who has difficulty coping with increasing demands. Dealing with cuts at the library level requires doing the right thing in the most effective way. Librarians should identify the most important tasks for the library, eliminate nonessential functions and processes (Schmidt), stop striving for absolute accuracy, optimize daily routines (O'Sullivan and Sweeny), and schedule staff effectively (Lannon/Holder). Libraries should also rely more on less expensive or free staff, including volunteers, interns (McIntyre and Kapraun/Sheppard), and students (Decker and Kapraun/Sheppard). Case studies include reorganizing circulation (Wells) and reference (Wesley). History buffs will appreciate the extended metaphor of the library as a feudal society (Owen).

Some principles apply to both the library and individual librarians. Building on core competencies is a good strategy for both (Dale/Kellam). Project and time management skills are needed to avoid overload. Project management focuses on successfully completing special tasks for both the library (Shomberg/Sizemore) and the individual (White). In one of the most original essays, Munro presents lessons from the National Novel Writing Month (NaNoWriMo), in which each author's goal is to write fifty thousand words in thirty days. The two essays on time management deal with tools (Dworak) and finding time to write (Weare). Picking your battles by selecting only those that can be won and are worth the effort to fight is another way to avoid dissipating energies (Hines/Farber). Gottfried puts it all together with practical advice on personal productivity through setting and meeting goals.

Lists are one of the more important ways to get organized (Troy and Selfon), whether written on the back of an envelope or created with the latest Web tools. Technology has created new challenges as librarians must cope with information overload (Selfon), e-mail (White), and social media (Fay). Libraries that adopt social media face the risk of having Twitter and Facebook become a time drain (Nardine).

Technology offers solutions. Librarians can save time by using asynchronous collaboration to complete library tasks more effectively and avoid time-intensive meetings (van Arnhem/Spiller). Similarly, working from home can reduce travel time and provide a more effective work environment (Nelson). Several authors focus on specific technologies or systems for increased productivity: Sigma tools for process mapping (Nelson), cloud-based portable memory to access information from anywhere (Mann), and Allen's "Getting Things Done" productivity methodology (Mann).

Beating budget and staff cuts shouldn't mean that librarians spend every waking moment working for the library. Gorman advises librarians on how to balance family commitments and child rearing with their professional lives. For Wade, time management and reducing stress require saying "no" more often to noncritical demands. Contrary to popular belief, multitasking isn't efficient, so having time for a personal life depends on focusing on the task at hand without distractions (O'Sullivan).

Time and Project Management Strategies for Librarians has productivity tips for all librarians, from the newly hired to the most seasoned veteran. Budget and staff cuts are part of the "new normal." This volume is a key contribution to helping libraries provide the same, if not better, service to their users and to showing librarians how to provide this service without losing their personal lives and their sanity.

Dr. Robert P. Holley, professor of library and information science, Wayne State University, Detroit, Michigan, obtained his doctorate from Yale University and his MLIS from Columbia University.

Introduction

Time and Project Management Strategies for Librarians is an anthology for public, academic, special, and school librarians, as well as LIS faculty looking for successful examples of time management when so much is changing in the profession: how to manage staff, time, boards, emergencies, finances, stress, patrons, technology, and related topics day after day with budget and staff cuts. It provides guidance on planning as well as execution. Time management is of vital concern for small rural libraries and libraries in large urban settings, and this anthology is for beginners as well as old hands, for solo librarians and those who are part of a staff. It includes thirty-three chapters focused on practical results by librarians making hard choices to provide the best service, such as "Time Management, Reducing Stress, and Getting Organized" and "Making the Best of a Reduced Staff: Utilizing Student Workers to Reach Library Goals." Rita Marsales, cataloger at the Menil Foundation Library in Houston, Texas, notes: "This book presents studies that will enable librarians to employ new technologies and new as well as proven ideas to better utilize their time and efforts in these difficult economic times."

Time organization is largely a learn-as-you-go process, as expressed by the librarians who have generously shared their experiences in this volume. You may have taken management classes, read books on management style, and attended workshops and webinars filled with well-designed organizational charts, but these chapters will provide on-the-job help.

Input was sought from practicing public, school, academic, and special librarians from various parts of the United States and Canada. Contributors were asked to write one or two chapters, totaling three thousand to thirty-five hundred words. Concise, how-to case studies, using bullets, headings, and sidebars, based on creative organization were sought. The chapters are arranged in eight parts: part I, "Management Strategies"; part II, "Working with Staff"; part III, "Students, Volunteers, and Interns"; part IV, "Monitoring Time and Projects"; part V, "Getting Organized"; part VI, "Using Technology"; part VII, "Work–Life Balance"; and part VIII, "Professional Development."

Dr. Robert Holley has written a foreword for this volume that begins: "*Time and Project Management Strategies for Librarians* focuses on solutions to the key challenge for the twenty-first-century librarian: doing more with less." The contributors' backgrounds are provided in the "Contributors" pages at the end of the anthology. The author/title/subject index ends the volume.

It has been a privilege working with contributors willing to share their experiences with fellow librarians. These dedicated and creative professionals have presented many facets of effective time organization—what really works in these challenging times.

The Coeditors

I

Management Strategies

ONE

Consult Your Stakeholders and Prioritize with Six Sigma Tools

Elizabeth Nelson

Coupled with the problem of having more to do with less staff, many in libraries are faced with competing claims on resources and no clear path to the correct prioritization that will create the biggest benefit for users. In addition, they struggle with how to provide quality resources and services without hiring more staff. One way to tackle these problems is by using tools that already exist. The Six Sigma methodology is one strategy that has long been used in business to improve processes, make decisions, and improve quality of results. Although not all of the tools originally developed for this program, which was intended for a manufacturing environment, will translate directly to the library world, several can be adapted and provide immediate benefits.

VOICE OF THE CUSTOMER

When setting priorities, it is crucial to get input from all the key stakeholders. In Six Sigma terminology, this group is referred to as the "customers," but in the library setting it includes library patrons (including faculty and/or employees, depending on the type of library), library staff, managers (including those at a dean or director level), board members, and anyone else who has a stake in the work being done by the organization. Getting the voice of the customer can be done in a variety of ways, including comment cards and information feedback or more in-depth interviews. One way that allows for immediate quantitative analysis is using a survey.

Using the template in figure 1.1, stakeholders can be surveyed to determine their level of concern with each project or issue being considered, as well as the level of satisfaction they have with the solutions that are already in place. Each stakeholder rates the importance of each issue on a scale of zero to three and their satisfaction with the current solutions on a scale of one to four. The resulting ratings would then be multiplied so the total "score" for the issue can be calculated as total = importance rating x satisfaction rating. This calculation results in total scores from zero (meaning the importance was rated as "not needed") to twelve (indicating that this issue is of critical importance and the current solution does not meet the needed standard).

In the complete Six Sigma methodology, tools like Voice of the Customer are used at the beginning of the process, during the "define" stage. Although Voice of the Customer can be used in libraries as a tool to help define a project, it can also be used on a larger scale to prioritize projects for goals and determine staff workloads. The quantitative nature of this tool makes it simple to apply and also straightforward to present to managers or board members as a justification for how decisions have been made. Because each issue has been rated on two factors and given a total score by each stakeholder, this survey tool can also provide insight into which issues are most important to each stakeholder or group of stakeholders, if the analysis spans several groups of people.

Voice of the Customer Survey Template

	ISSUE	IMPORTANCE 0 = Not needed 1 = Nice to Have 2 = Important 3 = Critical, Must Have	SATISFACTION 1 = Very Satisfied 2 = Satisfied 3 = Needs Improvement 4 = Impediment	Total = Importance x Satisfaction
Stakeholder #1	Issue #1	☐	☐	☐
	Issue #2	☐	☐	☐
	Issue #3	☐	☐	☐
	Issue #4	☐	☐	☐
Stakeholder #2	Issue #1	☐	☐	☐
	Issue #2	☐	☐	☐
	Issue #3	☐	☐	☐
	Issue #4	☐	☐	☐
Stakeholder #3	Issue #1	☐	☐	☐
	Issue #2	☐	☐	☐
	Issue #3	☐	☐	☐
	Issue #4	☐	☐	☐
Stakeholder #4	Issue #1	☐	☐	☐
	Issue #2	☐	☐	☐
	Issue #3	☐	☐	☐
	Issue #4	☐	☐	☐

Figure 1.1.

The tool can shed light on conflicts that may not have been obvious, as in the case where library patrons give vastly different importance or satisfaction ratings than library staff or managers. It can also show the similarities between stakeholders if one issue consistently rises to the top in total score. This situation might indicate a quick win, whereas the previous example may require further examination to determine the cause of the discrepancies between stakeholders.

PROCESS MAPPING

Once priorities have been set, evaluating the process is the next step. In Six Sigma there are two ways to think about a process: "as-is" and "should be." The distinction is necessary, because when it comes to documenting a process, it can be very tempting to put on paper the steps that should be taken in a perfect world. To really understand the workflow—and therefore allow improvements to be made in the process—it is necessary to record the process as it exists today. Any improvements that are generated can go on the "should be" process map.

Any workflow can be evaluated through process mapping, from cataloging and the acquisitions process to activities like creating library cards and shelving books. Many tasks have evolved over time based on personal preference and because "that's how we've always done it," and actually putting the process down on paper can help in getting past all the assumptions. Figure 1.2 shows a very simple process for a document delivery request. To create a process map, list the steps of the process in order. For a more complete map, especially useful for a more complex process, list the inputs and outputs for each step. This can help show how resources are being used or where time might be lost to inefficiencies. The final step is to determine if each step is value added (VA) or non-value-added (NVA).

To determine whether a step in the process is VA, simply ask: "Does the customer care?" If the answer to that question is yes, then the step is VA. If the answer is no, then no matter how important that step might be to the process, it is NVA. When completing a map, it is common that many of the steps in any given process are considered NVA. This is where there is room for process improvement, because these are general-

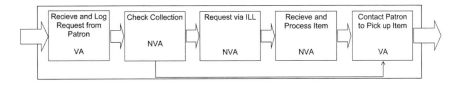

Figure 1.2. Example Process Map for Document Delivery Request

ly the behind-the-scenes steps in which the library magic happens. Because the customers do not see these steps, they do not care how they are completed. In the document delivery example, once the patron has requested an item, he or she does not know or care what happens behind the scenes—whether the book or journal was retrieved from the shelf or storage, if a new item was ordered, or if it was requested from another library—only that the item is received in a timely manner.

The presence of many NVA steps can also signal that the process is overly complicated or needs to be streamlined. If there are many approvals in a process, or if work must go through several departments to be completed, perhaps those steps can be reordered or consolidated so work can move more quickly. If this version of the process map does not give enough detail, it may be helpful to create a value stream map that also includes information about the time it takes an item to move through the process. This can be very useful in departments such as cataloging, where there are students, paraprofessionals, and librarians working on different steps in the process. You may find a logjam in the process that can be resolved to get patrons what they want faster.

FAILURE MODES AND EFFECTS ANALYSIS (FMEA)

No discussion of Six Sigma tools would be complete without mentioning failure modes and effects analysis. "FMEA" is an intimidating initialism for a very simple idea: to think through a process and determine where problems (failure modes) might occur and come up with a plan to make sure they don't. The idea behind the FMEA is to analyze each step in the process with a cross-functional group of participants. The group members should be people who can see different aspects of the process and brainstorm all the possible points of failure. Subsequent steps require rating the severity of the potential problems and then developing actions to resolve these potential failure modes.

Although this can be done as a very stringent process, it may be easier to implement as a more informal discussion of failure points when introducing a new process or reviewing an existing one. However, the key to using the FMEA effectively is to make sure the actions are assigned to a staff member who has the authority and responsibility to follow through on the corrective actions recommended.

Budget and staff cuts usually mean trying to do more with less or making difficult decisions about what to accomplish and what to let go, but using these tools can make it possible to do more by being more efficient. Starting with the projects that are quick wins for your patrons will create support for future programs and funding, while carefully examining each process or workflow will keep library staff open to continuous improvement in how they do their work. But completing this exercise is just the first step. The reason Six Sigma has worked for businesses is that the last component of the methodology is "control," or how the process is monitored to ensure that progress that was made is retained. The goal is to create value for library patrons and the library by focusing on the most important aspects of a process and then putting ownership of that process into the hands of those who know it best so they can make changes and improvements to give the customer, or the library, the best experience possible. Doing more with less should not have to result in doing a job with any less quality, and using these tools can help focus on reducing the time and effort spent on tasks that do not add value for the customer or stakeholder, while increasing the resources for those that do.

TWO

Daily Operations

Pamela O'Sullivan

The realities of daily operations for most academic libraries include short-ages—of staff, materials, and time—while demands on the library have both increased and changed. Breaking down silos and introducing work-flows that cut across traditional departmental lines can make it easier to do more with less while providing exceptional customer service. Priori-tizing and having good data will allow you to accomplish more with the resources you have.

The quotidian routines of the average academic library have changed dramatically over the last several decades, yet, in some ways, librarians and library managers ignore the reality of the changed workplace envi-ronment and run variations on decades-old workflows. Even where new service styles are introduced, parts of the workflow may still be tied to outdated ideas of what a library should do or be.

How does an institution break habits that have worked for years and offer the safety of familiarity, especially when it seems that there is no time to investigate, much less institute, new initiatives?

BREAK DOWN THE SILOS—OR AT LEAST PUT DOORS IN THEM

In my experience, this is sometimes the hardest thing to accomplish, yet it can yield the greatest returns. Proximity does not always breed familiar-ity; people can work ten feet apart and not know the specifics of their colleagues' tasks. The results of this kind of segregation of knowledge include duplication of effort as well as time wasted trying to find the correct information.

Look at your organization as a whole and make logical pairings. Examine workflows and consolidate where possible. Don't be afraid to stop doing something that no longer makes sense. Reduce the number of people who have to look at an item or handle a piece of paper. Wherever possible, eliminate the paper in favor of online resources: blogs, wikis, and the like.

For example, circulation and interlibrary loan are combined in some institutions. Students can be cross-trained to cover both circulation and ILL functions, reducing idle time at the circulation desk while at the same time expediting the document delivery process and freeing up the ILL librarian for more complicated searching.

DON'T TRY TO REINVENT THE WHEEL

Take a look at the library literature. Many academic libraries have already tried new service models and new workflows. Keep an open mind, but be realistic. For example, at my institution, we wanted a more accurate way to keep statistics, one that required less time to analyze and produce reports. We looked at various ways of doing this and decided to start with a free, open source software application called LibStats. We could customize it to yield the categories of statistics we needed, and I was able to use it to pull up on-the spot analyses to justify changes to staffing patterns that could be made immediately, rather than having to wait until someone compiled all the statistics at the end of the semester.

Another service upon which we have begun to rely more is instant messaging. One way we are using it is to have the circulation desk staff send an instant message asking for help from available librarians if someone needs reference assistance at a time when no one is at the reference desk. It saves time over using the phone and creates a better impression than having a staff member run from office to office in search of a reference librarian!

PRIORITIZE, USING DATA TO HELP YOU

The goal for most academic libraries is to have a librarian available whenever needed, but particularly at peak times. Using a program like LibStats enables you to track questions by time of day and day of week. There may be times when it makes more sense to have the reference librarians operate out of their offices, whereas at other times there may be a high enough volume of reference questions that you feel a librarian should be front and center.

Each institution is different, and though it may be tempting to borrow a reference model that worked well somewhere else—particularly if you are a manager who feels some pressure to make changes of ANY kind—

take time to step back and discuss with others the pros and cons of changes you are thinking of making. Whereas single service desk models have worked well for some institutions, others may find challenges to that model simply in the layout of the library.

In our library, we have gone from five service points to two. Circulation and reserves remain a service point, as they have for many years. However, IT, reference, and writing assistance, which were formerly in three locations on our main floor, have been brought together successfully in a single, highly visible location.

DON'T SET THINGS IN CONCRETE

Today's society is characterized by a high degree of fluidity. Library "routines," on the other hand, have often become static and unable to reflect the constantly shifting context in which we work. Pilot projects can be a good way to get your feet wet without committing a large amount of staff or resources. Set up pilots using what you have; rearrange furniture and devices as needed. Tweak service as needed during the pilot, and make sure to analyze and decide on its future in a timely fashion. You don't want a pilot that isn't working to continue simply because no one thought to say, "Hey, it's not working—let's try something else."

For example, three years ago, my institution wanted to introduce late night and weekend writing assistance. Our student learning center wasn't open past 9:00 PM, nor did it have weekend hours. My students worked as late as 11:30 PM and filled an observed gap in service very nicely. Their schedule and location in the library has been adjusted each year based on usage and feedback. The service has grown in popularity each year and has reduced the amount of time reference librarians spend on the mechanics of writing. This enables them to schedule more in-depth reference consultations in the evenings, a time popular with students who work or have classes all day. It also allows us to have times when we have a "complete package" at the desk: writing assistance, IT assistance, and a professional reference librarian.

CONSIDER BABY STEPS

Yes, sometimes it works to throw out everything and start from scratch, but there are times when the disruption would be too great. That doesn't mean you stay frozen in place. There can be many reasons to opt for small changes over a defined period of time. For one, if you introduce new workflows separately, you can gauge their success separately before adding another change. This can prevent "throwing out the baby with the bathwater" syndrome; you know which things are working for certain.

Baby steps aren't always favored by those above you, but you know your staff and students best and can use that knowledge to make a case for a series of gradual changes better than anyone else. If you are in a situation where you have to make a large change quickly, plan the steps out anyway; this will give you a fallback if something doesn't work out as expected.

SOMETIMES DISRUPTIVE CHANGE IS THE ONLY THING THAT WILL WORK

There will always be times when the only way to institute a change is abruptly. That doesn't mean with no warning; you should by all means prepare your staff, students, and faculty as thoroughly as possible. However, if the change is needed and would not work well introduced in stages, then set your date firmly and work out your strategies and back-ups to support it.

When my institution decided to begin charging for printing in the labs, informational sessions were held for lab managers and other interested parties, and all students, faculty, and staff were contacted. The day that printing quotas went into effect, that was it; there was no free printing in any labs, including the library. Graduate students were hardest hit, as they were used to printing out reams of articles, but the actual problems and complaints were fewer than we expected.

GET THE INFORMATION OUT

Use social media to let your constituency know about changes that are coming and the reasons behind those changes. Enlist the support of your students and faculty by demonstrating to them the advantages to be gained through new workflows, such as shorter waiting times for electronic document delivery.

Using steps such as those I have listed here have helped me manage my time and my staff's time more effectively over the last three years. Whether they will work for you is something that only you can decide. This is by no means an exhaustive list, but prioritizing and employing good data are two simple factors that you can use in trying to keep up with the reality of today's library world.

THREE

Feudal Society of the Stacks

Eric Owen

Most public and academic libraries in the twenty-first century exist in organizational cultures that rely as much upon the relationships among and obligations of individuals to one another as upon strict adherence to a proscribed hierarchy. Force of personality and charisma can be far more effective instruments of leadership than the authority of position alone. Our ability to cooperate and team build among disparate parties with varying agendas and duties has been a hallmark of our profession. Added pressures from budget shortfalls and staffing cutbacks have increased workloads while often shortening deadlines. What organizational structure might we comb for assistance or ideas, and how might individual librarians survive (and hopefully thrive in) this age of uncertainty? One anachronistic model with several structures similar to those of many libraries today is the millennium-old feudal system of the European Middle Ages. Analogies can be drawn between aspects of the medieval world and our current feudal society of the stacks.

A feudal library is populated by a diverse variety of folk. Student workers and pages, clerks, technicians, and various paraprofessionals fill the modern ranks of serfs and sergeants of the feudal stacks, completing many of the day-to-day business operations of the domain, with duties ranging from shelving books to managing units. The upper echelons of feudal society—the classes of knights and nobles—best describe the librarians, department and division heads, directors, and deans of the library today. In some work environments many or all of our library personnel may be members of one or more unions, a modern construct built on a framework created by medieval guilds.

As librarians, our position places us in a central role, working directly with most of or all the other members of our institutions. Our duties range from subject experts and selectors to instructors, and from technical and computing specialists to supervisors and mentors. Our obligations to and relationships with diverse ranks, from pages to provosts, require that we confront many of the pressures described below. This parchment records such wisdom as I can convey as a chronicle outlining some of the challenges facing the feudal librarian: places, pressures, and cycles, as well as a few tools and techniques that may help to speed thee on thy quests through the Byzantine realm of the modern library.

MANOR/FIEF (PLACE)

The feudal system of the medieval world was based on fealty and homage, concepts that encompassed personal loyalty and obligation in return for land (called a manor or fief) and thus position and responsibilities. A library domain will often be divided into numerous smaller units and departments, in effect manors or fiefs. In most cases a noble will be responsible for a fief and the duties and work of all those who fall within it: the barony of instruction, county of cataloging, shire of systems, or earldom of reference. The larger the initial fief, the greater likelihood that authority, duties, and obligations will be further distributed by a noble to create discrete subunits under his or her vassalage: the duchess of technical services provides supervision and control over a cataloging county, as well as baronies of acquisitions and serials, with each of these in turn representing a smaller fief.

TITHES (BUDGET CUTS)

In the Middle Ages, tithes were a regular tax on agricultural and craft production. Special tithes were also levied to raise funds in support of wars or large construction projects under the auspices of a ruler or the Church. In the library realm today, a constant stream of tithes seems to flow from our coffers. State support for public libraries and public institutions of higher education has steadily declined. Even in libraries unaffected by diminished state and federal funding, shifting institutional priorities may result in the levying of tithes by a local magnate. Local tithes may support new campus or municipal facilities, strategic cost-saving measures, enhancements for athletics programs, or support for more "vital" departments. A final tithe, which no library can escape, is the relentless annual inflation of material prices, for both print and electronic resources.

THE PLAGUE (STAFFING CUTS)

Major epidemics of bubonic plague ravaged Europe in the early and late Middle Ages. The Black Death in the fourteenth century killed so many people that a shift in social and cultural practices occurred as a result of the decreased population. Today, personnel cuts are the pox of the library world. Often in tandem with the tithe, staff payrolls remain precarious in many library settings. Even when a library escapes an outbreak of rampant layoffs, the pandemic of position eliminations and retirement attrition has taken a toll on personnel. Regardless of the cause, the plague in libraries today has started to alter our structure. Decreased staffing has forced a narrowing of collections and services, increased the workload for remaining personnel, and renewed efforts to obtain greater efficiency in our remaining endeavors.

CRUSADES (NEW LEADERS–NEW DIRECTIONS)

The Crusades were military expeditions (both political and religious in nature) launched in the late eleventh century and continuing until the late thirteenth century. During the time of the Crusades, papal and secular authorities repeatedly mobilized substantial forces by claiming that they were attempting to "free" (capture or retake) the Holy Land from Muslim control. The motives behind the Crusades varied over time and among the participants. The Crusades in the library world of today are those shifting priorities and programs (internal or external) that often disrupt ongoing operations and services. Many a crusade has been called by a provost or university president, mayor or city manager looking to make his or her mark in a new position. Crusades often impose new tithes on library budgets and sometimes introduce another outbreak of the plague. Although innovative ideas and reinvigoration of established objectives can result from the occasional visionary campaign, these grand ventures often seem more disruptive than beneficial.

SEASONS OF THE FEUDAL WORLD (A TIME FOR EVERYTHING)

In the Middle Ages, time for most people was best described in terms of seasons. The agricultural basis of medieval society followed repeating cycles of planting and harvest. Overlaying and interspersing these cycles were additional periods of taxation following harvests, and the "campaign season" for warfare between sowing and harvesting crops. Reigns of succession provided another common means for recording and recounting time on a larger scale. A reign could be brief or might last for generations, and the transition from one ruler to the next was as often a time of trepidation as of celebration.

The library realm has its own repetitive cycles. The student season is the longest, stretching from early fall until the beginning of summer. In academic and public libraries, the student season has distinct terms, which vary among institutions, each having its own ebbs and flows of frenzied activity and tranquil toil. The library calendar also contains annual intervals for subscription renewals. The fiscal year flip marks an omnipresent if not celebrated event on most libraries' annual timetable. With the continual contraction of external support for many libraries, the "appropriations season," as state and federal funds are curtailed or redistributed, has become our "campaign" season: a time when we must bolster our resolve for the next assault on our bottom line. We also see periodic turnover of our top-level administrators and politicians, although few now reign in one position for decades. A transition could signal a resurgence of crusading fervor, the establishment of new tithes, or an outbreak of plague. Therefore, it is wise to prepare for these eventualities and plan how best to position the library domain within the realm. While seasonal activities dominated life in the Middle Ages, daily regimens were not ignored. Medieval nobility might turn to a book of hours (medieval devotionals), which could include a daily schedule of liturgical duties and prayers from matins to vespers (morning to evening). For the feudal librarian of today, a guide to our daily duties remains important. Knowing where you are supposed to be, and where others in the realm might be found at a particular point in time, is vital. If you are trying to coordinate meetings, develop staffing schedules, or advertise your availability to library users, an online calendar is a must. Regardless of the product—Google Calendar (http://www.google.com/calendar), Groupwise (http://www.novell.com/products/groupwise), Zimbra (http://www.zimbra.com), or Microsoft Outlook (http://office.microsoft.com/en-us/outlook)—whether an individual account or part of an enterprise-wide system for a college campus or larger organization, and whether free or for a fee, the ability to create, maintain, and share calendars must be considered. The more complex the individual schedules and more distributed the domain, the greater the potential gain following adoption of a shared online calendar. A caveat with these systems is the importance of universal acceptance and use within an organization. If entire classes of library society or key individuals choose not to participate, the value of the tool quickly diminishes.

MANOR ROLLS (STATISTICS)

The wealth and business of medieval fiefs were commonly recorded in documents called manor rolls. More massive surveys of entire realms were also attempted on occasion, with the Domesday Book of William the Conqueror being the most famous. Written in Latin, the universal language of the Middle Ages, these rolls and surveys listed accounts and expenditures, land and livestock, and were used by the nobles, magnates, and rulers to determine the economic health of their domains and the extent to which taxes were being properly assessed and collected. Statistics are the Latin of the modern library domain. All librarians are familiar with calls for data to justify changes in services, additions or cancellations of resources, and adjustments in hours of operation. Although advanced analysis and data manipulation is beyond most of us, the use of some basic tools and knowledge of a few sources of comparative data can provide a solid statistical foundation.

Collection of statistics is often a shared undertaking. Individual fiefs may be expected to provide rolls outlining services and operations that fall under their purview. This can require aggregation of input provided by many people for an area, such as reference transactions or instruction sessions, or it may be the job of an individual yeoman, sergeant, or knight to gather more centralized measurements such as gate counts, circulation figures, website views, interlibrary loans, or books added to the collection.

The proliferation of electronic resources has increased the complexity of data collection and analysis efforts over the past decade. During this period standardization initiatives such as COUNTER (http://www.projectcounter.org) and SUSHI (http://www.niso.org/workrooms/sushi) have been developed to allow more accurate and easier comparisons of usage provided by different products and vendors. Compliance with one or both of these standards should be an important consideration when reviewing electronic resources for your library collection.

Once your rolls have been gathered, how can you make sense of them? Advanced statistical packages such as Minitab, SAS, and SPSS are powerful, but they require considerable training and expertise to use. If you have a statistics sage in your realm, take full advantage of his or her numerical wizardry. For the rest of us, the fundamental tool is the spreadsheet program. Microsoft Excel (http://office.microsoft.com/en-us/excel) has become a fixture in many offices today and is available for both Windows and Macintosh operating systems. Excel has one feature in particular that can be quite helpful in doing some basic statistical analyses: PivotTable. A pivot table allows one to perform common calculations, filters, and summaries of data without needing to know how to apply all of the functions and formulas that perform these operations. Current versions of Excel also have PivotChart, which expedites graphical representations of PivotTable analyses. For those lacking access to Microsoft Excel (due to expense or perhaps having a Linux OS), two similar open-source spreadsheets also have pivot table features. The OpenOffice software suite (http://www.openoffice.org) has a spreadsheet component called Calc, which contains DataPilot (a pivot table function), as does a scion suite called LibreOffice (http://www.libreoffice.org); its

Calc spreadsheet has pivot table functionality (called DataPilot or Pivot Table, depending on the version). Both of these free software packages run on Windows, Mac, and Linux systems. When faced with a statistical task, it is worth your time to become familiar with spreadsheets and pivot tables.

Library nobles and magnates often are asked to provide data for comparison with similar institutions when responding to tithes, plagues, and calls for crusades from their superiors. The American Library Association (ALA) collects figures on various types of libraries (http://www.ala.org/research/librarystats). Within the ALA, the Association of College & Research Libraries (ACRL) compiles metrics and measurements specifically on academic libraries (http://www.ala.org/acrl/publications/trends). Many of these resources require memberships, subscriptions, or a purchase. For those without access to such proprietory dossiers, there are publicly accessible free statistics from the National Center for Education Statistics (NCES) Library Statistics Program. The NCES provides online tools to compare academic libraries (http://nces.ed.gov/surveys/libraries/academic.asp) and public libraries (http://nces.ed.gov/surveys/libraries/librarysearch/index.asp); data comparing public and state libraries since 2007 are available from the Institute of Museum and Library Services (IMLS) website (http://www.imls.gov/research/data_sets.aspx).

For some of us, the immediate issue is collecting the rolls of data in the first place. Two tools for commonplace areas such as service desks and websites are noteworthy. LibStats is an open source online application (http://code.google.com/p/libstats) designed to collect statistics from public service desks and export this information for manipulation in a spreadsheet. The data entry interface can be customized to allow implementation across several fiefs, with the capability to track variations in people and types of services. The design is flexible enough to allow an assemblage of statistics in varying levels of granularity, from the equivalent of a virtual hatch mark to full transcripts of reference interactions with questions and answers.

Reports on website traffic and usage are another customary component in the chronicle of a library domain. Google Analytics is a free online service (http://www.google.com/analytics) that reports on any website it is tracking, registering the number and type of users, frequency and duration of their visits, the technology used to access, and the information and patterns of how users may find the library's online presence or to which digital destinations they depart.

VIRTUAL HERALDS (COMMUNICATION: RESEARCH GUIDES AND INTRANETS)

In the later Middle Ages the position of the herald was created to assist the interactions of the nobility in a formal, structured manner governed by complex protocols and historical precedents. Serving as historian, interpreter, and mediator, a herald facilitated communication among the various classes of medieval society, as well as between members of similar rank who differed in customs, practices, or language. Effective communication remains a central goal for the feudal society of the stacks. Today, certain technologies can act as an effective intermediary. These virtual heralds may serve as a conduit for transferring knowledge between librarians and researchers at any time and place or as a means of sharing institutional memory among members of the library domain.

Today's libraries rarely see expansion in their cadre of instructional knights, but the quantity and nature of requests for research assistance are expanding. As the complexity and variety of information resources increase, the ability of average users to determine how and where to meet their research needs decreases. Well-designed online research guides are an efficient response to this conundrum. Homegrown guides are always an option, but for those libraries (and librarians) with extensive and dynamic teaching loads, a purpose-built research guide product is worth the added expense. Springshare's LibGuides is one such tool (http://springshare.com/libguides). The product can be used for statical presentations, assisting a researcher, and can allow the incorporation of dynamic polls and quizzes for real-time interaction in an active instructional setting. Components of these pages can also be readily reused in other guides created by librarians within the institution and beyond.

Although the particulars of status and proof of lineage do not apply in the feudal society of the stacks, an intranet can serve as a virtual herald for larger organizations, providing a means to collect and communicate shared institutional knowledge (policies, procedures, schedules, minutes, reports, contact information) among numerous and distributed personnel. Intranets are often developed using a content management system (CMS). Microsoft's Sharepoint (http://sharepoint.microsoft.com) is an example of one such commercial intranet product; many open source CMS systems exist (a good overview of the open source market is available at http://www.opensourcecms.com). Several different programming platforms are used by both fee and "free" products, among them ASP.NET, Java, PERL, and PHP. Although the features afforded by a successful intranet implementation are valuable, the cost of installation and maintenance of these systems, even with an open-source option, is a significant investment of systems staff time, if not of real dollars for a commercial turnkey application.

"FREE" COMPANIES (OUTSOURCING)

In the Middle Ages, the cost of equipping, training, and maintaining a large force of skilled soldiers became increasingly problematic. The system of military obligation underlying the feudal structure proved inadequate to provide sufficient numbers of competent combatants for the various skirmishes and wars of medieval magnates. In response to this pressure, rulers accepted from their vassals monetary payments in lieu of specific numbers of knights, men-at-arms, and peasant levies. In turn, these new funds would be used to hire troops of professional soldiers, often called "Free Companies," to fight their wars. When such wars ended, so did the expense for the rulers. The use of these mercenaries was controversial in the Middle Ages, and in the feudal society of the stacks, outsourcing remains a contentious topic.

The "free" companies of the library world today are certainly never free, and their use is contested; however they can provide vital assistance to organizations with depleted and overworked staff. Among the many types of available outsourcing services, three have served my own institution well as we have weathered repeated cycles of tithes and plagues: approval plans, hosted computing, and cooperative chat reference.

YBP Library Services' GOBI (http://www.ybp.com/gobi.html) and Coutts Information Services' OASIS (http://www.couttsinfo.com/services/oasis.htm) are two of the major book approval plans. In various configurations, these plans can offer considerable time (and in some cases cost) savings. At basic implementation, individual selectors can receive digital slips to assist them in vetting the universe of print (and electronic) books. While such plans will not cover all subjects or include all types of publishers equally, they can make materials selection more efficient. Taken to the maximum extent of their capabilities, approval plans can be elaborated to completely automate selection for monographs in any or all subject areas in a library, with catalog records generated and shelf-ready processing performed off-site.

The ubiquity of computers in the modern library domain creates a dependency on costly equipment. Even when sufficient local expertise exists to administer and maintain technology, funds for replacement of servers and individual workstations are rarely forthcoming. Many commercial vendors offer hosted products. The outsourcing of responsibility for server administration—including backups and patches, as well as the expense of regular hardware upgrades—substitutes an annual subscription payment to a vendor for local investment in staff and equipment. A library domain within a technically sophisticated realm, say a large academic institution, may be able to gain many of the advantages of hosted products by having the campus IT division "host" some library systems. This strategy will often require trading some library control to gain "free" infrastructure support. Likewise, some "turnkey" systems require little local maintenance but cannot be customized.

Although most "free companies" act as replacements for plague-ridden populations or as more cost-effective or efficient responses to changing technology, real-time chat reference has become a common service and user expectation in many libraries. To offer sufficient coverage in a virtual reference environment, a library often must join a consortium. Few libraries can staff extensive hours for chat reference alone, and none has been identified that provides 24/7 availability, except as part of a cooperative venture or subscriber to a paid service. QuestionPoint (http://www.questionpoint.org) is a leading example of a cooperative chat reference service. Access to certain features like 24/7 assistance may require a commitment of active participation from local librarian ranks in addition to membership fees.

HEARTH, HEALTH, AND HAPPINESS (LIFE BEYOND THE STACKS)

In a feudal structure, great importance is placed on relationships and obligations among various members of society. The tools and techniques described throughout this chapter can assist a librarian in meeting some of the challenges we face in the feudal structure of the twenty-first-century library. One critical component remains to be addressed: life beyond the stacks. Avoidance of the obligations of hearth and home can sabotage one's overall quality of life. No less important is the maintenance of good health. Few modern office professions incorporate regular physical exertion, so it is essential to make time outside of work for physical activity to exercise and strengthen the body. And yet, a tidy hearth and robust constitution will mean little if one's relationships with friends and family members are deficient. Spouses, significant others, children, and perhaps pets, all demand (and deserve) affection and attention. Professional achievements are commendable, but a happy home and a rich web of social connections are the truest marks of success in life. That is one precept that has not changed over the ages.

FOUR

Necessary Sacrifices

LeEtta Schmidt

The idea of organizational reengineering came with a cloud of process thinking and employee development. The goal is to streamline processes and maximize use of resources so that an organization can do more with less (Champy 2004, 172). However, doing more with less often happens because there is less available. Fewer people doing more work is not any type of reengineering, improvement, or success; it leads to burnout and low morale. Yet this situation is one in which many libraries have found themselves. We hear and throw around catch phrases such as "do more with less." Eventually those phrases describe "the new normal." How do we cope and succeed when all our resources are disappearing? The new normal is like a growing mountain. It encourages us to climb so we don't get buried, but it never lets us reach the top.

Management and business literature, library related or otherwise, does not touch much on the failures we have to endure in order to succeed. Nitty-gritty sacrifices don't show up much in "how we did it" articles. We trumpet our successes and attempt to cover missteps, even if those missteps got us where we are now. Strategic management of resources includes sacrifices and mistakes as much as triumphs. In a basic sense, organizations are just like households. When the chips are down, luxuries are cut in order to afford what's necessary. Each household has different ideas of what make up necessities and luxuries. The necessities and luxuries of the academic interlibrary loan (ILL) department of the University of South Florida (USF) at Tampa are examined here to illustrate how strategic sacrifices can be applied in a library.

Improving the way things are done can help buy the time needed to absorb workload. Any process has redundancies that can be trimmed to

23

save time. New technology ensures that this is a never-ending cycle. Each advance in a system brings new possibilities. Trimming redundancies is a small sacrifice, but it requires a great deal of time to do successfully. Because of this, process thinking is often pushed aside as something to do when we have more time. The ground that can be gained by reevaluating processes is too valuable to put aside for another day. It is well worth the sacrifice that must be made to acquire it.

SACRIFICE YOUR TIME AND PRODUCTIVITY

The first steps of any real process improvements are evaluation and assessment, which take time (Cook 1996, 57). Giving time will be hard. Take a deep breath and put everything on hold for a moment. Have others in your team do the same. Brainstorm. Talk about the work. Chances are there are already valuable ideas for improvement ready to be utilized.

Sacrificing enough time to get it right means you will fall behind. You will lapse in your turnover goals. You will be buried by the mountain of the new normal. And because no process exists in a vacuum, you will infringe on other people's and department's time.

Once you have managed to assess and develop a new idea of how your processes and productivity could be helped by change, you have to enact that change. Don't expect this to happen immediately. Permanent change is not enacted quickly. Forcing a rapid overhaul can alienate staff and lose resources. The whole point of rising to the challenge of making the most out of limited resources is to keep what resources you have.

At the end of assessment and application, you will have to pay for the time lost. Your improvements will cut time and waste, but you are already buried. Be patient. The profits gained in time will help you catch up eventually, but may not really be evident until later. As seen in table 4.1, the days required to complete regular tasks fluctuated during the improvement process in the USF Tampa's ILL department. Attention was first paid to serving patrons in the library, the work of the borrowing side. Then the focus was turned to serving patrons of other libraries, the lending side. Recovery after time lost was slow and happened over the course of years. Making permanent real process improvements is planning for the long term, and the difference will be seen over time.

SACRIFICE YOUR QUALITY CONTROL

Consider how many of your daily tasks are done simply to check for errors and how much process planning is spent worrying over the task not being done right if it is not done the same way. Now stop. Sometimes faster and cheaper is the only option available. Maintaining control over every step in a process might not be the best way to provide the best

Table 4.1.   Days to Complete a Request

	2007	2008	2009	2010	2011
Borrowing	7.25	8.02	8.21	7.21	6.29
Lending	1.55	1.18	1.53	2.92	0.86

Note: Statistics gathered from University of South Florida interlibrary loan department request system.

service. If you are worried about other libraries providing less-than-perfect chat answers to your patrons, don't be. If you are worried about electronic articles being delivered to your patrons by other libraries with images of thumbs and black borders, don't be. If you are worried that students could not possibly provide quality service at your service desks, don't be.

In interlibrary loan, this can translate to allowing the unmediated delivery of articles to the patron, a task that would have waited for staff members to handle it during working hours. It can also mean trusting the system to handle requests and saving follow-up for down times. Both of these automations are employed by the USF's ILL department. Each library operation has aspects of its processes that are more quality than quantity. Temporarily cutting quality-driven tasks can buy time.

Yes, some patrons will not get all-inclusive information in chat or at the service desk. Some articles will have thumbs. Your customer population will be accepting of these little failures for the most part. Yes, there will be some dissatisfied customers. But as we witnessed at the USF, these customers will be the exception.

SACRIFICE YOUR SAFETY NET

Don't plan for the exception. Organizational awareness, common sense, and a little collaboration are all that's needed to solve most problems, whether or not they have been planned for in advance. Considering the exception often brings about the downfall of process planning. Learn to identify it, and stop it when you see it.

SACRIFICE BEST PRACTICES

Many best practices are simply not made for hard times. Sending a follow-up message to your patron to make sure he or she was satisfied is good business. Recording each issue of your journal subscriptions as it arrives is good business. Scanning document delivery requests in color is good business. Cleaning out your databases and taking inventory of your stacks is very good business. All of these activities take time that can be put to better use elsewhere when time is of the essence.

Assessment of services and request follow-up was the first to go in the ILL department at the USF Tampa. Following up on requests that should have been delivered but were never received was too time consuming when new requests flooded in every minute. This resulted in a small number of requests falling through the cracks. Of the requests lost, only a few patrons followed up on their own, and even fewer complained. Similar to what happened with the sacrifice of quality control, dissatisfied customers were the exception. Every other activity, like the scanning and delivery of articles, was done favoring speed over quality. The most basic need of the customer was met: legible and usable information. Colored and high-quality image requests could not be handled in the time allowed.

Although it is potentially embarrassing to admit to peers, playing messy for the sake of speed will get you by. One of the most useful attributes of best practices is that they will always be there as goals. Better still, they will be there as unquestionable goals. Best practices are created and understood to be points of aspiration.

SACRIFICE EGALITARIANISM

Start playing favorites. In the course of your planning and fat trimming, you have identified services that are not necessary. Services like document delivery, paging books, and chat and e-mail on weekends may face the chopping block. Any cut in service will result in complaints. If you have not already done so, consider restricting some of these services to your most powerful patron group. Faculty-only services in academia are not unusual. Request-per-week limits are also not unusual. Restricting instead of eliminating services will ensure that those services can one day return in full.

Given more elbow room in the future, our ILL department might provide document delivery to graduates as well as faculty. It may also remove the twenty-requests-per-week limit on services to all patrons. The restrictions in place control a workload that would expand at a faster rate if not contained.

SACRIFICE YOUR IDEA OF WHAT IT MEANS TO WORK IN A LIBRARY

Although the ideals of librarianship are far from those of Wall Street, libraries are just a different type of business. They have to act more businesslike in slim times to ensure their own survival. Part of this is documenting your profits to defend your processes. A library's profits are measured in patron satisfaction. Its good business is measured in effective use of resources.

Never assume that any activity is beyond question. Although information literacy education may have been accepted as rote, you will need to defend it. Circulation may have been seen as a library's life blood, but you will have to explain why. Reference may have been seen as a foundation; you will have to quantify its efficacy. This translates into more assessment, research, and time. Figuring out what information is needed and then locating it will be the most time consuming. Once that task is done, upkeep of the data will be easier. You will find that having all the information at hand will enable you to take advantage of any situation with more ease.

The first sizable interlibrary loan assessment project at the USF during the four years examined did not look for user satisfaction. It was all about cost. Your costliest and most used services can be used to defend all related activities. Mary Jackson's average costs for ILL borrowing and lending of $18.62 and $10.93, respectively, have been used to explain budget requirements by interlibrary loan and access services departments across the country (Jackson 1997, 1). When analyzed in the same way, the costs of each request at the USF were $10.20 borrowing and $4.19 lending. A comparison of the amounts illustrates good budget management. However, costs alone don't paint a complete picture. A valuation of service was estimated based on what it might cost to obtain similar materials via commercial document delivery sources. The estimated value of $24.78, when paired with an estimated cost of service, shows how effective strategic management of resources can be.

SACRIFICE YOUR REVENUE

This seems counterproductive, but it can save you time and money. Libraries are not usually known for service charges. Our services are provided for the greater good of the communities we serve. Still, there are several monetary transactions associated with library service. The act of billing is an expensive endeavor. It is fraught with government-imposed standards that require upkeep, double checking, and huge amounts of staff time.

A $5 charge for copy services just covers the staff time taken to fill the order. Extra time is spent creating the bill and sending out any follow-up bills. Still more time is spent processing the payment when it arrives. Staff time is money. You are functioning at a deficit. Your choice here is to cut the service or give it away for free.

SACRIFICE YOUR REPUTATION

One of the most stressful features of doing more with less is trying to make it look like nothing has changed. We all do it, and we all have been put in positions where we are expected to do it well. As unpopular as the idea may be, transparency can be a great friend.

You might not expect it, but asking your customers for help can make them feel great, when it is done with care and judiciousness. For example, the USF ILL department previously did all it could to verify citations and locate resources on patron requests, no matter how little information the patron had provided. It is no longer feasible to devote the same amount of time to a growing workload. When the information cannot be located quickly, the patron is notified that the request can go no further without more information. This has two outcomes. Patrons who don't really have that much invested in their request will give up, lessening the load. Those who want the material will become involved in the process of finding it. This establishes more face-to-face communication and makes the customer feel integral.

This practice can also develop your patrons into your business allies. Establishing a face-to-face bond with a patron is the best way to make him or her care about what happens to you. One of these very same patrons could be the vote that keeps your funding from being cut again.

Being honest about what you have to let slide is also the best way to ensure that you get some resources back once the economic downturn is over. Too many departments have been left in dire straits after the danger is over because they managed to make do too well. You should balance the demands upon you with your real ability to continuously fulfill them. What you end up with is a give and take of time and resources that will enable you to meet new demands without abandoning the old ones.

MAKING NECESSARY SACRIFICES

All of these ideas were applied to the University of South Florida at Tampa's ILL unit over a course of four years. The result is a unit that can process fifty-four thousand combined requests per year with only 3.5 full-time employees, three students, and a manager. This is a fraction of the one FTE per fifty-five hundred borrowing requests and one FTE per ten thousand lending requests recommended by the Greater Western Library Alliance (Leon et al. 2003, 425).

The statistics in table 4.2 also pinpoint drawbacks to playing fast and loose. The sacrifice of time and productivity to plan process improvements pays off indefinitely. Automated requests will always be beneficial to the unit. However, letting database upkeep slide in favor of managing the workload at hand should be a temporary solution. After four years, the fill rate for supplying requests from other libraries indicates that staff are spending too much time on requests they cannot fill. This has become a waste of time and is no longer an aspect of business that can be ignored.

Given more resources, this department could follow up on deliverables to guarantee receipt. It could spend more time on quality and fill rate while still maintaining speed. When a deficiency was identified, the department could divert resources to investigation and correction. Staff members could expand the department's reach to patrons by assessing services and following up on requests universally.

IMPLEMENTATION

Deciding about the benefit of any sacrifice begins with assessment and planning. Before you start chucking processes and services out the window, you must take a hard-nosed look at what you are losing. Apart from planning, here are a few more keys to successful sacrifice:

- Communicate
- Involve
- Celebrate
- Be positive
- Document

Communicate with your staff and your managers about changes and sacrifices. Talk about the need for them. Middle managers sometimes face the pitfall of being agents of someone else's change. When overseeing operations with little resources, every order from above is negotiable. Helping the organization starts with helping your boss. This means keeping him or her fully informed of all the sacrifices necessary to accomplish any one goal. You must be up front about the needs of your staff when facing new challenges. Managers and administrators would rather hear "we can do that if" than "we can't." Likewise, your staff will be more accepting of imposed changes if they are aware of the organizational need. They rely

Table 4.2. Interlibrary Loans: A Four-Year Comparison of Requests

| | Non managerial Staff | Total | Fill Rate | | Turnaround Days | | Cost of Transaction |
			Patron	Library	Patron	Library	
2007	4	42,072	70%	59%	7.25	1.55	$7.33
2011	3.5	54,921	78%	48%	6.29	.86	$6.70

Note: Statistics gathered from the University of South Florida interlibrary loan department request system.

on the organization for livelihood. They should know that it relies on them in the same way (Jennerich 2006). Give them as much information as you can. Let them decide which of it doesn't interest them.

Involve your staff in the planning. They will feel the loss of every process step they are asked to sacrifice. They will also feel the burden of every extra task they are asked to take on. They will be afraid of losing their positions. Give them a voice. The more opportunities to contribute that you offer them, the greater the chance that they will see contribution as a way to control their situation. A little control can help them feel steady amid the change. This is key to maintaining morale, and morale is key to maintaining your staff. Never forget that your staff is the most important resource you have.

Celebrate your efforts and results. This can be as simple as a thank-you or as elaborate as a party. Congratulations and celebrations make people happy. Happy people produce more results. This isn't a new idea. We have heard about whistling and spoons full of sugar since we were kids. Adding a little fun to the day will help with that ever-important morale. Management involves a cycle of challenge, facilitation, and recognition. Recognizing those who help the organization will make them feel integral. Public recognition will encourage others to do the same.

Be positive about the opportunities presented by the current challenging situation. For every sacrifice the department makes, point out a trade-off gained. If you can offer your staff one bit of positive thought, any loss will be a little easier to bear. This may be one of the most difficult things to manage. Positivity suggests taking ownership. Looking for the silver lining is active participation. It is far easier to bellyache over losses than to turn them into some kind of gain. Positivity is also contagious, which is what makes it so powerful. Your positivity will rub off on those you manage as well as those you report to.

Document your assessment, planning, sacrifices, and outcomes. Share the documentation with your manager and your staff. Keep records of the best and worst resulting statistics. This information will help you trumpet your success. It will also help you argue that you can do even better with more resources.

CONCLUSION

It is easy to perfect a process plan on paper and forget the people involved. Some might say that the perfect process is devoid of people. However, process improvement and reengineering do not happen without people. Library services are not provided without people. The perfect process is one that takes this fact into consideration from the beginning, and the most effective organization is one that considers people from the beginning (Crainer 2004, 193). If you do not consider the people involved, your plans will fail.

Using process improvements and reengineering to do more with less is intrinsically linked with managing people. When you are improving the way things are done, you are really improving the way people do things. Each sacrifice you make to ensure organizational continuation requires your staff to participate. Each change made to services requires your staff to implement them. You will need to develop, communicate, and involve your staff.

Strategic management of processes and people will help you gain footing on the mountain of new normal. It will also help you identify the give and take necessary for long-term success. In reality, you cannot do more with less. It is impossible to use fewer ingredients and make more soup. What you can do is shift the resources you have to make better use of them. This involves sacrifices. Of all the sacrifices you may make, good people management should not be one.

WORKS CITED

Champy, James. 2004. "Why Execution Is the Source of Competitiveness." In *MBA in a Box: Practical Ideas from the Best Brains in Business*, edited by Joel Kurtzman, with Glenn Rifkin and Victoria Griffith, 171–179. New York: Crown Business.

Cook, Sarah. 1996. *Process Improvement: A Handbook for Managers*. Brookfield, VT: Gower.

Crainer, Stuart. 2004. "The Well-oiled Machine: Organizational Models That Work." In *MBA in a Box: Practical Ideas from the Best Brains in Business*, edited by Joel Kurtzman, with Glenn Rifkin and Victoria Griffith, 188–193. New York: Crown Business.

Jackson, Mary. 1997. "Measuring the Performance of Interlibrary Loan and Document Delivery Services." *ARL: A Bimonthly Newsletter of Research Library Issues and Actions* 195 (December). http://www.arl.org/resources/pubs/br/br195.shtml (accessed May 15, 2012).

Jennerich, Elaine Z. 2006. "The Long-term View of Library Staff Development: The Positive Effects on a Large Organization." *College &Research Libraries News* 67, nos. 10–11: 612–614.

Leon, Lars, June L. DeWeese, Carol Ann Kochan, Billie Peterson-Lugo, and Brian L. Pytilik Zillig. 2003. "Enhanced Resource Sharing Through Group Interlibrary loan Best Practices: A Conceptual, Structural, and Procedural Approach." *Portal: Libraries and the Academy* 3, no. 3: 419–430.

FIVE

Productive to the Core: Core Competencies and the Productive Librarian

Jenny Dale and Lynda M. Kellam

Before you start this chapter, we have an exercise for you. List three of your own personal core competencies. It does not matter if you have no idea what this term means. Just interpret it however you like and jot down the top three that come to mind.

1.
2.
3.

Now that you have that short list, take another few moments to write down the three things you spend *most* of your time doing at work.

1.
2.
3.

Do your competencies and daily work match up? When I did this exercise, the following competencies came to mind:

1. Teaching
2. Building relationships with campus partners outside of the library
3. Design

I spend most of my time at work on these three things:

1. Teaching
2. Going to meetings
3. Working with campus partners

The fact that my perceived competencies and work match up fairly well is a sign that I am in a position that is a good fit for me. Although this is not a very scientific method for identifying core competencies, self-perception is an important part of this process. Keep these short lists at hand while you read this chapter. Do your ideas about your own core competencies change as we delve more deeply into this concept?

In the face of shrinking budgets and resource cuts of all kinds, "do more with less" has become an almost constant refrain in libraries across the United States. Unfortunately, doing more with less is a problematic and ultimately unsustainable model if we hope to continue providing high-quality services and resources for our users. There is only so much "more" that we can do with "less" before employees become stretched too thin and burn out quickly. These employees are unlikely to be able to provide the level of service that users expect, leading to a dissatisfied customer base. In addition, larger workloads may lead to increased turnover. Although "doing more with less" has become a common mantra, we could be doing a disservice to both our patrons and our institutions.

This chapter offers an alternative to this model, one that makes the best use of human resources in libraries. We discuss the concept of *core competencies*, an idea with strong roots in the business world, and discuss how you and your organization can leverage your core competencies to keep productivity high even in times of economic crisis.

CORE COMPETENCIES 101

In 1990, two academics, C. K. Prahalad and Gary Hamel, introduced the world to their concept of core competence in a *Harvard Business Review* article, "The Core Competence of the Corporation." The authors identified three defining factors of core competencies: a competence 1) can be applied widely to provide access to various markets, 2) "should make a significant contribution to the perceived customer benefits of the end product," and 3) "should be difficult for competitors to imitate" (Prahalad and Hamel 1990, 83–84). Prahalad and Hamel provided numerous examples of companies that were effectively leveraging these competencies at the time of their writing. One of the examples was from a company whose success is still based on investment in a core competence: 3M. According to the authors, 3M's success with products ranging from Post-It notes to photographic film is based on a single competence in sticky tape (Prahalad and Hamel 1990, 82).

Prahalad and Hamel linked core competencies closely to competitive advantage, claiming that "in the long run, competitiveness derives from an ability to build, at lower cost and more speedily than competitors, the core competencies that spawn unanticipated products" (1990, 81). In other words, corporations that focused more on developing core competencies that could be broadly applied were more successful than those that focused resources on developing very specific skills and technologies. The first group was able to take those competencies and innovate in new markets, whereas the second group was tied more exclusively to the specific products they developed. A contemporary example that comes to mind is Apple, a company that has built a competence in user-centered design that has led to an expansion beyond the personal computing market into mobile computing and digital media markets.

Throughout the authors' exploration of core competencies, there is a clear message that they are critical for innovation. According to Prahalad and Hamel, "The skills that together constitute core competence must coalesce around individuals whose efforts are not so narrowly focused that they cannot recognize the opportunities for blending their functional expertise with those of others in new and interesting ways" (1990, 82). This is at the heart of the distinction between competencies and the basic skills required to do a particular task and can also be a stumbling block for large corporations. Using GTE as a business example, the authors described a corporation that devoted resources to identifying important technologies, but "senior line managers continued to act as if they were managing independent business units. Decentralization made it difficult to focus on core competencies" (Prahalad and Hamel 1990, 81). True investment in and support of developing core competencies makes good business sense for these large corporations, because, as the authors pointed out, "Unlike physical assets, which do deteriorate over time, competencies are enhanced as they are applied and shared" (Prahalad and Hamel 1990, 82). Core competencies appreciate in value.

Our introduction to core competencies was not the most traditional. We first learned about this business world concept in a book about time management. In *168 Hours: You Have More Time Than You Think*, Laura Vanderkam takes the concept and applies it at the personal level. She argues that "people, like companies, can have core competencies too. The same Hamel-Prahalad three-part definition can still apply. An individual's core competencies are best thought of as abilities that can be leveraged across multiple spheres. They should be important and meaningful. And they should be things we do best and that others cannot do nearly as well" (2010, ch. 2, location 557). This concept is really at the heart of Vanderkam's approach to managing time, and she shares a number of examples of core competencies. Many of these examples are in the form of case studies or profiles of various individuals, like Roald Hoffman, a remarkable man who has "leveraged his core competency of patient observation" as both a chemist and a poet (Vanderkam 2010, ch. 2, location 562).

"THE CORE COMPETENCE OF THE LIBRARIAN"

The previous section was a quick overview of a complex concept that has been sparking conversations in the business world and beyond for decades. There is no shortage of literature about core competencies that explores various applications of the theory, and if we had more room, we could look at those applications in more detail. The point of this chapter, though, is to apply core competencies to the library world.

One could take the title of Prahalad and Hamel's article and substitute any number of things for the word "corporation." In the library profession, the application of core competencies exists at two levels: the organizational and the individual. Theoretically, we might expect libraries as organizations to be able to develop competencies in a similar manner to corporations. But most libraries are not corporations. They are knowledge organizations that serve a specific community. Our library, for example, is focused on serving the educational mission of our university and providing quality resources to students, faculty, and staff on our campus. As a state institution, we serve the public as well, but our main "customer" base is comprised of these campus constituents. Because this is the case, library resources and services are necessarily duplicative. We have many of the same books as a library down the road, for example, but our students can't always easily access those materials. We run a popular chat reference service, and so do many other libraries in our university system. That doesn't mean we should give up our chat and direct users to those other services; they are looking for a customized experience.

Still, libraries as organizations can identify and support core competencies. Some academic libraries have invested significant resources in becoming technology leaders, developing innovative technology solutions that can then be shared with other libraries. In our local area, North Carolina State University is known for technology innovation. They have a thriving Digital Library Initiatives Department (http://www.lib.ncsu.edu/dli/projects/) that produces projects as varied as citation builders (http://www.lib.ncsu.edu/dli/projects/citationbuilder/), historical walking tour apps for mobile devices (http://www.lib.ncsu.edu/dli/projects/wolfwalk/), and data visualization (http://www.lib.ncsu.edu/dli/projects/dataviz/). Other libraries have focused more on providing innovative customer service experiences, like Yale's Personal Librarian Program (http://www.library.yale.edu/pl/index.html) and Stanford University's Library Concierge Project (http://lib.stanford.edu/sulair-news/concierge-project-training). Still others have developed in the area of technical services. But at least in the case of academic libraries, technology, customer service, and technical services are all functional requirements, so it is not possible to outsource one of these divisions of your library to another organization. Focusing on an area of strength, however, can help libraries strategically allocate resources throughout the organization. One example of this is the trend in academic libraries to move away from staffing reference desks with only professional librarians. Staff members and students often can help fill in desk hours, freeing up reference librarians to develop other core competencies in teaching or outreach. We see significant opportunities for libraries to leverage the idea of core competencies, even if they are not able to divest themselves of particular functions. But that is a topic for another discussion.

Individual core competencies are what initially got us interested in this idea, and in these competencies we see significant potential for librarians to work smarter rather than harder or longer. Vanderkam states this idea best in her pithy explanation of individual core competencies: these are abilities that are not limited to a single sphere, that are meaningful to you, and that you do better than most people could (Vanderkam 2010, ch. 2, location 556). We use our own experiences in this chapter to illustrate what we mean. Jenny's primary role is to be a first-year instruction librarian, and she has spent her career honing a core competence of teaching. Though this competence is critical in her day-to-day work teaching first-year students, it isn't limited to that sphere. She also leverages her competence in teaching to create online learning objects, teach users in a more individual setting at the reference desk, and train colleagues.

Lynda's primary job as the data services and government information librarian requires that she spend a large amount of time in consultations with individual students and faculty. She has developed a core competence in one-on-one public service by developing strong relationships with her students and faculty, which has helped her become more embedded in their daily lives. She also has a core competence in project management and often serves in that capacity on committees.

APPLYING CORE COMPETENCIES TO YOUR WORK LIFE

You may identify one or two of your core competencies without much thought, but you likely have more than you realize. Vanderkam takes a holistic approach to determining core competencies. She suggests starting with a detailed time log and analyzing the results of that log to break time into rough categories. After looking at those categories and estimating the time spent, Vanderkam suggests asking yourself two questions: "What do I do best that other people cannot do nearly as well?" and "What things do I spend time on that other people could do, or could do better?" (Vanderkam 2010, ch. 2, location 773). Having gone through this activity ourselves, we can attest that it is critical to keep an open mind when looking at your core competencies. Jenny, for example, is a classic introvert. It initially seemed strange to her to look at the work that she was doing, and that she did best, and to realize that it all had to do with performing in front of or interfacing with people. When you look at the work that you do, try to let go of preconceived notions about your own personality or even your job responsibilities. Often our work evolves over time, so the reality of your day-to-day work may not match up directly with your position description. One way to avoid approaching this process with preconceived notions is to work through it with a partner. You can share your time log with that person and have him or her categorize your activities from a different perspective.

Determining your core competencies is a reflective process, but it must lead to action if you want to leverage these competencies to change your work life. According to Vanderkam, there are three choices for divesting yourself of all the work that does not align with your core competencies: ignore it, minimize it, or outsource it (2010, ch. 2, location 410). This may be a good time to note that Vanderkam, at least at the time of this writing, is a self-employed freelance writer. Those of us who work in organizations may have a harder time simply ignoring non-core-competency work. If a liaison librarian with collection development responsibilities realizes that selecting materials is not one of her core competencies, she cannot simply ignore it. (She can, but there would likely be negative consequences.)

As librarians, our best bet is to hone in on core-competency-related work and to either minimize or outsource the rest if possible. There will always be tasks that must be completed that are not our favorite ones, or that are not core competencies, but it is possible to sharpen focus on those tasks that we do best so that the "right" people are doing the "right" jobs. In the example in the previous paragraph, the librarian who lacks the competency associated with collection development could work within her organization to find someone else who *does* have that competency. In our own department, for example, we have an unofficial collection development guru. Something in her wiring makes her much better than either of us at collection development. If our goal is to maximize efficiency, it makes sense for us to "outsource" these responsibilities to her. At the crux of this issue is managing time and effort: this guru could almost definitely do a better job ordering books for some liaison areas, and in less time than it takes the current liaison. In turn, another liaison who has a core competency in teaching might take over some of the guru's teaching responsibilities. Brokering these types of deals is, of course, not always as easy as it sounds on paper. But we do think that it can be done, and done well.

As the example above indicates, simply looking over your time and identifying some competencies doesn't mean that you can sit back, relax, and enjoy increased productivity. Pinpointing your competencies is always a useful undertaking, but to really make changes to your work, this process cannot happen in a vacuum. You have to be able to communicate with your colleagues, and especially your supervisor, about how these competencies fit together. Such open conversations can lead to real change within an organization, or even a department or unit. For the exchange in the scenario above to happen, you would need support not only from your colleague (the collections guru), but also from your supervisor(s). To get such support, it is important to approach colleagues and supervisors with a solid plan for changing responsibilities. Telling your supervisor that you do not like collection development is not a good way to leverage your core competencies; explaining that it is not an area you consider a core competence and that it takes a significant amount of time away from the work you do best might be.

Another reason that supervisor or administrator buy-in is important is that core competencies can be developed. If a library has a goal of providing excellent customer service, it makes sense to invest time and resources in training staff to do so. In addition, some employees are better suited for frontline public service, whereas others may do better behind the scenes. The contributions of both groups are still valuable, but to best use employees we should enable them to be in positions where they can provide the best service.

A problem that can occur when core competencies come into play is that sometimes we might take on work in a core competence area that is outside the scope of our position descriptions. When Jenny began working as the first-year instruction coordinator, she inherited coordination responsibilities for a library game night, a successful outreach event started by the librarian previously in that position. This type of event happens to align with her core competencies of relationship building and outreach beyond the library, but that might not be the case for the next person in this position. We recommend that, especially in the current economic climate, organizations build some flexibility into professional positions. Perhaps some responsibilities are best matched with *competencies* of an individual who fits well within an organization rather than *positions* that the organization has designed in advance. Often the overlap will be significant, but there will always be additional responsibilities, those "other duties as assigned," that librarians take on based on interest and competence rather than position.

CONCLUSION

Though we find the idea of core competencies intriguing and have found that this helps us organize our work into areas to emphasize and areas to minimize, we are keenly aware that it is not a magic bullet. So much of the success of an undertaking like this one lies in the individual and the organization. If you are considering the core competency approach to managing your workload and your time, here are some questions to ask yourself:

- What are your core competencies?
- Have they changed over time and between positions?
- How do they fit into your organization?
- Are there ways you can leverage these core competencies to save yourself and your colleagues time and energy? Are there activities you can outsource? Are there activities you can stop?
- Will your supervisor be supportive of these changes?

As mentioned, this isn't a magic bullet. There will always be tasks to complete that do not align with your core competencies. If your library abandoned shelving books because no one claimed it as a core competency, your library and its users would suffer. Instead, consider core competencies a strategic approach to thinking through how you spend your time and where your time is best spent. In a world where we are often asked to do more with less, librarians need to be strategic about how and when we use our time so that we can work smarter and continue to provide high-quality services and resources for our users.

WORKS CITED

Prahalad, C. K., and Gary Hamel. 1990. "The Core Competence of the Corporation." *Harvard Business Review* 68, no. 3:79–91.

Vanderkam, Laura. 2010. *168 Hours: You Have More Time Than You Think*. New York: Portfolio. Kindle edition.

SIX

Rural Librarians, Farm Out Your Work

Michelle A. McIntyre

Small and rural libraries live up to their name. The library is rural, and the facility is often small. However, a rural librarian has immense responsibilities. It is not unusual for the librarian to be the director, the custodian, and the only full-time employee. Support staff typically are one or maybe two part-time staff persons. The rural librarian is frequently the person waiting on patrons, doing collection development, processing and cataloging books, and completing reports and paperwork. Just because the library closes its doors for the day does not mean the librarian's work is done. Rural librarians are often seen in the evenings attending meetings, staffing information tables at community events, or making presentations to potential funders. As you can imagine, the librarian is busy every minute of the day.

Small and rural librarians need to have exceptional time management and organizational skills. The librarian must assess every task and consider his or her amount of involvement. Can I ask a volunteer to step in and help at a community event? Does this assignment need my full attention? Can an intern perform research for this project? Is it possible to send a board member to a township meeting? It is difficult for a rural librarian to delegate tasks, because there is often no one to whom to delegate. Feeling comfortable with assigning tasks is crucial for any librarian to have a successful library. With proper planning, the librarian will be able to delegate tasks to volunteers, interns, and even board members.

VOLUNTEERS PROVIDE OPPORTUNITIES

Historically, librarians have utilized volunteers as support services in the library. Often used as story time helpers, book processors, or circulation assistants, volunteers play an integral part in the success of any rural library. Librarians agree that these traditional volunteer opportunities exist in almost any library setting. Due to staffing shortages and dwindling financial resources, librarians rely on volunteers now more than ever. They are always looking to lure skilled volunteers to their programs.

Small and rural libraries are typically staffed by only one or two people. The librarian is often the only qualified staff person performing clerical and professional duties. This person is tasked with providing quality services and library programs for all ages, while keeping the doors open. It is an enormous responsibility for just one or two people. Volunteers can play an integral role in the success of such a library.

Volunteers come to a library with a specific goal in mind: they are committed to making a contribution of their time to help the library. These individuals may possess skills that could increase the efficiency of the librarian. Librarians are now taking a proactive approach, assigning volunteers to jobs that match their skills. Skilled volunteers can effectively perform specific tasks. Individuals with experience in a particular area are pleased to utilize their talents, knowing they are making a meaningful contribution to the organization.

Structured volunteer programs that are properly planned and organized provide effective assistance for the rural librarian. The librarian must take a proactive and purposeful approach to the library volunteer program. Assessing a potential volunteer's skills and talents takes time, but done properly, it can greatly benefit the library. A small investment of time early in the volunteer process can save the librarian time in the future.

A rural public library should have a comprehensive volunteer program with the following components:

- Volunteer orientation and training
- Volunteer policy
- Volunteer application
- Volunteer job description
- Volunteer recognition

Volunteers need a library *orientation* so they will know what is expected. The orientation should begin with a brief overview of the library and its mission and vision. Discuss how volunteers are currently impacting the library organization. When a librarian uses volunteers to lighten the workload, guidelines are an essential part of the program. The training should include an outline of library *policies and procedures* that volunteers are expected to abide by, including dress code, tobacco use, and confidentiality of patron records. Discuss with volunteers their roles and responsibilities, as well as any expectations the library has about their volunteerism. These can include keeping a time log, calling off when scheduled, and obtaining the proper background clearances. A detailed volunteer *application* can assess an individual's skills and interests. Application questions may inquire about the individual's interests, specific abilities, and computer skills. Inquiries should be made about how many hours a week the person wishes to volunteer and which days he or she is available. Volunteers often want to help out, but do not know what type of opportunities exist. Volunteer *job descriptions* can be as simple as a sentence describing simpler tasks, such as taking care of the plants or straightening shelves. But being a story time leader requires a more complex and specific skill set.

There are a number of ways to utilize volunteers:

- Adult volunteers can be story time leaders, copy catalogers, book processors, or circulation desk assistants; they can also perform clerical tasks.
- Teen volunteers can be story time assistants or summer program reading assistants, or perform program preparation and cleanup.

Every so often a librarian will have the opportunity to work with volunteers who are assigned a project and choose to do it at the library. It is not uncommon for a scout group, church group, or service organization to contact a library looking to complete a volunteer project as part of its mission. These groups can perform larger tasks that would take solo librarians months to complete.

Our library has participated in United Way's Day of Caring for over ten years. Each year the library submits projects such as grounds clearing and mulching and collection cleanup for consideration. Volunteers from local businesses are assigned to complete projects at the library. The local business compensates its employees for the day, and the library provides lunch and a tour of the facility.

Scouting troops have completed numerous projects at the library. An Eagle Scout and his troop refaced cabinets and built shelving to house the professional collection. A Girl Scout troop looking to complete a requirement for a Silver Award took on a much larger task. Along with their troop leaders and parents, the girls renovated a vacant basement room to be a community meeting space. The girls cut and installed a sheet rock ceiling and built boxing around exposed pipes. They then plastered, sanded, and painted the area. This project was completed with funds raised by recycling aluminum cans and storm windows. Our local Boy Scout troop assisted with the removal and recycling of old library radiators, which in part also helped to fund the room project. Now the Girl

Scouts have a place to meet, and the library has a functional community room.

Some volunteers are assigned to the library through the judicial system. These individuals are nonviolent offenders who are offered the opportunity to give back to their communities in lieu of imprisonment. These adult volunteers are concerned with privacy, so it is important to be discreet and integrate them into your regular volunteer program. Our library has been associated with the court-appointed community service program for several years. During this time we have had tables built by a carpenter, murals painted by tattoo artists, and rooms redesigned by interior designers. Others have performed data entry, prepared bulk mailings, done clerical tasks, and processed books for sale or recycling. Some enjoy the experience and continue to serve after their assigned hours; they have become valued library volunteers.

Rural librarians have to be skilled in many areas, not just library work. Networking at community events can procure volunteer services. If business owners or professionals support the mission of the library, they are often willing to donate services. A number of employers are now requiring their employees to perform volunteer hours in a nonprofit organization. In some instances these individuals can contribute a specialized skill to the library. Sometimes a volunteer with professional skills will surface because his or her employer downsized recently. The individual is interested in keeping a current résumé and professional skills, as well as utilizing his or her talents to better the community. These volunteers can save the librarian time by providing professional skills and services in areas where the librarian's knowledge is limited. Our library has been fortunate to procure various professional services at no cost:

- An event planner to oversee a fund-raising occasion
- A makeup artist as a face painter at a local community event
- A strategic planner to assist the library board with developing mission and vision statements, as well as goals and objectives
- A chef to plan a menu and prepare appetizers for our open house

Other professional services to consider getting from volunteers are the following:

- A Web designer to create and maintain a website in return for being able to use it in his or her portfolio
- A fund developer to assist with contacting and procuring donors
- A lawyer to assist with an endowment program
- A grant writer to do research and write to foundations to procure funding
- A photographer to capture images that can later be used as stock images for library brochures
- A financial planner to assist with gifts of stocks and bonds

Periods of financial distress and budget cutbacks are an excellent time to consider a structured volunteer program. Establishing a volunteer program is a worthwhile investment of time for any librarian. You will never be able to count the ways in which volunteers enhance the library and its services and help you administer an efficient facility.

INTERNSHIPS

Internship programs at small and rural public libraries are not all that common. Many librarians feel they do not have the time it takes to develop and oversee an internship program. A structured internship program takes less time than you might think. Internships provide the opportunity for a student to perfect a skill, gain on-the-job work experience, and be mentored by a professional. In return, the library will gain an intern who brings fresh ideas to the table and develops new opportunities for the library.

A successful internship offer should include a brief description of the library and its services, as well as its contact information. The intern should also know the library is a nonprofit agency. A library offers an intern a unique opportunity to learn how a nonprofit is run and the chance to be part of an organization that provides a community service. The intern's duties and responsibilities, as well as goals and objectives, should be defined. Address student qualifications, dress code, start and end dates, and whether there will be any compensation.

Consider building in an opportunity for the intern to perfect a skill. A mechanism for evaluating the intern's performance is usually provided by the school. Also include an agreement between the library and the intern that any work product becomes the property of the library, but it can also become part of the intern's portfolio. Supervising an intern is an intense responsibility. Be aware that you will need to schedule time to supervise and assess the intern's work and fill out required paperwork. An investment of time in the internship can reap lasting rewards. If the experience is positive, some will stay on as volunteers until they find employment.

Approximately five years ago, the Roaring Spring Community Library began accepting interns. We looked at them as a way to supplement our staff and make our library more efficient. Our first interns were elementary education students, a perfect fit working with story hour, summer reading, and outreach. They also assisted patrons and performed minor clerical duties. After our library went through a strategic planning process, we quickly realized the potential existed to seek interns to work in various capacities in the library. At this time we did not have a defined internship program. We accepted anyone who was willing to work at the library. As we became savvier about seeking out interns, our program became more professional. Today we have the Intern@Your Library program. Our library has developed internship opportunity descriptions for marketing, outreach services, administrative professional, and youth services. To attract potential interns, we notify the intern coordinators at local and nearby vocational and technical schools, colleges and universities, and business schools about our program. Although there may not be universities close at hand for a rural library, students home on break may be looking for an internship site. In an effort to make the process as easy as possible, information on all of our internship opportunities, as well as guidelines and an application, are available on our website.

The library is fortunate to have had some wonderful interns pass through its doors. An administrative assistant intern developed a grant-tracking spreadsheet that keeps a running total of each grant and separates our purchases according to numbers required for reporting purposes. Our signature fund-raising event is a silent auction. This same intern was able to develop a spreadsheet for tracking all donated items and created a booklet template and bid sheets by using various merges. The same spreadsheets were used to track donors and send thank-you cards. The year before we had the intern, two library employees had to key in every booklet entry, prepare each bid sheet separately, and address all thank-you notes by hand. Because our intern was so proficient in using spreadsheets and merges, she was also able to develop a tracking program for our memorial program. Previously we had logged memorials in a book, typed bookplates, and handwritten acknowledgment cards. Today, all the information is placed in a spreadsheet, and, by using different merges, labels are generated and acknowledgment cards are printed and ready for mailing. The same intern developed templates for annual appeals letters and tax receipts, as well as spreadsheets for tracking donations over several years. The investment of time in a six-week internship was well worth it for the library; we continue to use the databases she developed for us.

Our library has also had the following services performed by interns:

- An early childhood education student assisted with youth services, preparing crafts and activities.
- Education students planned and delivered story times based on educational learning standards.
- Marketing interns developed marketing plans, wrote press releases, and prepared media kits.
- Administrative assistant students performed clerical tasks.

Consider these other possible intern placements as well:

- Interior designers can draw floor plans or design and change library spaces.

- Web designers can maintain the website, upgrade its look, or become webmasters.
- Those with expertise in Microsoft Office can create databases for annual appeals.
- Graphic design interns can design logos, templates for flyers, and newsletters.
- Horticulture interns can landscape and care for library grounds.
- Carpentry students can build furniture or do repairs.
- Warehouse and distribution interns can perform inventory of collection or supplies.
- Culinary students can plan menus for events, prepare food, and be servers.

Successful internship programs bring numerous advantages to the library. Interns can lay the groundwork for new programs, nurture partnerships and business relationships, and best of all, make your library efficient. You will be surprised just how useful the addition of an intern with fresh ideas, innovative thinking, and proficient skills can be to your rural public library.

WORKING BOARDS

In a small, rural library, board members can provide a support system for the librarian. They can play an active role in the library while allowing the librarian to manage its day-to-day operations. Move board members to a working team by asking them to assist with the following tasks:

- Write thank-you notes for donations
- Attend community meetings as a library representative
- Process fund drive donation responses and tax receipts
- Contact donors and follow up with a personal thank-you when donations are received
- Organize a fund-raiser to benefit the library
- Oversee a program or series of programs in the library
- Serve as a greeter and host for library events

Having board members engaged in the library creates a sense of ownership in the organization. Delegating tasks to board members allows them to feel a sense of accountability for the library's success. When ownership in the library is created through continued contributions, board members are more inspired by the mission of the organization.

To keep board members invested in the library, it is important to properly prepare for a board meeting. Make sure all of the information you need the board to review is provided at least two weeks in advance. If possible, all information should be in one e-mail in PDF format to eliminate the need to resend files. Providing information to the board in a timely manner will prevent rush visits and last-minute phone calls to board members to have items signed and approved.

The board meeting e-mail should contain the following:

- Minutes from the last meeting
- Policy drafts that need approval
- Documents requiring signatures
- A calendar of events
- The current agenda
- A calendar of fiscal responsibility
- The corresponding secretary's report

At the beginning of each year, provide board members with a calendar of important events. Having this information will give them time to plan how and when they wish to volunteer. Try to plan recurring events at the same time each year so that board members become accustomed to when their assistance is needed.

A library calendar of events eliminates the need to call board members at the last minute to attend an event or ask for help. Consider asking your board members to represent the library at meetings. This eliminates the need for the librarian to always attend various community meetings. The calendar should cover the following:

- Programming at the library
- Friends of the Library meetings
- Board of trustee meetings
- School board meetings
- Borough, township, or city council meetings
- Community events at which the library has a presence

FINAL THOUGHTS

Do you ever feel you could use a few extra hands around your library? Volunteers are the answer. For years librarians have been relying on volunteers in times of lean budgets and staff cutbacks. Whether they are individuals with free time or professionals wanting to impact an organization, volunteers invest their time in the library because they want to help.

Board members can be volunteers, too. Playing an active role in the library makes them realize the amount of time and work the librarian devotes to the organization. Board members who are involved and enthusiastic about the library are eager to invest their time in making the organization successful.

Interns can breathe new life into the library organization. They are not only looking to fulfill a graduation requirement, but also eager to put into practice newly acquired skills. With budgets on a shoestring, rural librarians can put interns to work. You may even learn a thing or two that will save you time.

Volunteers provide a rural librarian with the support needed to accomplish any number of tasks. Volunteers, board members, and interns bring new skills, opportunities, and connections to your library. Balance work and fun with your pool of volunteers and recognize their efforts with a show of appreciation. Always remember, they are willing to assist with accomplishing goals because they believe in the library and want to see it grow. So rural librarians, stop feeling overwhelmed and start farming out your work.

II

Working with Staff

SEVEN

Circulation Staffing

Kimberly Wells

As circulation staffing stays the same while the number of customers served and materials circulated at libraries continue to rise, efficiently scheduling the staff to meet the library's needs is one of the most challenging functions of management. To provide these services, managers need to reevaluate procedures and schedules, as well as possibly redistribute staff and use temporary workers or volunteers.

The circulation staff are a highly skilled workforce. They are knowledgeable about a large number of policies and procedures, know many of the tricks of a complicated ILS system, run lists for a variety of materials (holds, claims returns, missing items), and, most important, are the face of the library. As the first and last person the customer encounters in the branch, the staff member's customer service skills and ability to solve circulation issues directly influence the customer's perception of the library. Consequently, these staff members need to be at the front, working with customers. The changes discussed in this chapter will help to optimize staff time spent working directly with customers so that they can best create a positive customer experience.

Change is not easy for staff to embrace. Any change may be seen as a threat. A supervisor may encounter the "this is the way we have always done things" attitude. It is important to explain why a change is being made and how it will benefit the circulation staff and the entire library. It is also important to announce a time limit on when you will seek feedback on reevaluating a new procedure. The staff might be quick to tell you that a change is not working, but if they are informed that you will ask for feedback in three weeks, you should not be bombarded with negativity on the first days of the new procedure. This will also give the staff time to get used to the change so they can provide well-thought-out responses.

There are five major areas to reevaluate in order to maximize the potential of a limited circulation staff:

- Scheduling
- Procedures
- Staffing—temporary workers
- Equipment
- Self-check technology and RFID

SCHEDULING

The weekly staffing schedule is rarely revised by library management. Many staff members may have been working the same schedule for years without change. Discussion of schedule changes can cause a high amount of stress among the staff. Communication is the key, letting everyone know why the changes are being made and asking for input about what is not working. Although this can be a highly charged issue, it is important to remind the staff that the mission of the library, providing the public with access to information, is the primary goal of the schedule.

A supervisor should go through the daily schedule hour by hour with fresh eyes. How many people are coming in early to open the library? If there are two people, ask yourself if it could be done by one. Because staff members who come in early usually leave before closing, reducing early-arriving staff could give you another person at closing. Are there two people coming in, just in case someone gets sick? A new procedure can be established so a backup can be contacted in case of an unexpected absence.

Many libraries also use traditional lunch times of 12:00 or 1:00 PM. Staff may not realize that they can have the option of going earlier or later. Some may prefer an 11:00 AM or 2:00 PM lunchtime, and that would keep the desk from being tightly scheduled when the public is rushing in for materials during their lunchtime.

It is important that you look at the branch statistics, determine when the busiest times are during the day, and black out these times for breaks. You should have an all-hands-on-deck approach during these busy times so that full coverage is available. Scheduled breaks are useful in that they let the supervisor know where everyone is at all times.

You should also look critically at the weekly schedule. Untraditional schedules are becoming more and more common. You may find that some staff members prefer to work at night, whereas others would prefer to work every weekend in order to have days off during the week. Conversations with the staff about their schedule preferences may open your eyes to possibilities in arranging the weekly schedule that had not been considered before. A half-staffed Monday might gain another employee because someone prefers to take Thursdays off instead.

PROCEDURES

The procedures manual at many libraries has grown to cover every possible problem that might be encountered. In many cases the manual may also include steps that were relevant when they were written, but now just slow everything down. Many of these problem procedures are well known to the circulation staff, but they may not realize that something can be done to change them.

Ask the staff to list all library procedures and then review the procedures that they believe are redundant, unnecessary, and/or time consuming.

Redundant procedures are usually the easiest to remove, but sometimes the hardest to discover. At a staff meeting, ask how various processes are handled. For example, have them chart out exactly what is done to the materials. You may find that materials are taken off a cart by one staff member and put on circulation shelving. Another staff member then takes them off that shelving and puts them on a cart to go to the fiction shelves. The important question to ask is "Why?" Why are these items being touched by so many staff members before they go out on the shelf? Was this procedure set up years ago when there was a shortage of carts? Is that still an issue? You may find out that time can be saved by changing the configuration of the circulation room.

Unnecessary procedures may take some evaluation. The library would not have created a procedure for no reason. However, that reason may be long gone or forgotten. Ask the staff to note what procedures they view as "unnecessary" so you can eliminate them or reinforce the requirement. For example, statistical information is sometimes gathered by the circulation staff that is no longer used by management. A staff member may be meticulously organizing paperwork that will never be looked at again because there are now electronic copies stored on the library computers. Evaluating the document retention policies of the library can not only free up staff time, but also open up much-needed storage space. There may be some seemingly "unnecessary" tasks that are very important: they may be done for compliance issues or to meet requirements for a grant. It is necessary to share this information with the staff so that they understand why something is being done.

Time-consuming procedures may need to be evaluated based on their overall benefit. There may be a high-priority requirement that all items on a library cart be double checked to ensure accuracy. However, if when checking in items on these carts a second time you discover that there are very few missed items, the question becomes: "Is that small level of error worth the extra ten minutes per cart to double check them?" Checking three carts could add an extra thirty minutes to the time before those items get on the shelf and before that skilled employee can be made available to help a customer.

A time-consuming library procedure might also be carts being organized before they go out to the floor in order to make it easier to shelve. If you ask the staff how long it takes to organize the carts before they go out on the floor, you might discover that several hours that could be spent shelving are being wasted on what was thought to be a time-saving task.

When you sit down to evaluate your procedures, you will want to choose those that occupy most of the circulation staff's time:

- Library card signups
- Pulling and shelving holds
- Checking in materials
- Missing/mismatched pieces
- Opening/closing the library
- Register and refund procedures

STAFFING

Many libraries have accepted the fact that because of the economic climate, adding new full-time employees to their staff will not happen in the near future. However, the number of customers using libraries and the amount of material being checked in and out will not be reduced, but will actually increase. The question is: "Where can libraries find the manpower for these increased tasks?" There are a number of options:

- Seasonal employees
- Community service volunteers
- University practicum students/interns

Although it might be impossible to ask for the funds to add a full-time staff person, a seasonal employee is a much cheaper option. Seasonal employees can be used during the busiest part of the year, such as summer, to deal with the large amount of shelving that suddenly overwhelms the circulation department. They can be hired at a much lower wage and do not usually have benefits packages. Since their employment has an ending date, it is very easy to calculate the cost to your system. All this makes them much more attractive when proposing hiring them to management. Many city parks and recreation departments hire seasonal employees. If you are looking to do this for the first time, that department may be a good resource for information about the process. These employees also provide an excellent selection pool for when you can hire full- or part-time staff, because you have been able to observe them closely for an entire season.

Community service volunteers are another good source of staffing. Often courts have ordered individuals to serve a specified number of community service hours. This community service requirement can provide you with workers who are motivated to work for a number of hours to complete their service. You may be concerned about using workers sentenced to community service hours, but you can establish a policy that the library will not take offenders who have committed offenses involving violence, theft, or crimes against children. Many citizens who have been given community service sentences have committed minor offenses such as traffic violations, misuse of alcohol, or even such things as hunting without a license. Although they have broken the law, they do not pose a threat to your staff or customers. These volunteers can be utilized for shelving, shelf checking, or setting up or breaking down meeting rooms. You would need to have specific guidelines for these workers and a contact on staff to deal with the paperwork that has to be filled out when working with community service volunteers. These volunteers may be directed to the library by a number of different courts. You can contact the local municipal court, the county courts, or the local juvenile court and ask that they direct community service volunteers to the library. One thing to keep in mind when using these volunteers is that, unlike traditional volunteers, who are doing the library a service by spending time at the library, the library is doing them a service by allowing them to work off their hours. The library is a much more pleasant environment in which to work than picking up trash or cleaning up at animal control. It is important that you set a minimum number of assigned community service hours, for example, forty, before you accept these volunteers. Training them will take up your staff's time, and that investment is not worthwhile for someone who only has to complete ten hours. It is important to maximize your resources. Also, unlike traditional volunteers, whom you have an incentive to keep as volunteers and should work with to see what job fits their skills, if community service volunteers are unable or unwilling to do the jobs assigned, they can immediately be let go. They were brought in to free up staff from shelving, but if the staff have to spend their time constantly correcting mistakes, then the community service volunteers should be told they would be a better fit elsewhere.

Many library school students are required to do a practicum or internship as a requirement for graduation. They may spend a couple of hundred hours at the library learning the day-to-day operations. They usually approach the reference department of a local library to see if they can be assigned a supervisor. The practicum may involve receiving training at the reference desk or working on special projects for the librarian. These students are usually very enthusiastic and willing to learn as much as possible about the library system. You may approach management and ask that they make part of the practicum duties spending a certain number of hours in circulation. These students should be able to work on more than just shelving. They can learn about book repair, pulling holds, missing/mismatched items, and a variety of other hands-on tasks that will benefit the circulation department. The student will also gain the advantage of understanding how circulation is handled and that it is not a simple system of just checking books in and out. This may also benefit you in the hiring process, as many college students are looking for part-time jobs while they are in school, and a library would be the best location for them. Evaluating their work ethic and performance while they are working as interns may help you decide whether you would want to hire them in the future.

EQUIPMENT

It is important to look at the equipment that your staff is using in its day-to-day operations and evaluate whether it is causing a slowdown at the circulation desk. Many libraries are using state-of-the-art ILS systems but at the same time a register that is over ten years old. You may need to look at what transactions are done on the register and whether it needs to be reprogrammed or upgraded. Some older registers will not void or override a mistake, so the staff member has to fill out paperwork to document every error. This is a waste of time if a newer version of the register would simply erase the mistake.

Printer costs have come down in the last few years, especially for label makers. If you are still using handwritten labels for holds or pulling them individually from a sheet, you should look at the new equipment to see if it will fit your budget. Technology moves so quickly that it causes prices to fluctuate. Equipment that may have been too expensive one year may be affordable within a couple of more years. Keep a list of items that you want to upgrade for the sake of streamlining staff processes and check on the prices for these items on a regular basis. This can be useful if you have extra money at the end of the year or get an offer from a Friends of the Library organization to purchase materials for you, or you can offer something from your list as a cheaper alternative if you are turned down for new staff by administration.

Equipment to Evaluate

- Registers
- Label printers for holds
- Scanners
- Demagnetizer for materials
- Paper cutter
- Self-check technology and RFID

The trend in libraries for years has been toward RFID and self-check technology. Many circulation staff members, perceiving this as a move toward replace them, have been concerned about their future. This technology should be thought of as a system to assist the staff instead of replacing them. The circulation department is the face of the library. They are assisting customers who need help, those who are filling out library card applications and others who have concerns about their accounts or questions about policies. These trained staff members do not need to be spending hours checking in mountains of books that have been returned if there is a technological solution. In these years of staff cuts and freezes, you need to take advantage of any opportunity that will free up time to help your customers. If your circulation and door counts have been growing and your staff shrinking, think of this technology as filling in the gaps instead of replacing the vital members of your team.

Bringing in an RFID system will not replace all of your procedures; it will just change them. Once the equipment has been installed and you have been trained in its functions, you will then need to develop a new set of procedures. You may need to map out exactly how material will travel through the circulation department and determine what changes need to be made. Staff who usually check in may be free to back up the circulation desk, run hold lists, or shelve more often. The new procedure may even require a change in the physical setup of the circulation workroom.

It is important not to create redundancies when working with this equipment. Some believe that because the machine might not catch every item that is checked in, the staff should recheck the items. If you do this you might as well not have the technology. It would not make sense to spend that amount of money on equipment and then keep doing the same thing, saving no staff time in the process. Troubleshoot to find out the best way to avoid problems; talk to the vendor and other libraries in the area to see how they are using their staff.

Self-check machines are popular with customers who are very busy. They grab their materials and just want to check out as soon as possible. When these machines are not available, they may end up standing in line behind a customer getting a library card or dealing with a complicated fine issue. This may give them a negative experience and lead them to believe that you have not staffed your desk adequately. Self-check devices have become popular at grocery stores, and many customers are comfortable with them. Many do not see them as a negative but rather as a convenience when they are in a hurry. If they want one-on-one contact, that option would still be available.

To best assist your customers and staff, the self-check machine should be close to the circulation desk, preferably in an area where the circulation or reference staff can assist customers if they have any problems using it. It will not be a time saver if someone constantly has to walk across the library to show customers how to use it. The machines should also be located close to the area where your holds are kept. Customers who put items on hold are usually among the most technology savvy and willing to use the technology when it is available. They will also view the speed of checkout as a positive experience. Many of the self-check machines now available will unlock DVD and CD cases; others will allow customers to pay fines and renew materials.

CONCLUSION

It can be frustrating dealing with a shrinking circulation department when the amount of materials pouring in keeps increasing, but this challenge can be met by communicating with your staff. Do not become locked into dealing with these new circumstances by trying to make things work the way they have always been done. Look at schedules and procedure with new eyes, look for temporary workers in new places, and embrace upgraded equipment and technology and make it work for you. Learning a new way to deal with these challenges will prepare you for the next big change, which is always right around the corner.

EIGHT

Going, Going, Gone: Management Strategies for Time and Staff When There Is Little of Either

Amber Lannon and Sara Holder

Many librarians in management positions are also serving other roles in the organization (often as department liaisons, as reference librarians, or in collection development). They are managing diverse staff groups such as a mix of librarians (tenure track and contract) and library assistants (often unionized), as well as students and volunteers. This chapter provides practical advice on how to organize daily operations, including the following:

- Organizing professionals in addition to paraprofessionals
- Long-term scheduling of shifts and vacations
- Creating in-house training and cross-training programs
- Prioritizing in extreme situations
- Balancing work and managerial responsibilities

Effective management is difficult work in the best of times. In the real world of doing more with less, it can seem impossible. The strategies outlined in this chapter will help you develop systems to streamline regular tasks and effectively deal with unplanned-for situations. In turn, this will free up more of your time and alleviate some of the stress that accompanies managerial duties.

ONE-AND-DONE SCHEDULING

Putting together the work schedule for your unit is probably not your favorite managerial duty. It is, however, a necessary and important one. Scheduling can be complicated by many factors, such as the following:

- Number of staff in the unit
- Variations in skill level, status, and seniority among staff members
- Rules and regulations related to union contracts and labor laws
- Nonstandard practices and special privileges applied by previous managers

If you have taken a job in a region or an institution that is new to you, take the time to carefully review employment rules and regulations that apply to your staff. Meet with your human resources representative to ensure that you fully understand how these will affect scheduling before you begin the process. It is likely that you are managing both professional and paraprofessional staff, perhaps multiple groups in each category. Typically, because of either position obligations or employment regulations (or both), scheduling practices will be different for these groups.

Librarians in your institution may be part of a union, may be tenure track or have faculty status, and may not have set working hours. In many units, both librarians and paraprofessional staff have multiple responsibilities (e.g., service desk hours, materials processing, teaching, shelving, research, committee work, etc.). All of these variables can affect scheduling, so it is best to have a clear picture of the position responsibilities and status of all members of your staff before you begin. Staff will also have commitments outside of work that you may be asked to factor into the schedule. Maintaining a good relationship with your staff is important; however, the functionality of the unit is your first priority.

If you manage a unit in the public services area, it will be important to ensure that librarians with flexible schedules are aware of the hours during which they are expected to cover the reference desk. Paraprofessionals are often part of a union and generally have set working hours, though these may vary to some extent (nine to five, eight to four, ten to six, etc.). The need for a strictly defined schedule for service desk coverage (for both professional and paraprofessional staff) will depend on the size and collegiality of the unit. More staff will necessitate the creation of a more complex schedule. If your unit is small, your staff may prefer to work out the shifts among themselves on a day-to-day basis. In this case you will want to monitor the situation to ensure there are no gaps in coverage and that the work is being shared equally.

Scheduling isn't fun. The best approach is to do it as little as possible. Many managers get into the habit of making a monthly or even a weekly schedule, but there is usually no reason for this other than precedent. Most organizations require that all staff submit vacation requests well in advance, often for the entire upcoming year. Take advantage of this and create a schedule that stretches as far out as possible. Instead of collecting your staff members' existing commitments for the upcoming week or month, assign regular, recurring weekly shifts with exceptions for vacations. Consider entering the schedule into a calendar program such as Outlook (if you have access to Microsoft Office) or Google Calendar. This will make it easy for staff to view and easy for you to input the recurring shifts. With a predictable schedule that is planned out for six or twelve months, it will be easier for everyone to see where other work and commitments can fit in.

As in many other managerial duties, fairness and collegiality are paramount. If there are particular shifts that are universally preferred or disliked, you will have to schedule staff in rotation to ensure equality. If it doesn't already exist, try to foster a culture of collegial shift trading so that staff members do not feel constrained by the schedule. This may be difficult at times, but it is important that professional and paraprofessional staff feel they are contributing equally. If either group feels that the other is receiving preferential treatment in scheduling, that will negatively affect the team atmosphere. If you think that this may be a problem in your unit, it may help to add the librarians' schedules into the calendar even if they function fairly autonomously.

TRAINING IN NO TIME

With ongoing rapid changes in the delivery of services in libraries, continued learning through staff development is essential to improving staff competencies and ensuring good service for our clients. The challenge for many library organizations is offering training opportunities when time is a limited resource for both managers and staff.

In addition to limited or nonexistent resources for training, you may also be dealing with staff who have had insufficient training for a number of years, feel stuck in the organization, or lack motivation. Your staff may also have a broad range of skills and abilities, making it difficult to develop a program that works for everyone.

For a manager charged with training staff for new job duties under these conditions, the first step will be to identify learning outcomes for the training program. A learning outcome is the particular skill or behavior that you expect your staff to exhibit after they have completed the program (see textbox 8.1 for an example). Learning outcomes define both the type and depth of learning that will result from the program. By basing your sessions around learning outcomes, you will be able to more effectively develop a session. Learning outcomes will also allow you to evaluate your program and then make appropriate adjustments for the next session, or to add to the program as you go.

* * *

Textbox 8.1. Learning Outcomes for a Twenty-minute Session on Basic Circulation

- Can address complex check in and check out problems and trouble-shoot to find solutions.
- Is able to edit date due and use judgment in editing due times.
- Understands and is able to explain all circulation policies.
- Identifies problems and makes appropriate referrals for complex problems.

Once you have the learning outcomes for your program, you can begin to develop your content. Because people's attention naturally decreases in the middle of a session, it works best to group your content into sections. This builds in a lot of beginnings and endings to hold your audience's attention. Punctuate each section with an active learning strategy, either an activity or a group discussion. This will help reinforce what the participants are learning and encourage them to ask questions.

If you are developing a program made up of a series of sessions, it works best to follow the same basic outline in each session. Participants will become used to the structure, and it will provide some continuity to your program. Table 8.1 shows an outline that can be used for a one-hour session.

Although your sessions may be short, you will still need to build in assessment. This will allow you to adjust your program and add to future sessions as necessary. Table 8.2 shows some simple but effective evaluation strategies appropriate for short training sessions.

To effectively kick off a new training program for paraprofessional staff, it is important to start with the overall vision. In any kind of train-

Table 8.1. Sample Outline for a Brief Training Session

Step 1	5 minutes	Brief activity, not related to the subject matter, that will energize participants. Also known as an "icebreaker." Example: participants describe their dream vacation.
Step 2	3 minutes	Learning objectives.
Step 3	2 minutes	Agenda.
Step 4	40 minutes	Deliver the content of the session, grouping the material into three sections. After each section, include a group discussion or exercise.
Step 5	5 minutes	Brief conclusion.
Step 6	5 minutes	Simple evaluation.

Table 8.2.   Evaluation Strategies

Muddiest point	Ask participants to write down the answer to the question: "What was the 'muddiest' point in the session?" (That is, what aspect or concept was the most confusing or hardest to grasp?)
One-minute paper	Give participants three minutes to answer: "What was the most important point made in class today?" and "What unanswered question do you still have?"
Stop-start-continue	Ask participants to write down something we should STOP doing, something we should START doing, and something we should CONTINUE doing in the session.
Multiple choice	Write four to five multiple choice questions to test learning outcomes.
Closing summary	Ask participants to write a two-sentence closing summary for the session.

ing that is necessitated by new job duties, the participants must have a vision for the future in order to be engaged. Librarians often take part in developing library strategy; however, paraprofessional staff are not always included in or even aware of these developments. You may either include this explanation in the first session of your program or hold an information session at which you introduce the vision and the training program.

If you are developing training for new job duties and the staff are unionized, there are a few things to consider first. You will need to consult with your human resources advisor to ensure that the new job duties fit within the current position descriptions. It may also be advisable to brief union leadership about your plans. In your sessions, it is helpful to tie the training back to the job descriptions. This will ensure staff are aware that what they are training for is in their job descriptions. In any kind of training for new job duties, communicate performance expectations as you go along and assure employees that making mistakes is part of the learning process.

For units that are time starved and that support public service desks, schedule short but frequent sessions. It will be easier to develop the content and liberate the attendees from your public service desks. Furthermore, this method makes it easier to reschedule or repeat an individual session if a staff member is absent, rather than having to rerun the entire program.

If you are having difficulty fitting in training opportunities for your staff, try the following strategies:

- Distribute the teaching time throughout your organization by having a mentoring program. Pair employees with someone who has experience with the job duties that you are training for. Mentors and mentees can meet after each of the brief training sessions to give the latter an opportunity to learn more on the topic. Mentees should be responsible for arranging the session and for bringing questions to the meeting.

- As you would for a regular staff meeting, build training time into your schedule and calendar as a regular appointment. Book the space you will need for months at a time.
- Add a ten-minute training portion to every staff meeting or send a weekly training e-mail with an exercise for staff to complete.

Cross training is also essential for libraries with limited staff resources, yet it is often overlooked. It is also a proven method for improving client service, because staff members become more broadly knowledgeable in all aspects of library services. To kick off a cross-training initiative, have staff create manuals for their jobs. The manual should include personal practices as well as passwords and contact information. (This can be a lifesaver in the event of a staff member's sudden, extended absence.) Then have employees shadow one another; shadowing is learning what a staff member does by working side by side with that person during a normal day. Training sessions in a classroom can also be added to your program.

Professional staff may be more accustomed to ongoing development. An approach that might work with this group when time is an issue is a Web conference or webinar. Most vendors and database providers offer these at no cost and will arrange them to fit your schedule. There are also many low-cost options available through the various library associations. Another strategy is to ask one of your professional staff to develop a training program and deliver it to colleagues. This provides a dual benefit, in that participants will be learning new skills and the staff member facilitating the program will also be gaining valuable experience.

HERE TODAY, GONE TOMORROW

Operating a library for a few days during a staff shortage due to illness or vacation is challenging. When the shortage must be endured for a longer period and the loss of staff is extreme—because of a strike or hiring freeze, or as a result of a retirement incentive program—the challenge can seem insurmountable.

In both situations, temporary employees, like students, can be a big help; however, most library organizations will not be able to deal with an extreme staff shortage with student and temporary help alone. In unionized environments, you may be limited to allocating a very small number of hours to temporary employees. Student workers are also limited by class schedules and are not always reliable. In a strike situation, they may feel uncomfortable crossing picket lines.

Thus, during an extreme staff shortage, most library organizations will not be able to do everything that is done under normal circumstances. In this situation, the organization needs to focus on core services: access to the library, shelving, the provision of information services, maintaining the library website, processing new materials, and interlibrary loans. Projects, cataloging of more specialized materials, digitization, and renovations must wait until the staffing crisis is over. Generally any task related to public services is a priority, and anything that is considered back office, such as internal processes and functions, is potentially something that can be put on hold.

In the case of a shortage due to a strike, use staff from other units to assist with core tasks. Where possible, be flexible about when they perform these tasks. Using a wiki to allow them to volunteer for these duties helps to build cooperation and community. Furthermore, scheduling in an extreme staff shortage is a critical duty and will often involve several units, if not the entire library staff. For these reasons, it is a task best coordinated by a senior manager.

Consider reducing your service hours while maintaining access to the library. If the building is open, clients can continue to use the space, log on to computers, return materials, and access the collection. If your budget allows, this can even be done strictly with security personnel. To ensure that this goes smoothly, develop a manual for the security guards or provide some training. You may want to consider restricting these hours to your core clientele by having security guards check and log identification.

During times of uncertainty, such as those brought on by extreme staff shortages, it will be important to expedite decision making. Senior management should meet daily to deal with problems as they arise. Having one person who is responsible for receiving information about operational issues and for communicating the decisions that arise from the daily meetings will prevent unnecessary delays. A dedicated blog for this purpose can be a useful tool for communicating and keeping track of this information.

Although it can be tempting to suspend regular meetings, they should be scheduled more frequently if at all possible. It is important to meet with remaining staff to develop procedures, answer questions, and address concerns. At a minimum, this should happen weekly, with daily updates posted on the blog. Communicating with frontline staff must be made a priority so that they can accurately communicate with your clients. In addition, your library website may need to be updated on a daily basis. Use any and all outreach tactics you have in your arsenal, including social media.

On the surface, an extreme staff shortage would not seem like the best circumstance in which to change workflows. But it can be the perfect time to take a hard look at existing procedures. When one person is doing the work of five, unnecessary steps and inefficiencies become obvious. This will not only alleviate problems in the short term, it will also ensure that the workflow is improved moving forward. Track all changes so that any returning staff can be quickly trained or you can train any new staff who join your organization.

To ensure that your library will not be caught off guard should an extreme staff shortage occur, implement a cross-training program immediately. If a key responsibility is held by only one individual, this is a red flag, and more cross training is needed. Improve documentation on processes—creating this documentation should be added to the goals of all employees and stored centrally. To create a better, more concrete understanding for you and your staff of what all staff do in their day-to-day functions, consider a shadowing program.

You should also consider how you would deal with managing an emergency during an extreme staffing shortage. In this situation, you will not have enough staff to follow normal protocol for dealing with the event as it arises. Create a kit with preprinted signs (e.g., "The library is temporarily closed") and caution tape, as well as general emergency supplies (flashlights, gloves, garbage bags, key phone numbers, etc.).

When the staff do return to work, the impact of the shortage is not immediately relieved. The reintegration of returning staff or integration of new staff will not be automatic. It is important to plan and make time for this. If, as in the case of a strike, staff return to work all at once, the chief librarians should meet with all staff, welcome them back, and provide an outline of changes in broad strokes. During the reintegration period, continue the heightened communications and regular meetings.

Before, during, and after this kind of crisis, the most important issue will be access to timely and accurate information. Maintaining consistent and open communication with employees and clients will avoid further complicating these difficult situations.

WEARING OTHER HATS

The position of manager brings with it the weighty responsibility of keeping your unit running smoothly, ensuring your staff are working to the best of their ability, and providing the best possible service for your clients. With this kind of mandate, it is often difficult to feel that you have done enough or that the work is ever finished. The truth is that your management tasks will expand to fill your workday as much as you let them. So how do you find time to devote to your other responsibilities? While you are working on becoming a master scheduler for your unit, take some time to look at your own calendar. Are there particular times during the week when you could block off one or two hours? Make appointments with yourself—complete with reminders—and honor them the way you would any other appointment. This works best if you can make the times consistent week after week, but it is not absolutely necessary.

Establishing fixed hours during the week when you work on nonmanagement tasks and projects will be habit forming (a good thing in this case!). It will also make it more likely that your staff will get into the habit of leaving you alone during these times. If you find that you cannot work (at least relatively) undisturbed in your own office, it may be necessary to find an alternate location. Getting out of your office may also help your brain switch gears away from management tasks so that you can focus on your other work. You will likely find that consistently making time to work on other tasks will help to lower your stress level and allow you to focus more fully on your management responsibilities for the remainder of your workday.

EVERY LITTLE BIT HELPS

Managing staff and facilities is time-consuming work, even when the stars align and there are no bumps in the road. Business as usual is often a lot closer to chaos. Following the advice in this chapter will not double your staff or cut your workload in half, but it will help you to work more efficiently and do more with less.

NINE

Staff-Level Management of Library Reference Services: Not Just Personnel Economy, an Enhanced Service System

Threasa Wesley

Libraries have been experimenting with tiered reference assistance for decades. Even before this service strategy was widely accepted, reference staffing by nonlibrarians was the common economic solution to staffing extended library hours. Whether using support staff in reference for economy or to enhance the service being offered, librarians are typically placed at the top of the organizational hierarchy, responsible for both operational management of the service and responses to complex reference questions. This chapter describes an organizational redesign of the reference program at Northern Kentucky University's (NKU) Steely Library, which removed librarians from that managerial role. The implementation processes, cost efficiencies, and most important, service enhancements, resulting from reimagining reference service as a program managed by nonlibrarian staff are discussed.

This structural reorganization was an outgrowth of experiments with tiered service at Steely Library. We readily saw the service advantages to layered staffing, as it supported no-wait responses to straightforward directional and ready reference questions, as well as referral of complex questions to librarians. However, discussions soon arose regarding whether this dual-tiered staffing arrangement, alone, maximized the service we could provide. Were both types of service, informational/ready reference and complex research consultations, being equally supported?

Did either this tiered system or our previous system of daytime librarian service and evening staff-level support maximize the success of both assistance levels? If not, could we afford the personnel resources necessary for excellence in both services?

UNINTENDED PRIORITIES: RESEARCH ASSISTANCE OR SERVICE MANAGEMENT

The first experiments with tiered reference service at Steely Library illuminated some of the unplanned choices that had been made in our programming over the years. Despite their best intentions, librarians had not been able to effectively provide both assistance and management of the overall service in either multiple- or single-tier service arrangements. When librarians had staffed reference prior to the implementation of a tiered system, more attention was devoted to managing the reception of questions and simultaneously assisting multiple users. A librarian on reference duty was always aware of the volume of pending questions and the importance of being visible at the service desk (or in the online chat window). He or she was constantly using techniques to move from one questioner to another. The realization that responses to complex research questions were frequently compromised for these more immediate management duties led to our tiered service experiments. Of course, removing librarians from frontline service positions meant that less attention was given to management and oversight of the responses being offered by the rest of the reference team. While the increased focus on enhanced research consultation was a desired outcome, the impact of librarians "stepping back" from on-the-spot management was not fully expected.

As we moved further into our commitment to multitiered service, we began to appreciate that we had lost perhaps as much as we had gained in overall service quality. In our library, the first service tier is staffed by student employees. No matter how conscientious these assistants are, or how thorough the training that we provide is, they remain part-time staff with high turnover. Certainly students form a less expensive workforce, yet costs lie in the fact that they have limited opportunity to build relevant experience and understanding of the complex range of information and research options. This lack of experience with the variety and depth of research assistance that can be provided has meant that our student assistants regularly tried to "answer" all questions. They would competently use the known-item and directional reference tools from their training for the questions we expected them to answer. However, most would also respond to other questions with basic "quick-and-dirty" keyword searching of the Web and one or two databases. Sometimes the student assistant and questioner would uncover information useful for the topic requested. When their efforts to browse through a variety of search result sets failed to satisfy the questioner, our assistants at last referred the question to the librarian. By this point the questioner had experienced inefficient, meandering searches, and had perhaps developed a negative impression of the expertise available in the library. Moreover, the goal of having quick, responsive attention to new questioners by the first service tier was often lost as other questioners waited while student assistants were engaged in trying to answer complicated questions.

To understand the obvious breakdown in the referral process, we held problem-solving group discussions with librarians and student assistants. As students described their experiences in helping users, we began to understand that the summary training descriptions of advanced research strategies that librarians could help questioners use had not been sufficient to encourage referrals. Our assistants had not been able to form a concrete mental model of the different path research could take as librarians applied their expertise. They did not have enough experience with research to anticipate that differing levels of precision in search results could be attained with more sophisticated research tools and strategies. At the same time, our students had connected wholeheartedly with the goal of providing prompt service response; however, for them, it meant that the best answer to a question was an immediate one. They shared in planning discussions a strong negative view of the need to refer a question. (Indeed, they were also communicating that to questioners. They reported that their introduction of referral options often was, "I'm sorry, but you will have to wait for a librarian." We had hoped to hear, "The librarian will be able to find very useful material. Would you like to wait a few moments, or would you like the librarian to call you when he is available?") We were also concerned that our students viewed making referrals as a negative reflection of their skill sets. They did not appreciate the value of skills for a positive reception and management of questions. None of the librarians wished these coworkers to be in a position in which they felt unprofessional and ignorant. Serious consideration of the students' referral performance led to a recognition that although we were still committed to the service potential of tiered service, there was an element missing, hindering the success of the program at Steely Library.

AN ENHANCED TIERED REFERENCE PLAN

During our discussions reviewing the tiered service pilots at Steely Library, two baseline principles were identified:

1. The depth and effectiveness of research assistance that librarians provided in a referral tier were significantly enhanced over what was regularly available when librarians were on the front line

managing the intake of all questions. We did not wish to return to the system that provided our best research assistance only when the questioner had the serendipitous luck to present a question when few other library users were also requesting service.

2. Expert management of the initial reception of user questions, analysis of the level of assistance required, and positive communication regarding referral services were at least equally critical for successful reference service as was expert librarian assistance.

We tried making several "tweaks" to our tiered plan, including training a few students for advanced information assistance and referral service, employing graduate library science students to provide frontline management of questions, and double staffing librarians during busier hours. None of these tactics successfully addressed the joint goals of enhanced research assistance and consistent management of the overall service. Both groups of advanced student assistants still were part-time staff and not able to build the experience necessary to adequately manage the first tier. Moreover, the effort to repeat advanced student training each semester as the staff changed was costly in terms of librarians' time. Likewise, our experiment with adding second librarians to the schedule during limited hours of the day was an expensive, unsatisfactory solution. We still had many hours of operation with only one librarian, and some late night hours with no librarians on duty. We could not fund sufficient librarian positions to elevate this scheme to more than a "sometimes" solution to the need for overall management of reference service. Double staffing librarians also had the negative effect of redirecting librarians' time from other valuable programs in the library.

The use of library science graduate students, some of whom had already completed courses in reference assistance, did, however, illuminate the type of skills critical for on-the-spot management of reference services. An academic knowledge of core reference tools and strategies was a plus, but the indispensable skills were 1) a mature communication style and positive customer service experience and 2) a detailed awareness of our library's specific personnel and service options. That public service demeanor and library-specific knowledge are most successfully built on-the-job: attending staff meetings, interacting with fellow employees at various levels in the organization, hearing referrals provided by more experienced colleagues, being a part of building organizational goals for customer service, and so forth. Fortunately our library had staff members in the circulation department who were familiar with our library's organization in this way and possessed proven public service skills. That group of four staff members joined the two staff assistant positions in the reference department to form the new managerial group for library public services. (The combination of staffs was facilitated by physically combining the two departments' service stations. Basic circulation and reserve service was added to the responsibilities of the first-tier student assistants, whereas service oversight and referral processes for both reference and circulation were assigned to these staff members.) The circulation staff had already been scheduled to manage their students during all library hours. With the addition of the reference staff members, the group was now able to provide management of both public service programs.

HOW THE NEW TIERED SYSTEM WORKS

In our revised tiered service system, student assistants remain on the front line, receiving questions in person, via phone, electronic chat, text, and e-mail systems. A staff manager is present physically at the service desks and observes electronic communication channels. This manager helps guide the direction of questions, oversees the responses students are providing, and intercedes as needed to ensure library users are being served efficiently and effectively. Librarians are available in "office hours" during the busiest hours of reference assistance, taking on referred in-person and electronic questions. During other library hours, the student assistants and staff managers arrange for the next librarian on duty to contact users with pending questions and have scheduling rights to set up appointments with librarians for anyone wishing that more formal arrangement. Because library staff members now manage the tiered service, we find that we are getting questioners to the appropriate level of assistance more promptly and more frequently. Regular data collection of reference interactions has shown an uptick in the percentage of questions answered by both students and librarians that fit into the service definitions established for each group. In addition, the performance level of our student assistant staff has been raised due to staff training efforts that take advantage of teachable moments that occur within the framework of real reference questions.

As noted, we operate within guidelines that define the type of questions to be handled by the first tier (basically circulation processes, as well as information, directional, and known-item requests) and the type of questions to be referred to a librarian or a circulation staff member (those requiring investigation in more than one reference tool, in which more than one concept element is in the description of the topic, that require a search taking more than three minutes, fee appeals, etc.). On a day-to-day basis, these service boundaries are flexible, and assignment of questions can vary. The number of concurrent questions being asked, the number of available student assistants and their individual training status, the expectations and demeanor of the questioner, and so forth can all affect the referral decisions made by staff managers. On occasion, a librarian may be asked to help with a ready reference question or to help a user find a call number, if the specific situation calls for that deployment of personnel. These redirections of front-tier questions are not common, and the staff manager works quickly to accommodate the pending questions so librarians can again be available for research assistance. The key operational principle is that the nonlibrarian staff member is in charge and will make the assignment of questions. When staffing service hours, librarians are a resource for and will take direction from the public service manager.

BENEFITS OF A STAFF-MANAGED REFERENCE SERVICE

Steely Library has found staff-managed tiered public service to be

- cost effective,
- an overall enhanced professional public service with positive representation of referral options,
- a structure that maximizes library users' access to all services,
- a more effective training and development structure for the student assistant staff,
- a means to foster increased production of research guides, and
- support for other areas of expanded library service.

Several benefits resulting from the implementation of this modified tiered service program have been described previously in this chapter. Other service growth and cost efficiencies came to light as well. Although staffing tier one with student assistants alone may have seemed to be the least expensive means to achieve the goals of tiered service, we actually developed a less-costly program by adding a middle layer of staff-level management. The combination of the public service responsibilities in circulation and reference allowed us to add this middle tier without adding staff positions. In addition, we were able to reduce the size of the student staff by more than one-third in this departmental combination. With a manager guiding use of referrals and providing more effective training, the number of students needed to respond to both circulation requests and basic reference questions was smaller than the staff size needed for separate service points. Using the student staff economy, we later added a second service desk on a lower floor of the library and extended morning and evening library hours.

Other, more direct user benefits have resulted from this organizational change. As mentioned previously, users with informational or ready reference questions are more consistently receiving prompt assistance from tier one, and more questioners with advanced research needs are being referred to librarians directly, without a preliminary extended general searching process. In addition, the involvement of staff managers who have knowledge of the specialized collections and personnel in our library has meant that some users are receiving direction to library programs that they may not have been aware of, such as archives, the curriculum collection, and media services. Removing the distinction between circulation and reference service has been also been viewed as helpful by many users. This separation was frequently an artificial one, based on library operations rather than the natural connections within an information need. We are looking forward to establishing in the near future a more direct operational connection to other specialized service centers in our library, with tier one providing scheduling and contact referrals as it does for reference librarians.

Another benefit for library users made possible by a better managed reference service has been an increased production of research guides. With staff members managing the daily activities of the tiered system and taking on the training of student assistants, librarians have tackled more interactive tutorials and webographies for NKU assignments and research areas. These Web-published tools, of course, extend the availability of librarian-level expertise, as more users can access and apply the materials than in individual reference interactions. Moreover, our staff managers bring greater awareness of the content in these research guides to the initial reference interview than our student assistants did on their own. More questions are satisfied without referrals. In this programming area, public service staff members are sharing management roles as well. They identify specific guides needed and provide clear feedback on the effectiveness of the produced resources. This direction from staff becomes a core part of the librarians' "to do" list.

KEYS TO SUCCESSFUL IMPLEMENTATION

Several aspects of the organizational culture at Steely Library led to placing nonlibrarian staff members in a key management role and formed the foundation for the success of that program as well. Three of the chief factors were

- a system-wide commitment to assigning elements of authority to staff-level positions,
- an established investment in staff development and training, and
- a proactive public awareness campaign communicating the multiple service levels available in the library.

The willingness of Steely librarians and staff to question the traditional management system for reference service was a reflection of global changes ongoing in our library. In recent years, Steely Library has significantly expanded the sphere and depth of library programming at NKU. (Examples of growing programming are an extensive online embedded librarian service, a library science bachelor's degree program, an online professional development series, a request-driven collection development policy and all-inclusive document delivery service, a focus on e-resource collections, and a groundbreaking model for accessible library websites.) Underpinning several program expansions have been new expectations for staff involvement. As new roles have been assigned to Steely staff members, new opportunities for advanced training and financial rewards for staff members who take advantage of these options have been instituted. The budget for conference and workshop attendance by staff has been significantly increased. We also encourage library staff to complete either the American Library Association's staff certificate or a library science certificate offered by a community college in our state. Upon earning either certification, the staff member receives a significant salary increase and the opportunity to hold positions of greater responsibility.

Within the reference department, additional team-building efforts were necessary to support the new role our staff were assigned. Some staff members were hesitant to assign questions to librarians; some librarians expressed concerns about reference questions referred to them that turned out to be simple issues. We held joint and separate review sessions for each group, asked everyone to engage in role playing and visioning activities to emphasize the potential benefits of the new system, set up training sessions for new librarians by staff members, and so forth. All these efforts were focused on building an appreciation of the central role played by staff managers and the complex responsibilities they were carrying. The early discomfort with the nontraditional role reversal soon abated. Librarians began to recognize the clearer details that were being conveyed in referral call-back slips and observed the efficiency evident in the service of multiple questions during busy hours in the library. We have seen a growing sense of ownership and confidence on the part of our staff managers. When hiring new staff members, experience and qualities important in management activities are required. We are exploring additional management tasks that it would be logical for the staff to take on, such as the determination of the librarians' office hours schedule.

While building an internal commitment to this managerial role for staff, we have also made concentrated efforts to raise public awareness of the multiple tiers of service available in Steely. It is a much more positive and productive referral interaction for our staff and students if questioners have a prior awareness of the varying expertise available in the library. Our webpage has live links indicating services currently available as well as upcoming schedules for services unavailable at that hour. During instructional sessions, librarians describe how the public service staff connect researchers to the needed library expertise. The head of the reference department and library director have discussed the new service tiers at university faculty meetings, explaining how this system facilitates advanced research consultation. Availability of referral librarians is noted on whiteboard signs at the public service desks and on menu banners in the electronic communication channels used for reference. These visual schedules have lent credence to our staff's offers of advanced assistance through referrals.

CONCLUSION

The establishment of a public service program with nonlibrarian staff managing the daily operations has proven successful at NKU's Steely Library. It is a cost-effective system that has supported both expansion of service options and more seamless access to available library expertise for our library's users. Economic resources have been maximized, as this system uses relatively low-cost student assistant staffing to provide information and ready reference responses throughout library hours. The effectiveness of these staff members is significantly augmented with on-the-spot supervision by professional library staff members. These managers, with mature public service skills and full knowledge of the service options in our library, are making sure that each questioner is connected to the appropriate library service. Finally, this system allows our most expensive staff, librarians, to be focused on assignments that require their unique skills: advanced research assistance, information literacy instruction in a variety of settings, and the development of research guidance tools for a wide range of library users. By assigning operational management of public services to professional staff members, both the first tier and the referral tier of our reference program are functioning more effectively, with enhanced guidance available to all library users.

III

Students, Volunteers, and Interns

TEN

Interns and Volunteers: Finding and Deploying Free Labor

Portia Kapraun and Beth M. Sheppard

Interns and other volunteers give freely of their time and are one way to fill the gap between available staff and an explosion of new library projects and services in the digital era that require librarians' attention.

Building a vibrant internship and volunteer program requires investments in infrastructure planning, time, skill, and perhaps even a small budget. In essence, no volunteer program is without costs. The rewards, though, are tremendous. Fortunately, one need not reinvent the wheel. The key strategies—nailing down logistics before beginning to host interns and volunteers, locating and recruiting this free labor force, providing training and supervision, and recording and recognizing their accomplishments—are each covered in turn.

NAILING DOWN LOGISTICS

When building a volunteer program from scratch or taking on the library's first intern, the first task is deciding what a volunteer program should accomplish and how it will complement the existing workflow of the library. An effective program creates a "match" between the library's ethos and its volunteers or interns in terms of the volunteers' availability, commitment to the library's mission, and dependability. Spelling out expectations in a "volunteer handbook" helps make certain that both volunteers and library staff are on the same page. It is important to clearly establish the following features.

Time Commitment

Interns enrolled in courses often have to fulfill requirements set by their academic institutions. For example, they may be obliged to complete eighty hours during a ten-week semester. The library must be willing to work with and accommodate the specific requirements of the educational program of the student. Other types of volunteers, however, may have widely divergent schedules and availability. It is important to be able to track when volunteers are coming and going, so projects may be assigned and completed according to library schedules and strategic plans. Mechanisms for managing volunteer schedules involve the following:

- Asking volunteers to sign time "pledge cards" and commit for a certain number of hours per week or a specific span of time.
- Setting minimum blocks of time for a volunteer shift to allow for project setup, a period of work, and cleanup.
- Using "active" and "inactive" library volunteer status designations to permit volunteer workers to temporarily suspend commitments without the need to sever the relationship with the library.

Prescribed Workplace Behaviors

Each institution has policies governing drug use, smoking, regular hours of operation, breaks, dress codes, and other stated and unstated rules for professional conduct. Many of these may be the same for volunteers and regular employees, but there may also be differences. Some libraries, for example, may require volunteers to wear special name tags so patrons can readily differentiate volunteers from regular staff. Others may not issue keys or certain equipment to volunteers. There may even be designated parking places for volunteers that are different from those of regular employees. When putting together a handbook, think through the "typical day" of volunteers from the time they drive up to the library until they depart. Then list or describe any policies that apply based on the visualized scenario.

Privileges and Perks

Are there special benefits that will be accorded to volunteers and interns for the work they do? These might include longer checkout times, access to a staff cafeteria or conference room, waiver of registration fees for library events, advance invitations to book sales, or other small benefits. It is better to know what a library is willing to offer up front to ensure all volunteers are treated consistently.

Reporting Structures and Communication

Having current contact information for volunteers is vital, as is having a designated supervisor or coordinator who is the main link between this category of workers and the library. Notifying interns and volunteers of snow days, emergency library closures due to power outages, and other events that affect their shifts is an important courtesy to perform for those graciously giving their time for free. Likewise, having emergency contact information, particularly for underage volunteers, is an absolute must should illness or accident occur while a volunteer is on library premises. The type of information that volunteers are expected to supply should be listed in the volunteer handbook.

Forms and Documents

The handbook should also include samples of all forms that volunteers are expected to complete. Examples of these documents have been provided by Sandy Dolnick on the CD that accompanies her book, *The Essential Friends of Libraries*. Such forms might include the following:

1. Time log of hours volunteered
2. Volunteer application
3. Emergency contact cards
4. Federal Education Rights to Privacy Act (FERPA) documents, or confidentiality statements, if required
5. Release for performing background check
6. Acknowledgment of receipt of the handbook
7. Other documentation

In addition to creating a volunteer handbook, volunteer programs require a budget. A library might incur costs related to

- fees for background checks;
- parking passes/tags;
- thank-you notes/small gifts to acknowledge contributions of volunteers;
- an annual volunteer banquet/party;
- supplies for special library projects that volunteers might undertake;
- ID cards;
- name tags;
- printing of handbooks, forms, and paperwork; and
- fees related to technology (user log-ons, e-mail accounts, a workstation for volunteers to use, etc.).

The coordinator of a well-structured volunteer or internship program is aware of these costs and has adequate funding to cover them.

Finally, library administrators should check into the legal aspects of running intern and volunteer programs. For example, library directors should learn whether volunteers are covered under the library's workers' compensation policy or liability insurance. In addition, they should be aware of specific state or federal regulations relating to honoraria or small stipends that are provided to interns or as scholarships to their academic institutions. An excellent resource to consult on these issues is Jan Masoka's *The Nonprofit's Guide to Human Resources: Managing Employees and Volunteers.*

LOCATING AND RECRUITING FREE LABOR

Once the handbook and basic program infrastructure are in place, it is time to recruit volunteers and interns. School libraries might solicit adult volunteers by advertising via parent-teacher associations or through boards of education. Principals' offices may consider assigning library service during free periods to student workers requiring mild disciplinary action or detention.

All types of libraries might locate volunteers by asking for the assistance of activity directors in retirement communities, religious leaders at local houses of worship, or presidents of civic organizations. These leaders generally know persons who have time on their hands and would love volunteering. Interns may be found by calling or e-mailing local colleges, universities, and library schools. Try to find the internship coordinators or the heads of departments that teach courses in nonprofit management or library science. These individuals often coordinate practicum experiences for their students.

SUPERVISING AND TRAINING

Gail Dickson, in a survey of 417 school libraries, discovered that of the 76 percent that used volunteers, half deployed volunteers in jobs that required minimal training, such as covering books, shelving, inventory, and book checkout (2011, 57). Possibly this was due to the numbers of younger student volunteers in the ranks, but college-age interns and adult volunteers may find job satisfaction in a variety of more complex tasks, such as copy cataloging, processing archives, digitization, and basic reference assistance. The trick is to match the personality, prior work experience, and interests of the volunteer with the tasks that need to be accomplished. Putting a retired computer programmer to work shelving books might not be the best use of that volunteer's gifts, even though it is easier to train someone to reshelve than to run statistical reports from the ILS. When it comes to interns, special supervision may be prescribed by their schools. This may include writing reports to the university, being willing to provide the practicum coordinator with a tour of your library, and making certain that the intern completes particular projects required by the educational institution's curriculum. Whether working with interns or general volunteers, the more time one invests in training and supervising them, the higher the level of fulfillment and engagement that volunteer experiences in undertaking library tasks. And happy volunteers are more likely to stick around.

ASSESSING THE PROGRAM AND SHOWING APPRECIATION

Regular staff members have built-in incentives to work, namely paychecks and periodic evaluations. Volunteers' and interns' contributions, though not rewarded in the same way, do deserve recognition. In addition, it may be necessary to report their valuable work to library advisory boards, trustees, or accrediting agencies. There are three basic ways to keep track of the significant aid that volunteers and interns provide to libraries for purposes of rewarding volunteers and reporting on their efforts. The first is to request each volunteer keep a record of labor hours contributed. This may take the simple form of a time sheet on which the volunteer lists date, hours donated, and a note about tasks undertaken. A second mechanism is to have the supervisor keep track of progress on particular projects. Many tasks are quantifiable or may be decisively marked as completed or at a certain stage of progress. Finally, it is important to solicit feedback from volunteers and interns themselves. A volunteer's experience may be improved if the program is adjusted so that it is beneficial and challenging to that person (see Tikam, 2011).

Record keeping also provides fodder for reward programs. Following are some popular ways of saying thank-you to volunteers:

- Promoting very dedicated or talented persons to special levels, giving them particular tasks, or granting them distinctive titles.
- Celebrating anniversary points, such as recognizing a specific number of hours contributed, completion of an exceptional project, or the conclusion of a certain number of months/years of service.
- Holding an annual volunteer recognition event like a picnic or dinner.

Volunteers and interns are an investment in the future of our libraries.

WORKS CITED

Dickinson, Gail. 2011. "LMC 1-Question Survey: How Do You Use Volunteers in Your Library?" *Library Media Connection* 30, no. 3: 57.

Dolnick, Sandy. 2005. *The Essential Friends of Libraries: Fast Facts, Forms and Tips.* Chicago: American Library Association.

Masoka, Jan. 2011. *The Nonprofit's Guide to Human Resources: Managing Employees and Volunteers*. Berkley, CA: NOLO.

Tikam, Madhuri. 2011. "Library Volunteerism Outcomes: What Student Volunteers Expect." *Library Management* 32, no. 8: 552–564.

ELEVEN

Making the Best of a Reduced Staff: Utilizing Student Workers to Reach Library Goals

Emy Nelson Decker

When the assistant curator of the Visual Resources Center (VRC) at the Lamar Dodd School of Art at the University of Georgia (UGA) announced in June 2008 that he was leaving to pursue another professional opportunity, I was disappointed to see him go, as he had been an essential member of our relatively small staff. It wasn't until several months later that I realized exactly how much of a setback his departure would be to our daily operations. It unfortunately occurred at the beginning of the recession, and we would be unable to fill the position because of a well-known, though not well-publicized, hiring freeze in the university. I had to reassess, regroup, and determine a course for the future.

The Visual Resources Center staff at the University of Georgia is traditionally comprised of a director, an assistant curator, at least two graduate student assistants, and two undergraduate work-study students. Each member of the staff reports on weekdays and fulfills an important role. Losing one member of the small team has a ripple effect through the entire staff and negatively affects the balance of our workflow. Each member of the staff makes an important daily contribution, and losing the assistant curator position also meant losing the student staff manager, quality-control overseer, and daily operations leader.

Budget cuts complicated matters. During the first few years of the recession, our operational budget was cut nearly in half. There was some improvement in following years, but to this day, we operate with about 75 percent of what we had during better economic times. In an average year, the operational budget monies ensure that projects and initiatives stay afloat. This is crucial because the Visual Resources Center is a stand-alone center, not a part of the University of Georgia libraries. The services we offer include scanning images and text for classroom presentation and study, digital media instruction, access to a growing image database shaped by faculty research, access to and tutorials for using scanning and image enhancement software, and use of a multicomputer scanning lab. As a "library-like" collection outside of the campus library system, the VRC is not technically under the aegis of the UGA libraries and does not benefit financially or organizationally from main library resources. Instead, it is a part of the Lamar Dodd School of Art and is dependent on departmental funding. Therefore, when there are cuts to the department, there are cuts to the funding of the VRC. There was already no extra in the budget, and having to trim it so significantly required a diligent eye for reusing and repurposing what we had while reevaluating what we could and could not do without.

The recession hit higher education hard, and not only campus-wide, but also university system-wide and nationwide. Though this is unfortunate, the one good thing to come out of it is that faculty, students, and patrons who had been apprised of the situation were helpful and understanding regarding our recent cuts and the almost certain changes in what the VRC could provide for them and in what time frame. To say that our patrons were, on the whole, patient and supportive, is an understatement. In fact, this spirit of cooperation inspired the staff of the VRC to work harder to reach the goals set prior to the staffing and financial damage the recession wreaked.

This chapter details how the staff of the VRC learned to make do with fewer workers and how those workers who remained stepped up to more responsibility. More specifically, it discusses how student employees can become a vital asset to collections hit hard by budget downturns. It provides key points for how to apply the lessons learned from this situation to another environment and encourages the reader to see staff and budget reductions as opportunities for positive change.

HOW TO HIRE AND WORK WITH STUDENT WORKERS

Student workers in the VRC at UGA are usually funded in one of two ways, either as college students participating in the work-study program or as graduate students working in the center as part of their assistantships. Both types of students bring skills to the table, and they also tend to work well together. Because of the configuration of our scanning lab, and given an overall student staff of four, two students usually work together at a time on each shift.

Horror stories abound about student workers being unhelpful, and there is an occasional tale of a student sleeping on the job, but generally speaking, student employees do good work. There are many advantages to working with student employees. Many self-select into the position because they want to work in a museum, gallery, or library upon completion of their degree, and working in the VRC is a great way for them to get the required experience while they are still students. Not everyone is cut out for library work, however. The difficult task is to find those in the pool of student employee applicants who are suited to it, so as to maximize productivity from a very limited staff. In addition to the typical interview questions, ask and determine why the student wants to work in the library setting. If the answer is, "I need a job," you may not have found your best employee. At the UGA, a student work contract lasts one academic year, and firing a student results in an unfilled position for the duration of the year, so finding the right student for the job is crucial. This is particularly true when there are so few students making up the staff.

Undergraduate and graduate students alike bring surprising amounts of enthusiasm, innovation, and creativity to daily tasks. More than once a student has made a suggestion or recommendation that overhauled our existing procedure and streamlined our workflow. Most students today are at least comfortable with technology. They may not be skilled with every computer program, but they tend to be quick to learn new computer skills, as they can draw upon a reasonably solid background in technology. It is important to note that whereas professional staff may not enjoy the most menial tasks, students usually do them with ease and rarely complain about it. Some have even noted that grunt work, such as scanning, provides a nice break from their coursework.

To maximize their contributions and enhance daily workflow with small numbers of staff, determine the unique strengths of each student. Foreign students, for example, may have great technical skills, so they would be primary candidates for scanning and then enhancing the scanned images in PhotoShop; however, their grasp of English may not be strong enough to enable them to translate from another language (German, French, Italian) into English for the metadata in image files. The daily tasks of an area of a library are diverse. Each student employee can find a niche within that area. Within weeks of hiring a student, it will become readily apparent where he or she excels. Use the students' strengths to the advantage of your operations and let the student who enjoys inputting metadata do so. His or her enjoyment likely also represents his or her strength.

Some students, particularly the younger undergrads, have little work experience, and some are more prone than others to making mistakes. Speaking strictly in terms of daily operations, there are several tasks that students, no matter how advanced or diligent, cannot do. It is important to be aware of these limitations. Quality control can be handled by a professional staff member of any rank, but it is not a task for a student. When the professional staff is cut down to one member, it is that person's job to oversee quality control. Ultimately, the work the students do will reflect well or poorly upon the professional staff. In other words, there is only one person to answer for poorly scanned images, incorrect metadata, or anything else that the students' contributions might include. Once student workers have submitted their finished entries, it is imperative that they be checked for content, spelling, clarity, format, and overall correctness.

Although student workers in UGA's VRC are often allowed limited-time "administrator" access to the database to rearrange image files or restructure sections in the database to make it user-friendly, they cannot be involved with design input or changes to the database code. Not only does this become a case of "too many cooks in the kitchen," but it can also become a problem of continuity when the students eventually matriculate and leave their college or graduate school jobs in the VRC.

Finally, although students interface with faculty, students, and staff each day, they are not suited to holding meetings with these patrons one on one. Accountability dictates that the professional staff member be the one and only official point of contact for patrons. This reduces confusion, maintains consistency, and promotes a better sense of stability in the environment.

There are a number of advantages to employing students:

- Many students are interested in learning new skills that they would not otherwise learn in courses (scanning, metadata, Adobe Photo-Shop, etc.).
- Many students want to return to the same job for the duration of their program (continuity).
- Students often select jobs that are within their field of concentration, so they bring some specialization to the job and learn more information on-site.
- Students contribute new energy and ideas. They can be very enthusiastic, innovative, and creative.
- Students are communicative: technologically literate and able to express themselves in multiple ways (verbal, social media venues, etc.).
- Students will do grunt work tasks without complaint.

There are also disadvantages to employing students:

- The library has to navigate their course schedules, school breaks, exam schedules, etc.
- They may not have much personal interest or "investment" in the job.

- They are not always detail-oriented enough and are prone to making data-entry mistakes.
- They have little "real-world" experience.

PRIORITIZING AND STREAMLINING

Faculty members were cognizant of our reduced staff situation, but their needs had not changed. Because we were already kept busy when we had a full staff, such a reduction actually meant that we all had to redouble our efforts to get everything finished by the deadlines. Some faculty members retired, and still others were hired as their replacements. Though this seems a straightforward change in personnel, it can introduce complications. Faculty members working in the same subject area often specialize in very different subtopics and use very different approaches. To the VRC, this means there is little overlap with our existing image sets and results in having to add needed materials upon the arrival of the new faculty member.

The daily tasks lists never changed, regardless of our dwindling staff and resources. Upon this realization, we endeavored to assess short- and longer-term needs and pursue them in order of importance. It is easy to become overwhelmed by the amount of work that needs to be done if it is not considered in a "parts that make up the whole" fashion. Even with the reduced staff, the same amount of work was accomplished, but we changed our approach quite a bit. A good example of this is the way we now handle rush orders. When we had a more robust staff, we could immediately add images to the database. With our reduced staff, we now favor scanning the images and giving the jpeg files to the faculty member who requested them so he or she will have them in time for the lecture. Later in the week, we complete the metadata and upload the images to the database.

This "just-in-time" approach requires coordinating student work so that faculty needs are met and means trusting that everyone is doing his or her job properly and that all the parts will come together eventually. Learning how to delegate is a fine art. For some people, giving up control is an unpleasant task. The key to not becoming fatigued is to not try to do everyone's job for them. When a staff is cut back beyond the "bare bones," everyone must put in more effort and accept help even when they would prefer not to take it. It can be nerve-racking to give student employees so much input, but when your professional staff is cut back, student work is essential to completing tasks and to running daily operations as smoothly as possible.

Though frightening and at times frustrating, delegation can have its benefits. When the idea was originally conceived to build an image database for the classics department on campus, the assistant curator was slated to be the main contact person between that department and the School of Art. His departure coincided with word that we had received grant funding for the project, and we ended up utilizing students in ways we would not have done, had we had a professional assistant curator at our disposal. Students came together, worked together, took our advice, and came up with creative solutions on their own over the course of two years; they were absolutely instrumental in bringing the project to fruition. Students scanned images, digitally enhanced and cleaned the files, contributed metadata from research, and adhered to a preapproved format, all with relatively minimal supervision. They relied on each other, their notes, and our instructions, and finished the bulk of the project within the time constraints of the grant. Necessity required us to work with what we had, but the results were so great that I would write student involvement into any future grant proposal. Although we were lacking a crucial staff member, the student employees enjoyed working on the grant-funded database project and surprised all of us with how well it turned out. Judging by the final product, it was difficult, if not impossible, to tell from the outside that we were "making do" with a severely reduced staff and missing a crucial member of the project team.

Prioritize short- and longer-term needs by doing the following:

- *Determine whether or not the issue at hand is a one-time need or an ongoing concern.* Ongoing issues require careful consideration so that time can be built in to handle them on a weekly, monthly, etc., basis.
- *Be flexible in finding new ways to get the same amount of work finished.* Just because something has been done one way for years does not mean it cannot be accomplished in a more simplified, streamlined manner. Allow for creativity.
- *Assess importance.* Is the need mission crucial to teaching, or is it something that can be on the "back burner" for a little while? Learn to differentiate between "need to have" and "would like to have."
- *Relinquish control and learn to delegate.*

ENCOURAGING STUDENT WORKER BUY-IN

Team spirit is crucial to success. Each student needs to be aware of the importance of his or her contribution, both why and how it matters. As an example, many students find tasks, such as data entry repetitive and boring. Sloppy data input full of typos and the improper use of standard terms creates more work for someone else later. Often, getting the best, most mistake-free product that a student can submit simply requires taking the time to explain that patrons depend on being able to use standard search terms, correctly spelled, to find the images that the student spent all day scanning. The responsibility of communicating this to students rests squarely on the professional staff. Without a direct explanation of why it matters that something be done a certain way, anyone would be reluctant to follow strict rules without taking some shortcuts.

It is important to cultivate concern for the project, explaining why it matters. Even giving background information about how the project got started, what the goals are, and how the student is personally contributing builds interest in and higher regard for the project. If a student employee knows what his or her contribution is, that student is more likely to invest time and energy in producing good work. Everyone must participate to the fullest capacity. This is crucial when there is a small team working on a large project.

Good attitudes among student employees are crucial to a high-functioning work environment. Some students bring a "can do" approach to the job regardless of the task; with others, it requires some gentle intervention. Some have such an upbeat demeanor that they become role models and can be paired to work a shift with more disaffected students, who could use a boost in their interest in the project and their enthusiasm. Never underestimate the importance of your own good attitude. Try to avoid letting students see you complaining or acting bored. It is up to you to cast the project in the most positive light possible.

A foundational tool for improving and maintaining worker attitude is incentive. Good student employees, as well as those who need to be reminded why they should care about any given task, benefit equally from rewards. By and large, most student employees will be compensated financially through work-study or a graduate assistantship. Occasionally, a student will request a unit or two of course credit for a semester of working, under the direction of a faculty member. In these cases, the student is receiving an evaluation from the faculty member as well as from professional staff, and with two "bosses" to impress, students tend to work extra hard. Other students, along with appreciating the "real library work" experience they are gaining, hope to request letters of recommendation upon their completion of the work period or school year. As this job represents their work in the academy, as opposed to coffee shop work that they will likely remove from their curriculum vitae, they are interested in securing letters attesting to their diligence, hard work, and suitability for projects requiring research, translation, metadata input, and attention to detail.

To get students to take pride in a job well done:

- Explain why the job at hand matters and why it is done the way it is done (unexplained "rules" can appear to be annoying obstacles that students will try to short cut or avoid).
- Give a history lesson: How did the project start, why, where is it headed, and how is the student contributing toward the library's goals?

- Ask the professional staff to set a good example by not complaining in front the students, speaking excitedly about the project no matter how repetitive it is, etc.
- Reward well-done work.

CONCLUSION

Professional staff cuts are never good news for any division of any library. The reality is that they have happened in the past and will continue to happen. It is the charge of the remaining staff to make the best of the situation and to be flexible enough to find new ways of carrying out daily operations with minimal interruption to the patrons. In our case, enhancing the role of our remaining student workers was the key to success. By learning how to excel with a team of student staff members, we were able to reach and exceed our goals, even in the face of reduced resources and money. Reevaluating workflow, prioritizing, and seeking intra- and extramural funding will ensure that your library will be in a better position to meet steadily growing demands, even in economic downtimes. Learning how to utilize the student workers you have is the crucial key to this success.

TWELVE

Student Workers on the Job: Maximizing Output

Portia Kapraun and Beth M. Sheppard

Maintaining a workforce of student labor can be seen as one of those "blessing and a curse" types of endeavors. Although it is great to have what seems like an endless supply of affordable labor, often the quality of that labor can be unpredictable. One student will naturally find work to keep busy throughout the workday, but another might be just as content to put in as little time and effort as possible. How, as a supervisor, can you ensure that all students work to their full potential? Keeping your student workforce motivated and engaged is the best way to ensure that everyone is pitching in whether you're watching or not.

Motivating a workforce can be achieved by keeping a few things in mind:

- Match talents with tasks.
- Create buy-in.
- Show confidence in your workers.
- Fill "downtime" with long-range goals.
- Assign tasks with achievable milestones.

MATCH TALENTS WITH TASKS

Working at a task that does not suit one's talents and personality can be frustrating and more often than not leads to dissatisfaction for both the worker and the supervisor. A circulation worker who appears to be too busy placing books on a reshelving cart to be bothered by patrons may

97

need a more structured work environment, whereas a shelver who seems too chatty might do better in patron services, where her outgoing nature can be put to use. Most students can thrive when placed in the right environment; it may just take a little bit of work on your part to discover what that environment is.

Often, when applying for campus employment, students are more concerned with getting a paycheck than with finding a job that is well-suited to their talents. A prospective employee will often put in applications all over campus with little thought to what the jobs may entail. You will find that most applications come in for "any available position" even though the posted positions vary greatly in assigned tasks and skills needed. When screening prospective student employees, remember to ask a few distinguishing questions:

Does the student prefer to work:

1. in a team environment where everyone pitches in to complete a goal?
2. alone on a single task seen through to completion?

Does the student do better:

1. in a fast-paced environment in which tasks and duties may vary from day to day?
2. knowing exactly what will be expected each day?

Does the student feel most productive:

1. with a variety of tasks to keep busy?
2. seeing one task through to completion before beginning another?

When faced with downtime, does the student:

1. look for ways to keep busy?
2. seek out a supervisor to assign a new task?

A student answering these questions with mostly "1"s is best suited to circulation and patron services tasks. These are your "service with a smile" students, who enjoy being helpful to patrons and fellow workers. They feel most useful assisting patrons and performing the multitude of tasks needed to keep things running smoothly. Students with mostly "2"s are generally "back of house" workers, assisting with technical services work, shelving, data entry, etc. They work best when assigned a single task that can be performed with little distraction.

Remember that some students come to university with no prior work experience and may not know what type of work is best for them. You may find, after a new hire has been on the job for a few weeks, that he or she might work best in another department. Putting a student in a position for which he or she is most suited will provide a more enjoyable workday for everyone and require less direct supervision on your part, allowing each of you to complete your work in a more timely manner.

CREATE BUY-IN

How can a supervisor ensure that a student is not only going to show up to work, but will also work diligently at the assigned duties? Matching talents with tasks is an important first step, but a student must also be made to feel that his or her tasks are crucial to the daily work and future of the library. When students feel good about the work they are doing and see themselves as vital to the success of the library, they are more likely to be invested in the work being done. Unfortunately, for most employees, students or not, buy-in doesn't just happen on its own; it must be cultivated from the very beginning.

Look for ways to create buy-in when performing the following tasks:

- *Writing job descriptions:* The text should not only accurately describe the assigned tasks, but also the role of each task in the life of the library.
- *Training new workers:* From the first day on the job, students should know that their work is valued. Be sure to mention the importance of a task and how it fits into the overall work of the library.
- *Assigning tasks:* Take note when students mention particular tasks they enjoy or for which they are particularly well suited. This not only makes students feel appreciated, but also helps get them through those tasks they find less appealing.
- *Making decisions that affect the work environment:* Something as small as asking which finish a student prefers on a new fixture can be helpful. Everyone enjoys feeling like a valued member of the team, and decision making is a role everyone can take a hand in.

Remember, many of today's students have a number of responsibilities, both on and off campus, pulling them in many directions. The best way to ensure that their jobs at the library will continue to be a priority is to help them understand that they are important to the success of the library and that their work matters.

SHOW CONFIDENCE IN YOUR WORKERS

Another benefit of having workers who are invested in the work they do at your library is that these students generally require less supervision and provide a higher quality of work. To maintain worker happiness and value, it is important to show confidence in their abilities. There is no point in matching tasks with talent and creating buy-in if the students will be micromanaged to the point of uselessness. Allow students to do the work for which they have been hired.

Student workers invested in their tasks will often seek out greater responsibility in the library or find new tasks to take on. Because they tend to interact with the most patrons, students are often the first to see a need or growing trend in their department. When a student worker notices a need in the library, instead of saying you will look into it, empower him or her to look for ways to complete the task or fill the need. This may mean that you will spend more time training that worker on a new task or helping to find a solution than you would spend resolving it yourself, but it will pay off in the long run, because the student will acquire important skills that will benefit the library in the future.

FILL "DOWNTIME" WITH LONG-RANGE GOALS

Every library has those projects that would be great to start or finish if there were just enough hours in the day and dollars in the budget. This might be digitizing a special collection, updating or creating local databases, converting older materials from a card catalog to an online catalog, or any number of other tasks that seem too big or expensive to take on. At the same time, students in public services may have long stretches of "downtime," especially at the beginning of the semester, during which they have little to do. With a bit of innovation, a large portion or even all of a "too big" project can be worked on, a little at a time, during the lull between daily operations.

To successfully implement a long-term task such as those mentioned here, knowing what will be needed and having a plan in place are incredibly important. For any such task you will need to consider the following:

- What equipment and software will be needed to enable students to work at their current workstations? Often, all that is needed is additional software for an existing circulation or reference computer.
- Can all of the work be completed by students during downtime? You may find that some parts of the process require large equipment or tasks that are best performed uninterrupted. This does not mean that the project will not work, only that the work will have to be divided up by where it can best be completed. For example, some digitization projects may require large scanners that won't fit behind a desk, but once the text is scanned, optical character recognition and proofreading can be completed with any desktop computer equipped with the right software.
- What training will be needed for the students to complete the tasks on their own? Before beginning, make sure all instructions are clearly written down and available at all times for workers to reference.

- Will there be resistance from students who have previously been allowed to do homework or read during downtime? Plan ahead for resistance to change. Remind students that workers in other areas of the library work their entire shift, and it is really only fair that everyone put in 100 percent.

These big projects won't be finished this week, this month, or maybe even this year, but with everyone working a little bit at a time, progress can be made without the cost of additional labor.

ASSIGN TASKS WITH ACHIEVABLE MILESTONES

Finally, look for ways for students to see the progress of their work and acknowledge when a goal is met. For long-term tasks that may not be completed until after current workers have graduated, break down the project into smaller tasks so that progress is visible for students and staff. Breaking down a large task into smaller sets with achievable goals keeps up the momentum for everyone involved. These smaller sets also allow you to celebrate milestones when they are reached. This doesn't mean you need to have a big party each time a milestone is reached, just something to acknowledge the effort put forth by your workers.

Ultimately, getting the most out of student labor relies on the culture of the library. By making sure everyone feels that they are playing a significant role in the success of the library, you are fostering a work environment in which students will be most willing to go the extra mile.

IV

Monitoring Time and Projects

THIRTEEN

Developing and Implementing a Project Chart

Jessica Shomberg and Daardi Sizemore

This chapter outlines how project charts were implemented in a mid-sized academic library. A project chart is a table identifying major projects that are under way or that are being planned for the future, along with relevant information, such as priority, project leader, timeline, and completion status. Some project management charts can be very complicated and high-tech, but the example provided in this chapter is a textual table in a Microsoft Word document, which makes it very customizable by different libraries.

This concept can be used differently depending on purpose, people, and leadership style. We are sharing our practices for using a project chart to achieve both library-wide goals as well as goals for the technical services unit. Project charts are a successful way to

- manage projects,
- prioritize activities,
- establish reasonable deadlines, and
- assess library goals and objectives.

RATIONALE

The library went through a comprehensive program review and also lost librarian positions as part of campus budget reductions. These activities were stressful and resulted in many projects being added to our collective and individual "to do" lists. In addition, we had several existing time management challenges that made it difficult to prioritize all of our goals, much less complete them.

The context of our library includes shared management with minimal hierarchy, both in making decisions and implementing them. The autonomy of the library faculty in day-to-day and long-term undertakings did not aid in setting library-wide goals, even before staff cuts. In addition, we lost momentum due to our summer schedules, resulting in a cycle of what a colleague refers to as "brainstorm ideas, forget, repeat." Add in the administrative directives to "do more with less" and to find the "new normal," and we knew we needed a new strategy and method.

We needed the following outcomes:

- To improve internal communication.
- To identify project leaders.
- To clarify the work assignments of individuals.
- To engage in more long-term thinking, while accomplishing immediate needs and respecting historical continuity.
- To identify which assignments and library priorities weren't being given enough attention.

PROCESS

Step 1: Write Down All Topics

To achieve the goal of maintaining historical continuity, the first step we took was to review the meeting minutes of committees from the previous year and write down all agenda items that had been assigned a progress status of "later" or "next year." These were specifically library-wide activities that involved multiple units and required reporting in multiple venues. The first draft of the document was more than three pages long.

Subsequently the same step was used by the Technical Services unit to identify unit-based projects. Although the project scopes were more limited, the steps the group followed were essentially the same as those followed by the library faculty as a whole.

Step 2: Get Buy-In for the Project Chart

The second step was to present the project chart as a draft to the librarians at the first meeting of the semester, something that could be adapted and utilized throughout the year. The library faculty discussed the outcomes that we as a group hoped to accomplish. Additional topics were added to the project chart as a result of brainstorming conducted during the initial meeting. This time, the ideas we brainstormed were not forgotten. Over the course of several meetings, librarians discussed the idea of the chart, agreed on general principles, and better outlined activities we knew we would need to devote a significant amount of attention to over the coming years. We worked together to fill in the fields as a group.

The Technical Services unit had already seen the benefits of the library-wide project chart and how easy it was to customize for different purposes, so buy-in was smooth.

Step 3: Deadlines and Priorities

The third step was to identify deadlines and priorities. After a brief discussion about what various priorities meant, it was important to spend a little time defining them and clarifying the difference between the priority level and the deadline. For each activity on the chart, librarians suggested priorities. Most of the time, the initial suggestion was adopted with minimal discussion. Acknowledging the priorities and comments that each librarian brought up was helpful in terms of getting continued buy-in, ownership, and collegial working relationships with regard to the project chart.

The deadlines were decided similarly. During initial discussions there was some confusion over start dates and completion dates in relation to the timeline box on the project chart. This was handled slightly differently in different groups. The library-wide chart focuses on the current academic year. It remains slightly nebulous whether we are referring to start or completion dates, but is broken down by months, which can be revised as needed. The Technical Services chart, in contrast, looks forward at least eighteen months. It also has separate columns for start and completion and refers to semesters rather than months.

The complexity of some projects necessitated breaking them up into subtasks with separate deadlines. Over time the groups became more strategic about dividing tasks into subtasks (objectives) with milestone deadlines.

After the initial review, it was helpful to revise some priorities; it seemed there might be too many "very important" or "essential" activities. It was necessary to clarify early on that because so many items were ranked as important, some might not be completed within a single academic year. Following discussions at several meetings, the librarians adopted the project chart as a working document for the academic year.

One of the benefits of this step was that it helped us to recognize our actual planning goals. For example, over the previous few years, work related to electronic resources had quietly and consistently expanded. Seeing the number of projects and names associated with electronic resources activities on the chart helped us become more aware as a group of our shift in focus. This helped us get more buy-in to support electronic resources work and in turn allowed more freedom to those already responsible for this work to negotiate their workloads.

Step 4: Iteration

The fourth step is to acknowledge that an essential part of the process is to look at and revise the chart as needed. Circumstances change, campus priorities change, and personnel change. Even the act of modifying the project chart, which is a helpful tool for synthesizing the many projects going on in a library, can adjust one's perception of the big picture. What may have seemed to be a workable deadline in September may no longer be feasible by January. The project chart is a working document and can be adjusted throughout the year. The document should be brought back to meetings for review, discussion, and updating throughout the year. Our activities in this area are addressed in the assessment section of this chapter.

WHAT TO INCLUDE ON THE PROJECT CHART

A variety of components could be included in the project chart. The following lists discuss and explain those components.

Essential Components

- *Activity: Identify what you plan to accomplish.* Be specific or general, whichever is appropriate and most helpful to your organization. We did both in our project chart. You may also consider using SMART goals to shape the activity. SMART goals are: specific, measurable, achievable, realistic, and time oriented. Activities can be made SMART as part of the iteration step. *Note:* We did not include ongoing library activities such as "Staff the Reference Desk" or "Catalog All the Things" in our project chart; we just included ad hoc projects and, occasionally, new initiatives that didn't already have an existing support structure. However, if, for example, one of your organization's priorities is to reduce the backlog of music scores to be cataloged, that sort of activity could easily be included.
- *Lead Person or Group: It is important to assign responsibility for the activities.* The person assigned to be project leader may sometimes be obvious, but not always. Whether you use individuals' names rather than library groups is likely to depend on the size of the library and how the chart is being implemented. In our library-wide implementation, we used both individual names and groups in the chart. For the Technical Services chart, we used individual names, primarily because of the size of the group. The benefit of

this component is that it helps others know whom to go to with questions about a specific project and creates a broader awareness of the number of tasks some individuals are already working on. As one colleague mentioned, "Knowing who's working on what changes my own expectations of their availability and helps me determine the relative priority of my own projects."

- *Timeline:* The group should identify whether the timeline refers to when the activity will be completed or when it will begin. Be realistic. Be aware of external factors that may necessitate changing your timeline. For example, if your activity is "Implement Streaming Video Service," nonlibrary entities may affect your timeline, such as contract negotiations, campus technology support, or disability services. Even if you are uncertain about the timeline at the beginning, adding an activity to the project chart with an open timeline can help, as it provides a reminder to include that topic in future meeting agendas so it is not forgotten.

- *Priority:* How important is this activity in relation to other items on the list and day-to-day activities? It is acceptable to have several items ranked at the same level. We used the words *essential, very high, high, medium,* and *low* to rank our priorities. If you are having difficulty assigning priority levels, go back to your library mission and goals statements. Your project chart should support your organizational priorities.

- *Status:* It is rewarding to look at the chart throughout the year and see the items that have "In Progress" or a checkmark in the column to denote completion. It is also helpful to monitor how an activity is progressing; you may need to add resources or adjust your timeline. In addition to monitoring the group's activities, the status column is useful when reporting to others (dean, director, colleagues) about progress on library-wide and unit activities. When we first started using the project chart, some people were hesitant about having their own projects included for fear of being judged for an "incomplete" status. Now, however, with more shared experience watching the status of some large, successful projects stay "in process" for months at a time, people are more aware of the social and professional benefits of having their projects included, so their peers have more opportunity to recognize the many activities they work on.

Optional Chart Components

- *Reporting Lines:* Identify to whom results and discussions are brought. This may depend on the organizational structure of your library. However, whether reporting lines are horizontal (like ours) or vertical, successful and timely completion of any project relies on communicating with the right people. Having the reporting lines listed clarifies for both project leaders and others where progress reports, discussions, and general questions should be brought.

- *Objectives:* Some activities are so big (e.g., Select an ERMS) that they should be broken up into more manageable pieces, with multiple timelines. This allows for more accurate measurement of timeliness, projected completion rates, and resource needs.
- *Notes/Comments or Resources Needed:* It can be helpful to have a field to reflect additional information relevant to the activity.

ASSESSMENT

It is important to assess the project chart throughout the year, taking a look at what you have done and what you have left to do and making any necessary adjustments. Therefore, the project chart itself can be considered an assessment tool. This may involve midyear reviews and updates, end of the year review, and beginning of year planning.

Your organization could set a different timeline, but this is the process we used for our first year with the project chart. We discussed progress every other month; during these meetings, librarians were asked to update the status on chart activities. A midyear update was presented, with check marks in the "done" category as appropriate. Librarians were reminded about the document and asked for progress reports, but no one was criticized for not completing an activity. At the end of the academic year, the library faculty were asked how effective the project chart was. Based on the comments received, minor changes to the design of the chart were made, but overall there was enthusiastic support for maintaining the concept.

For the second year of using the project chart, we added to the process slightly. Now when we review the project chart, we are looking at whether a project can be done in the time we proposed, what has already been

Library Topics from AY10 for AY11 that the Library Faculty recommended working On (updated 5/5/11 by DS)

This is a working document. It is also a flexible document and can and should be adjusted throughout the year.

Activity	Where did this come from?	Who is the Lead?	What is the faculty priority for this project?	Deadline / Outcome Deadlines usually refer to when the activity will begun.		Who should this be reported to?	Done!	What Resources are needed?
Revisit the 5 Year Goals document that was compiled for the Program Review report.	F-5/7/10 F- 8/19/10	Planning	Low	September	Review document	Faculty	✔	
				April	Review w/ Progress Update		✔	
Review the brainstorming activity that was included in program review.		Personnel and Planning	Medium	October (Personnel)	Review and consider how it should/could be used this year		✔	

Figure 13.1.

done, what needs to be added, and whether we need to change anything. As mentioned previously, "Step 4: Iteration" is an important and ongoing part of the process.

The response has been overwhelmingly positive. The librarians liked the following:

- The list of "done" items at the end of the year and the sense of accomplishment and pride that brings
- Clearly stated priorities, which help us stay focused and negotiate when new project ideas are brought up
- The group awareness of what we have been working on, which demonstrates our priorities in action
- Peer support for the major activities that many librarians were involved in
- Bridging activities and discussions from one year to the next, that sense of historical continuity that is so important for maintaining momentum
- Looking at activities holistically, which provides an opportunity for active reflection
- Using the project chart concept as a time management tool for individual tasks
- Giving the chart a humorous name, which reminded everyone that the chart was a guide rather than a mandate

CHALLENGES TO IMPLEMENTATION

Challenges to implementation will vary based on a library's organizational structure. We have a system of shared management, a horizontal structure, so the way we implemented the project chart was through collaboration among library faculty to manage and report our work better. We could see potential personal and professional benefits from using this tool, even if we did not always agree immediately on the details. If it had been implemented differently, the results may have been very different.

Challenge one: Establishing deadlines and priorities. This is easy when we have an external push (e.g., our primary vendor is going out of business in six months; therefore, our deadline for finding a new vendor will be six months from now). When dealing with an internal demand, conflicting agendas may make it more difficult. In addition, sometimes we conflate deadlines with priority levels. Because any activity we decide to take on is important to someone, we tend to automatically assign everything a high priority. It may only be when we are in the moment and have to make a decision between having staff work on a licensing project rather than cataloging training that we really have those conversations. Part of what makes this challenging is discussing these priorities as a faculty, balancing organizational priorities with personal priorities. Clarifying priority levels before a potential conflict ensues is preferred. However, as helpful as the project chart is, it is still just a tool; it's not a replacement for the ongoing communication and incremental adjustments required by real life.

Challenge two: Establishing the lead person or group. Position descriptions often do not change as fast as might be optimal. If positions remain static, but the work itself changes, it may be difficult to identify the appropriate lead person without changing the existing organizational structure. This may lead to miscommunication, turf battles, and other conflicts in the workplace that may not be immediately resolved. Although this is an ongoing challenge, we have been successful at realigning work assignments in some areas of the organization to better reflect library goals and needs. In fact, we may not have been able to get to that point as quickly without the use of the project chart process. As a group, we are now more focused on collaboratively accomplishing activities that support our goals.

Challenge three: Transparency can be a difficult adjustment. Identifying perceived work gaps on a shared document means that sometimes things that people don't want to address are publicly highlighted. If work is getting done, but no one knows about it, this could mean that there are other issues to be addressed. If work is not getting done, the person ostensibly responsible for that area (if there is anyone) may feel targeted. This transparency can lead to necessary but uncomfortable conversations about changing position descriptions, job assignments, or even library goals. The benefit is that this process identifies where support is needed, even though that may be threatening to some. In our situation, because of the explosion in electronic resources over the past few years, the person with that job title initially felt threatened by a perceived imbalance in the project chart toward electronic resources projects. However, over time, it became apparent to everyone that the problem was structural rather than personal. Although it was challenging at times, we were able to realign duties in such a way that rather than feeling attacked for perceived deficiencies, the person responsible for electronic resources felt that her contributions were more recognized than they had been in the past, at the same time that her workload was adjusted to be more reasonable in the future.

The project chart is helpful in managing time, but it does not replace honest and respectful communication. At this point, we have increased transparency among library faculty, which has aided internal communication. It has also been very helpful in reporting our activities as a group to others while still allowing us to push ourselves, without individuals taking the full burden of risk they may have previously felt.

CONCLUSION

Because the project chart was primarily meant as a time management and communication aid, so far it has only been used as an internal document among the librarians. It allows us to track progress, workload, and coverage gaps in relation to goals and accomplishments. As a colleague stated, "This has helped us move forward as an organization with a better understanding of the historical continuity of our activities. We've stopped reinventing the wheel."

As we continue to use this chart in the future, it may have more implications for collegially assigning and taking on work projects and letting other projects fall off the priority list. It may also allow us to be more flexible in modifying our own job assignments to acknowledge the changing needs of the library.

FOURTEEN

How Many Hours in My Day? How Many Slices in My Pie? Personal Productivity for the Busy Librarian

John C. Gottfried

In recent years, nearly every librarian in every library has struggled daily to meet the confusing demands of an ever-changing work environment. This bumpy state of affairs should, however, come as no surprise. As early as 1959, management expert Peter Drucker predicted that the twenty-first century would be marked by a jarring change from manual work to knowledge work. Not coincidentally, librarians are a good example of Drucker's knowledge workers, and he predicted that such workers would face difficult hurdles in their complex new jobs. In the world of the knowledge worker, he warned, just determining which tasks need to be done may be a daunting challenge. Effective knowledge workers must be self-managing, ready to set their own priorities and overcome obstacles independently to make a positive contribution to their libraries and their communities.

Fortunately, this type of self-management need not be a difficult or involved process. To be clear at the outset: the underlying message of every item in this chapter is simplicity. Each tip and technique is a variant on the theme of taking what has become unnecessarily complex or irrelevant about your job and reducing it to its purest, most efficient form. Like the old story about a sculptor describing the creation of a beautiful marble horse—"I just cut away everything that isn't horse, and this is what remains"—let's see if we can remove all that is not horse from your work.

HUMANS BEING

To begin at the beginning, librarians are, after all, people. They cannot be plugged in and left to spin indefinitely like department-store escalators. Consider a dog moving across a field: it darts back and forth, stops to bark at squirrels, sits to enjoy a passing smell, and lets the wind blow its fur in the breeze. For all that, it still gets to the other end of the field, and probably faster than the person walking it. Advanced degrees and lofty goals notwithstanding, in this sense at least, librarians are just big mammals. Like our four-legged friends, we perform best in little spurts. People who take frequent, short breaks from their work normally produce more and better output than their nose-to-the-ground comrades (Allen and Schwartz 2011). Plan your day in thirty- to ninety-minute segments. Allow time for pleasant chats with your colleagues or little walks around the building. Take a moment occasionally to let your fur blow in the breeze. You will still get to the end of the field, but you will enjoy the trip so much more! We cannot constantly expend our physical and mental resources without taking time to replenish them. Eat well, be active, and get lots of sleep—most of us know what we should be doing to take care of ourselves, but too often we don't seem to make the crucial connection between proper maintenance and high performance.

In a similar vein, as there is a natural rhythm to our daily activities, so there is a natural pattern in our movement toward goals and objectives. When charting our performance over time, we might like to see the pattern shown in figure 14.1.

Sadly, however, life does not normally follow such a tidy path. Even if you are moving in a positive direction, an accurate chart of your achievements would most probably look more like figure 14.2.

These are the jagged teeth you will face on the difficult road to accomplishing major goals. Every path will inevitably include its ups and downs, and there is little you can do but gracefully accept setbacks as learning opportunities. Velcro, potato chips, microwave ovens, and Play-Doh were all unintended inventions resulting from fortuitous accidents. If scientists and inventors can profit from their failed experiments, then why shouldn't librarians?

FIRST THE MAP, THEN THE VOYAGE

Abstract notions about the wellness of the whole being will not be very helpful if the whole being doesn't know what it wants to make of itself. If you are lucky, your leaders and supervisors will give you an idea of your library's general direction and goals, but you will be far more effective as a librarian—and ultimately more highly valued by your superiors—if you can create and clearly articulate your own viable strategy for contrib-

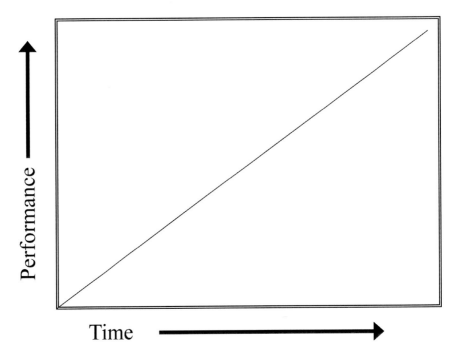

Figure 14.1.

uting to the library's goals. Although nothing is simpler than making a "To-Do" list, nothing is more difficult than doing it well. What follows are some useful tips collected over the years for making your personal plan a vital, effective roadmap for each day's journey.

Begin with the End in Mind

There are few investments you will ever make that will pay bigger dividends than the time and effort you put into developing a meaningful set of personal and work goals. What are your library's goals? What is the mission? What are the biggest problems your library faces? Write down the answers, then consider the three most important things you could do to make things better. This is the time to think big—take on what the authors of *Built to Last* (Collins and Porras 1997) refer to as "Big, Hairy, Audacious Goals (BHAGs)." BHAGs, the authors point out, help energize you and everyone around you by offering the hope of a making a real difference to your organization and its patrons. Always remember, though, that even the most humble contributions can turn out to have a far greater impact than you might imagine.

It is equally important to follow a similar procedure in identifying your personal goals. What is really important to you? What do you need

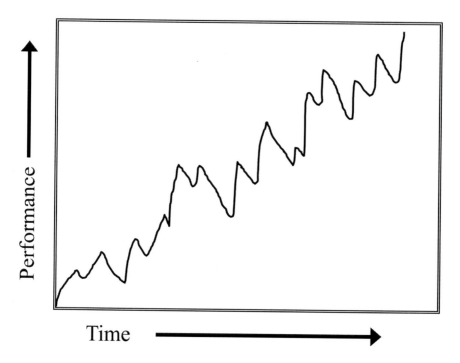

Figure 14.2.

to do with your time in this world? Take this process seriously. Your personal goals and the needs of your job may not always be perfectly aligned, but if the two are truly in conflict, this could at least indicate that some serious self-reflection is in order.

One Step, Then Another

Having established these major goals as your ultimate destination, it is easier to map out the daily activities that will get you there. The method you use to do this is a highly personalized choice. Many people are reluctant, for example, to have anything at all to do with daily activity lists and appointment calendars. Well and good, but for such people it is all the more important to keep the big goals in mind and arrange daily actions accordingly. I advocate creating a thoughtful plan each day—in writing—and I encourage you to faithfully record your appointments. Whatever your preferences, there are good books to help you get started (see the suggested reading at the end of this chapter). Just be aware that none of them will answer all your needs. Good personal planning is an art to be developed over time through trial, error, and revision. Toward that end, following are some helpful tips I have accumulated along my own path to productivity:

- *"SMART" goals are best:* Specific (define your goals clearly, for yourself and others), Measureable (define what success would look like, as objectively as possible), Achievable (Can you really affect the outcomes necessary to reach your goal?), Realistic (a goal should stretch your abilities, but it should not be mere fantasy), Time (there should be clear timelines and completion dates for your goals).
- *Multiple roles, multiple lists:* Our modern lives include many roles (work, family, spirituality, fitness, and so forth), and each role may well require its own list of goals, feeding into its own daily lists.
- *Break objectives into doable pieces:* If the pieces are too big, break them down again.
- *Make everyone aware of your plans:* Be able to express objectives clearly, quickly, and persuasively.
- *Have a firm plan,* but keep it flexible enough to adapt to the unexpected.
- *Invest quality time in planning,* perhaps the night before a workday or at a quiet time in the morning.

Tools: All That Glitters, Beeps, and Boasts

At every bend in the path to productivity you will be tempted by a seemingly endless selection of customized tools, gadgets, software applications, and expert consultations. There are many sweeping claims, some hefty fees, and worst of all, the implication that one cannot plan a trip to the candy machine without the assistance of an involved planning system. The arsenal may include daily planners, smart phones, tablet computers, self-help books, workshops, websites, and any other crazy notion the human mind can hatch. This is not to say that such aids are not helpful, and some may even be worth something near to the price you would pay for them. I do, however, advise caution and frugality. Reflecting on your life goals and planning your daily activities need not be a complicated undertaking. Some of the most tech-savvy people I know still keep track of tasks and appointments by nontechnological means. Paper planners, sticky notes, and even the venerable pencil are all still perfectly useful planning tools, adaptable to the needs of effective, successful individuals.

A similar decision must be made with regard to consultants, workshops, classes, and gurus. In the same way that some of us are comfortable setting up a simple exercise and diet program at home, while others prefer a professional gym and a personal trainer, so some of us arrange our own personal goals and activities, while others derive great benefits from expert advisors. This may amount to anything from spending a dollar on a used book to hiring a personal coach for thousands of dollars. The choice is yours, of course, but make your decision prudently; the real magic beans are far rarer than the advertisements would have you believe.

If, on the other hand, you favor a more modernist electronic approach, you need not necessarily spend a fortune to enjoy the fruits of the digital age. One of the most popular online calendars, for instance, is Google Calendar (www.google.com/calendar), a free Web-based system that allows you to access your appointments on any Internet-connected device. To keep track of tasks and projects you can use another free service, Remember the Milk (www.rememberthemilk.com), which allows you to track and prioritize your activities, and, as an added benefit, allows you to create and edit tasks from within Google Calendar. This is, of course, only tip of the iceberg. There are thousands of free online services to help you manage everything from citations and bibliographies (Zotero) to complex projects (Zoho) and online file storage (Dropbox). Then there are the endlessly fascinating but boundlessly expensive electronic gadgets. New mobile phones and computer devices offer an enormous variety of handy functions and services. As with the other methods, make your selections carefully and only after considerable research and trial. Take advantage of sites offering impartial reviews, such as *CNET* (http://reviews.cnet.com/) or *PC Magazine* (www.pcmag.com). And always keep in mind that, although smart phones and smart pads are exciting and loads of fun, smart *people* are the real source of productivity.

JUST DOING IT

Thomas Edison once said, "Opportunity is missed by most because it is dressed in overalls and looks like work." To this point in the chapter we have focused on the importance of setting meaningful goals and laying out the steps necessary to reach those goals. None of this, however, is of even the slightest value if we don't roll up our sleeves and get the work done. This is certainly the simplest and most straightforward piece of advice—get to work!—but for many it is the hardest to carry out. Here are a few basic tips to help you keep the train moving down the track:

Base your activities on need and priority, not mood and preference.

- When you do need a break from high-priority, difficult tasks, "pick the low-hanging fruit" by focusing on tasks that have meaning but can be quickly completed.

Important, immediate, or both?

- If the task is important and needs to be done immediately, do it quickly and move on.
- If the task is important but not immediate, plan time to do it right.

- If the task is unimportant, put it aside or delegate it to someone who is not doing anything important.

Play to your strengths.

- Understand how you produce your best work and stick to that method.
- Experiment with new methods and tools, keeping what works and discarding the rest.

Right time.

- Most people are at their mental peak from mid- to late morning—a good time for tough, important tasks.
- Most people are physically at a peak in the late afternoon—a good time to exercise.

Right place.

- Eliminate clutter and organize your space efficiently (seek help from books or consultants if you can't manage it yourself).
- Some people work better in silence, some with soft music playing, and some with energetic music playing—use earphones if necessary (and permitted) to create the optimal "audio environment" for yourself.

Overcoming Distractions

In our hurried, overcrowded, instant-access world, finding time and space to work without constant interruption seems, at times, like sheer fantasy. The ideal solution, of course, would be to just shut it all down—lock the door, unplug the phones, lower the shades, and turn off the Internet! In reality, though, no librarian is an island. We can no more cut off communication with the world than we can cut out our central nervous systems. With a little determined effort and diplomacy, however, we may be able to mute and deflect some of the most disruptive annoyances.

- E-mail has been identified as the most challenging form of workplace distraction. Set specific times to check e-mail, allotting only a specific amount of time. Perform triage by prioritizing using subject lines, senders, and e-mail addresses. Do not send e-mails unnecessarily; above all, avoid contentious or long-winded e-mail debates that are better handled in person. Manage old e-mails efficiently by creating as few folders as you can, then using the e-mail search function to find what you need.
- Social networks are to be avoided at work unless you absolutely have to. Even if you do, you don't have to post and answer inces-

santly. Budget a time slot for social networks if they are really a job responsibility. If not, save them for leisure time at home.

- Telephone calls can collect on voicemail; check it at specified times.

No ... Just. Plain. No.

No one likes "no." It is harsh. It is final. It is the ultimate negative. But if you are to reach your real potential, you must eventually master the fine art of No. Put simply, when you don't have the ability to say no, you will forfeit the right to say yes. "Maybe" just means you'll have to deal with the issue all over again in the future. Certainly you want to be as agreeable as you can in the workplace, and you should always seek to negotiate a favorable solution. Sometimes, though, the only responsible reply is a negative. When this is the case, try the following:

- Base your decision on job requirements and priorities, not personalities.
- Speak to the person face-to-face if possible, or by phone—do not use e-mail.
- Be ready with reasonable alternatives.
- Explain why you are saying no, in the most honest yet polite manner possible.
- Be reasonable and respectful, but firm.
- When all reasonable attempts to resolve a conflict fail, you may have to consider documenting the situation, along with your attempts to correct it, with an eye toward further action.

Multitasking

Most people believe that multitasking describes the process of working on several tasks at one time. In reality, we don't really multitask. We actually switch back and forth among separate tasks quickly, and with each change we lose some time in readjustment. Several studies have shown that it takes more time to complete each separate task when multitasking, resulting in lower productivity overall (e.g., see Appelbaum, Marchionni, and Fernandez 2008). Therefore, to work more efficiently it is advisable to avoid multitasking whenever possible.

There are times, though, when multitasking may be a necessary evil. Most reference librarians, for example, are familiar with the necessity of catching up on tasks and chores while serving at the reference desk, stopping sporadically to deal with library patrons. Certainly these librarians could complete their work more efficiently if they didn't have to stop and start their projects over and over. It would also be convenient if those same librarians could answer all the reference questions for the day, one after the other, without pause. But patrons are rarely so predictable. Everyone reading this passage can supply positive examples of multitasking. Research shows, in fact, that organizations whose employees are comfortable with multitasking tend to be more successful (Souitaris and Maestro 2011). The best advice, then, is to avoid multitasking when you can, but do not shun it altogether.

Librarianship as a Team Sport

Team dynamics and group performance are fascinating topics in themselves, but they are well beyond the scope of the current discussion. Nonetheless, a few words about working well with others are in order, as your personal performance is almost always tied, to a greater or lesser degree, to that of your colleagues and coworkers.

- Form solid alliances with positive, productive colleagues.
- Always discuss expectations, timelines, and objectives up front.
- Confirm and restate conversations, in an e-mail or even in writing when possible.
- If you are in a supervisory position, delegate work with the goal of making your subordinates shine, not sticking them with the dirty work.
- Make the investment—spend time getting to know a bit about the people you work with.
- Be gracious and grateful for the contributions of those around you.

CONCLUSION: YOU, MANAGING YOU

We have covered many aspects of personal productivity and time management in this short chapter. Despite all the twists, turns, tips, and tricks discussed, I return to my main point: keep it simple. Working hard and being productive is rarely complicated. No matter the situation or environment, it is always—always—a matter of respecting yourself and your time as the priceless resource you are. You, moreover, are the primary steward of this resource. Self-management is at once a burden and self-liberating: what happens is your fault, and your triumph, and you are answerable for making the very best of the gifts you have been given.

In this spirit, be a good manager of yourself. Make sure you are doing your best work. Check in often to be certain you remain inspired and gratified by the work you do. If not, look for new opportunities and challenges that will help you grow. Perhaps you can give yourself something akin to a formal review periodically, looking over your goals and your progress toward them, making readjustments as needed. Reward yourself for successes, and consider new directions and strategies to deal with shortfalls. There is no doubt about it: with a boss like you, you cannot help but succeed!

WORKS CITED

Allen, David, and Tony Schwartz. 2011. "Being More Productive" (interview). *Harvard Business Review* 89, no. 5: 82–87.

Appelbaum, Steven H., Adam Marchionni, and Arturo Fernandez. 2008. "The Multi-Tasking Paradox: Perceptions, Problems and Strategies." *Management Decision* 46, no. 9: 1313–1325.

Collins, Jim C., and Jerry I. Porras. 1994. *Built to Last: Successful Habits of Visionary Companies.* New York: HarperBusiness.

Drucker, Peter F. 1959. *Landmarks of Tomorrow.* New York: Harper.

Souitaris, Vangelis, and B. M. Marcello Maestro. 2011. "The Case for Multitasking." *Harvard Business Review* 89, no. 10: 32.

SUGGESTED READING

Allen, David. *Getting Things Done: The Art of Stress-Free Productivity.* New York: Penguin, 2002.

Bregman, Peter. *18 Minutes: Find Your Focus, Master Distraction, and Get the Right Things Done.* New York: Business Plus, 2011.

Forsyth, Patrick. *Successful Time Management.* rev. ed. London: Kogan, 2012.

Tracy, Brian. *Eat That Frog! 21 Great Ways to Stop Procrastinating and Get More Done in Less Time.* 2nd ed. San Francisco: Berrett-Koehler, 2007.

FIFTEEN

A Librarian's Time Management Toolkit

Ellie Dworak

I'm sure that all of you have had "the conversation." You know, the one in which somebody asks what you do, then comments about how peaceful your job must be, surrounded as you are by quiet study and tomes of learning. Whether this stereotype was ever accurate is the subject for another book, but it is certainly not true today. Librarians and library staff of all stripes are busy and getting busier. Along with tight schedules and varied responsibilities, many of us are coping with shifting organizational and community needs, budget cuts, and reduced staffing levels. Add the strain of keeping up with rapidly changing technologies, and it's no wonder that librarians regularly experience job stress and burnout (Harwell 2008). Without a doubt, excellent time management is a survival skill for the contemporary library professional.

Everybody is different, and there is no formula for how to most effectively manage your time. For example, some people work best by focusing on one project at a time, while other people's brains don't function well without the stimulation of shifting from one task to the next. Personality type, organizational culture, job duties, stress, and the flexibility of your time are just a few factors that impact the best time management strategy for you. Rather than presenting rules, this chapter offers a set of tools and suggests ways to incorporate them effectively into your unique situation.

TOOL NUMBER 1: INVENTORY AND ITEMIZE

The starting point for managing your time is to get a handle on how the hours in your day are currently being used. One way to do this is an activity log, but if you have the time and wherewithal to write down everything you do every minute of the day for several days, you can probably stop reading this chapter. Further, many library responsibilities are seasonal (e.g., a public library may hold a summer reading program), so a daily log will likely not accurately reflect your responsibilities. Instead, I recommend a workload inventory, which is less scientific but faster and more inclusive.

Create a Rough Inventory

First, make a list of your projects and major job duties. This is my partial list:

- Reference desk, chat reference
- Instruction sessions
- Liaison and collection development
- Conference planning committee chair
- State library association membership committee chair
- Book chapter or other writing
- Search committees
- Review LibAnswers FAQ
- Reference desk schedule
- Research skills class

Not every activity on a given day falls neatly into a project category. Most of us spend at least an hour a day responding to e-mail, for instance. Rather than try to sort out which e-mails fall into which job duty, I added a category called "general."

Track Your Time

Next, notate the list with an estimated number of hours (or range of hours) per week that you need to spend on each item. This does not need to be exact, and it's all right if some tasks overlap, such as doing collection development at the reference desk. Just try to impart a sense of how you spend your time. This is my annotated list:

- Reference desk, chat reference 12–16
- Instruction sessions 0–12
- Liaison and collection development 0–4
- Conference planning committee chair 4–8
- State library association membership committee chair 0–2
- Book chapter or other writing 2–8

- Search committees 1–20
- Review LibAnswers FAQ 2
- Reference desk schedule 0–6
- Research skills class 0–12
- General 7–14

Next, dig up and review your job description and other goal-setting documents, perhaps written as part of your evaluation process. Check your list against these documents to see what is missing. Are there activities that are not currently getting your attention, but should be? If so, add them.

Review and Adjust

Finally, review the list to see if there are items you can stop doing, spend less time doing, or pass on to somebody else. If so, make a note of this, and of any steps that you need to take. This is what I ended up with:

- Reference desk, chat reference 12–16
- Instruction sessions 0–12
- Liaison and collection development 0–4
- Conference planning committee chair 4–8 (step off this committee in April, after the conference)
- State library association membership committee chair 0–2 (delegate monthly reminder e-mails to another committee member and concentrate on coordination; pass gavel in October)
- Book chapter or other writing 2–8
- Search committees 1–20
- Review LibAnswers FAQ 2
- Reference desk schedule 0–6
- Research skills class 0–12
- General 7–14
- Library assessment planning and projects 3–15
- Professional development (reading, classes and workshops, learning new tools) 5–10
- University-wide committee involvement 0–5

This list will be your master document for the next item in our toolkit and is also a helpful reminder of how you should be spending your time. You can also transpose the information into a spreadsheet and roughly log how you spent your time at the end of each day. This will help to align your actual daily workload with your goals and responsibilities, as well as possibly uncovering new duties to add to your list. Finally, this is an excellent list to use for discussions with a supervisor about goals and achievements.

TOOL NUMBER 2: TAKING TASKS TO TASK

Now that you have broadly identified how you spend your time, let's take a look at managing the details. I expect that everybody reading this already keeps a task list of some sort, but perhaps not as effectively as possible. Here are some tips for getting the most out of this important time management tool.

Choose a Task Tool

The first step is to find a task list system that works well for you. A paper list is fine for grocery shopping, but is usually not ideal for work. An online tool is more flexible and useful for optimizing time management. If possible, select a task list manager that allows you to do the following:

- Create multiple lists and interfile or view them separately.
- Create recurring tasks.
- Set a priority level for each task.
- Sort by due date or priority.

I use the task manager Remember the Milk, available at http://www.rememberthemilk.com, but there are others that meet the criteria outlined above, such as those discussed in Andre Kibbe's article for WorkAwesome (Kibbe 2010). Of course, there are many criteria to consider when selecting your tool, so think about what other features you would find useful. For example, do you want to sync your to-do list with your smart phone? Will you always be at an Internet connection, or do you need to be able to work offline? Will you want to be able to view completed tasks? It's worth taking some time to find the right tool for you.

Although I prefer the flexibility of an online task management system, paper is very portable, and there is no risk of server downtime (though paper *can* get lost, wet, or left in a locked building). If you do prefer a paper notebook for recording tasks, find a good one. Levenger's Circa agenda (http://www.levenger.com), with annotation tabs and task pads, is an excellent choice, as the pad pages and individual, item-sized tabs can be resorted or moved from day to day. The Franklin Planner (http://store.franklinplanner.com) is another popular agenda and planner, although it doesn't offer the flexibility of physically moving tasks from day to day. What really matters is that you find a tool that you can (and will) use effectively.

Once you have a task management tool, the next step is to use it to your advantage. The following techniques take advantage of options available in online tools, but they can be modified for paper.

Create Lists Based on Projects or Roles

Go back to your workload inventory (the final product from tool number 1) and use it to create a list for each of your major projects or roles. Create multiple lists, one for each item on your inventory, so that you can interfile them or view each list separately. Being able to review all of the tasks that you need to do today or this week is important, but so is being able to review what is coming up on a particular project. Don't forget to add task items for those areas in which you have decided to cut back. For example, one of mine is "step off ACRL committee when term ends."

Include Recurring Tasks and Small Tasks

Some tasks have to be completed daily or weekly. Although it may not seem necessary to list "check the comment box" as a daily item or "grade class assignments" as a weekly task, there are two reasons to do so. First, when you get busy, these sorts of tasks can fall through the cracks or get pushed to the end of the day. Why work late when a simple reminder would alleviate the problem? Second, research suggests that the human brain can only keep four things in working memory at a time (Buschman et al. 2011). Writing things down clears your head so that you can focus on actually doing your job, not on remembering to do it.

Add Due Dates

It is intuitive to record a task's due date in the "due date" field, because that's what it says. However, some tasks take two minutes and some take three weeks. If you arrange items in the order they are due, rather than in the order you need to work on them, large tasks may not pop to the top of your list until it's too late. A solution is to record the day you need to work on the task in the "due date" field, and to include the due date, if needed, in parentheses. For example, one item on my list is "reference desk coverage during librarian meetings (9/13 forward)." Although I have completed the reference schedule through 9/13, I need to start thinking about this task in August, so my "due date" is August 1. For items that take more than one day (such as writing this article), I either create a repeating task or click "postpone" to move the item to the next day, after I have worked on the task for the allotted time.

Record Preparation Time as a Task

In a fast-paced environment with competing priorities, it is easy to forget to prepare for a meeting or class until the last minute. Of course when this happens, everything conspires to make it even harder: the copy machine jams, your toner cartridge runs out of ink, and your laptop battery dies. Arriving at an appointment frazzled is no fun, and the problem is easily remedied. Record time to prepare for events as a to-do item. This takes care of this problem and gives you time to sweet-talk the copier.

Review Your List Daily

The best task list in the world won't do you a bit of good if you don't use it. Review your compiled list each morning and adjust it as necessary based on how much time you will actually have to complete tasks. Each evening before going home, take a few minutes to review and adjust again. It's a good idea to scan a few days out, to see if there are things that you should do sooner (such as a major deadline that you forgot to allot time for) or could push out to a later date to make room for other work. Once a week or so, I look at each project and responsibility task list individually, to see if I'm missing anything or should adjust due dates to create balance.

Use Priority Levels

Most online task management tools will let you sort by date or priority level. You may find the priority option helpful, in which case use it, but I find that *everything* in my list needs to be completed. I use priority labels as sort of a project management hack, to sort complex projects that I am in charge of, but to which other people are contributing. For example, I am chairing a conference planning committee. I label all tasks that I need to complete personally as priority 1, tasks that committee members will take care of as priority 2, and things that we need outside people to complete as priority 3. This allows me to see only the tasks that are on *my* plate by doing a priority sort, but I can also see tasks that others are responsible for by date and send reminders if needed.

Break Big Projects into Small Tasks

Being overwhelmed by big projects is a common complaint and a frequent cause for procrastination. This can be stressful and result in unprofessional, even disastrous, consequences. Rather than listing an entire project as a task item, break every assignment into the smallest possible items. For example, the idea of being in charge of an entire library conference is overwhelming. However, I know that I am capable of calling a caterer, checking on laptops for the presenters to use, or sending letters to potential vendors.

Breaking projects into small tasks has the added benefit of making it easy to use time between one appointment and the next productively. I could hardly plan an entire assessment survey in the fifteen minutes between my reference desk shift and a meeting, but I could certainly write an e-mail to the person in charge of campus assessment to request a random sample of students for the survey. Having already recorded the individual steps needed to complete a project makes it easy to pick one and check it off your list, so begin every project with a detailed breakdown.

Record E-mail To-Do Items

Another source of overwhelming work for many people is e-mail. I have seen colleagues' e-mail inboxes with thousands of e-mails in them. They are saving those e-mails because they require action, but in order to take action, they have to reread the e-mails. I think that this is a time drain, as well as being the electronic equivalent of having a cluttered desk. Clutter doesn't bother some people, but if it is a problem for you, I suggest that you either act on each e-mail that day or create a to-do entry that more succinctly indicates what action to take. Once you have recorded an action item, delete or file the e-mail.

TOOL NUMBER 3: ADMINISTERING YOUR AGENDA

Calendars and task lists go hand in hand, so the methods for managing them match closely. Anything with enough space to record your daily agenda is fine, including the Levenger and Franklin planners noted previously, although I am partial to online calendars for a number of reasons. An online calendar is accessible from anywhere with an Internet connection. Many will also sync with a smart phone for easy and portable offline access. In a work setting where everybody uses the same calendar system, it is easy to invite others to a meeting and to see when people are available. Finally, scheduling recurring events is easy, as is moving items to a new time slot.

Record Recurring and Future Events

Record recurring events well into the future. This will keep you from double booking yourself, as well as simply acting as a mnemonic. Also record future events when possible, so that you don't have to look up things like when that conference will be held in 2013.

Set Aside Time to Prepare and to Work on Projects

It seems that open spaces on a calendar attract appointments. This can create problems getting ready for meetings, classes, or other events that require preparation. It can also leave you with no time to work on projects. Supplement the reminders in your task list by blocking off preparation time in your calendar. During extremely busy times, you might even want to schedule breaks and time at the start and end of each day to review your task list and agenda.

Review Your Calendar Daily

As with your task list, spend some time reviewing your calendar each evening before leaving work. The two go hand in hand: as you review your calendar, be sure that everything you need to accomplish for the next several days is listed in your task list. As you look over your calendar to see where you are supposed to be when, note whether you'll have time to complete the items on your task list. Make adjustments where necessary.

TOOL NUMBER 4: SPOTLIGHT ON FOCUS

Many people, especially those in fast-paced professions, have a difficult time focusing during quiet times. Those of us who teach know how much easier it is to get students involved in an activity than it is to get them to pay attention to a lecture. It's not just students, though; the majority of people prefer action to concentration, and most people who work in libraries get more practice with juggling multiple activities than with quietly directing their attention to one thing. Following are some techniques that can help with focus.

Set a Timer

This method is great for tasks that you tend to put off or that fall through the cracks. For me, professional reading is a chore I often procrastinate about. I would simply rather be doing almost anything else. I have a book about statistical analysis on my desk right now, where it has been sitting for three days, unopened. Today, and every workday for the next three weeks, I have set aside twenty minutes to read. Twenty minutes isn't very long, so my brain won't launch a full-scale rebellion, and one of two things will happen. Either I'll get through the book twenty minutes at a time, which is slow, but much faster than not reading at all. Or I will become interested in the book and keep reading after the timer goes off. Either way, I win.

Take Notes

It is always a good idea to take notes while reading or while listening to a lecture, webinar, or training session. This helps keep your mind from wandering and creates a record of important points. Perhaps more important, it turns a passive activity into an active one, which stimulates the mind. Having paper and pen is also helpful, because if something unrelated to your current task comes to mind, you can take a quick note and then return to the matter at hand. This technique is often used by people who have trouble sleeping due to anxiety, and I have a friend who used it to train herself to meditate. Getting things on paper gets them out of your head.

Limit Distractions

My library purchased iPads for all of the librarians, and they are great in many ways. I don't have to print documents to bring to meetings. I can add things to my task list, look up pertinent information, and take notes that are easy to edit and send as e-mail. However, I don't carry my iPad in situations where I know I will have a hard time concentrating. Having the Internet at my fingertips is just too distracting when I should be watching a webinar on assessment techniques. Similarly, if I have professional reading to do on an airplane trip, I don't tempt myself by also bringing the latest Carl Hiaasen novel.

YOUR OWN TOOLKIT

Using the entire list of ideas in this chapter exactly as written may work wonderfully for you, or it might make you feel strangled. Miserable people are not productive, so it's important to select tools and routines that work for you. As you determine what will work for you, keep in mind the basic criteria for managing your time:

- Get a handle on how you *currently* spend your time.
- Map how you *should* spend your time, based on your responsibilities and goals.
- Generate tasks based on this map.
- Create the time and habits to accomplish your tasks.

Best of luck in building your own successful time management toolkit!

TIME MANAGEMENT TOOLKIT REFERENCE

For quick reference, here is the entire toolkit in outline form. You may want to photocopy this page and use it to record notes and your own ideas.

Tool Number 1: Inventory and Itemize

- Create a rough inventory.
- Track your time.
- Review and adjust.

Tool Number 2: Taking Tasks to Task

- Choose a task tool.
- Create lists based on projects or roles.
- Include recurring tasks and small tasks.
- Add due dates.
- Record preparation time as a task.
- Review your list daily.
- Use priority levels.
- Break big projects into small tasks.
- Record e-mail to-do items.

Tool Number 3: Administering Your Agenda

- Record recurring and future events.
- Review your calendar daily.

Tool Number 4: Spotlight on Focus

- Set a timer.
- Take notes.
- Limit distractions.

WORKS CITED

Buschman, T. J., M. Siegel, J. E. Roy, and E. K. Miller. 2011. "Neural Substrates of Cognitive Capacity Limitations." *Proceedings of the National Academy of Sciences of the United States of America* 108: 11252–11255.

Harwell, Kevin. 2008. "Burnout Strategies for Librarians." *Journal of Business and Finance Librarianship* 13: 370–390.

Kibbe, Andre. 2010. "10 Online To Do List Manager Solutions to Get Things Done." http://workawesome.com/productivity/10-online-to-do-list-manager-solutions-to-get-things-done/. (accessed February 1, 2012).

SIXTEEN

Nimble Project Management for the Time and Budget Challenged

Erin White

This situation may sound familiar: you are a new manager, a team leader, or a team of one; you are working on a variety of projects that differ in complexity, scope, and importance; and you're drowning. There is too much to remember, details are being overlooked, timelines are not being followed, priorities are unclear, and there is no way you have time to learn about how to manage all these projects.

This chapter outlines one solution: a lightweight framework for busy managers of small to medium projects. It includes a flexible, transparent way to document project plans, milestones, and other requirements, using tools freely available on the Web. This methodology has been used in varying iterations at Virginia Commonwealth University (VCU) Libraries for Web project management since 2010. Although the examples in this chapter are Web application projects, the principles and techniques can easily translate to non-Web projects as well.

A DISCLAIMER ABOUT PROJECT MANAGEMENT

This framework is helpful for managers of small to medium projects who are not formally trained as project managers. Larger-scale, enterprise-level projects that rely on large implementation teams are an entirely separate undertaking. In those cases, it may be helpful to bring in a dedicated project manager. There is probably an abundance of literature in your own library that addresses project management techniques. For more robust techniques specifically for libraries' unique business models,

Web Project Management for Academic Libraries (Fagan and Keach 2010) offers instruction grounded in theory and practice. The book's methods can also extend to non-Web projects.

A NOTE ON USING WEB-BASED TOOLS

The techniques in this chapter use Google Docs spreadsheets as the primary repository for project information. Web-based document management software allows several actions that non-Web spreadsheet editing software cannot. With Web-based software, managers can do the following:

1. Edit documents from any computing device with an Internet connection and a browser, at any time.
2. Embed or link to documents from other web pages without requiring readers to download files or launch separate applications.
3. Share documents with team members, who can use the documents for reference and update the documents with their progress on tasks.
4. Share documents with stakeholders, who can see the project requirements and work status and understand overall project priorities.
5. See past revisions to documents.

If you or leaders of your organization are hesitant to store documents on third-party servers, a Web-based solution may not work for you. Some organizations may expressly prohibit storing work-related documents on another organization's servers, while others may proscribe certain software packages for document management. Because the documents in this chapter are spreadsheets, any spreadsheet application will do, but Web-based tools offer easy collaboration, flexibility, and transparency that non-Web software cannot.

PRIMARY TOOL: THE MASTER PROJECTS LIST

If you use nothing else in this chapter, build a master project list. This spreadsheet will be the go-to document for your team and the key element in your toolkit.

What Is It?

The master project list is a combined spreadsheet of all the projects on your team's radar, from small to large. The list should at the very least include a name for each project, its priority in comparison to other projects, and its status. At a glance, you, your team, and others in your organization should be able to see which projects your team is aware of, which projects you are working on, and which are most important.

Why Have It?

- *It keeps stakeholders in the loop.* Project owners, your supervisor, your team members, and others in your organization can check in on the status of their pet projects or others' projects.
- *It helps you field new projects.* When a new project request comes in, there is a framework for understanding where that project will fit in with other projects.
- *It gives a general idea of your team's workload.* This 30,000-foot overview can help when you need to readjust the priorities on the list, give others a realistic idea of timing for new projects, or lobby for new team members.
- *It helps you and your boss determine your priorities.* Assigning priorities together with your supervisor will help align your work with the larger needs and goals of the organization.
- *It manages your time in the short and long terms.* The project list can serve as a dashboard for you, allowing you to track your team's progress and plan into the future.
- *It tracks your successes.* A list of completed projects helps you assess your team's accomplishments, write end-of-year reports, and demonstrate value to your organization.

What's In It?

For each project on the list—remember, no project is too small—you can include any or all of the following information, presented here in order of importance:

- *Project name:* A short, descriptive, novice-readable name that will help you identify the project in communications to your team and the rest of your organization.
- *Short description:* A brief description of the project and the business need.
- *Link to project plan:* A connection to a separate project plan for this project (covered in the next part of this chapter), if you have developed one.
- *Priority:* How the project stacks up against others. How priorities are named is up to you. VCU uses A/B/C, but you could also use high/medium/low; critical/urgent/whenever; or any other scheme you'd like. Developing some rubric for assigning project priorities, informal or formal, will help save time when assigning priorities in the future.

- *Status:* Your team's progress on the project. VCU uses pending, administrative review, under way, complete. This field can also be used for more specific notes on where the project is. For example, "Underway" = ready for departmental test.
- *Project lead:* The person on your team who is responsible for carrying out the project.
- *Project owner:* The person who initiated the project or is most impacted by the project; record name and e-mail address.
- *Category of project:* What type of project it is; categories are up to you. Depending on the size of the project list, being able to filter or sort by the project category may be helpful.

SECONDARY TOOL: THE INDIVIDUAL PROJECT PLAN

Depending on the complexity of individual projects, you may want to develop a separate project plan document for each one.

What Is It?

The project plan is a document for each project that covers the basics of the project, its business need, goals, requirements, and stakeholders. For more complex projects, the document may be made more complex to include timelines, tasks, and milestones, and to serve as a working document for you and your team.

Why Have It?

- *It clarifies the scope and business needs of the project.* Setting the project goals and scope early on can prevent scope creep in the future.
- *It helps you understand dependencies.* Very few projects exist in isolation. Understanding projects' impact on other systems, processes, or users early on helps prevent headaches later.
- *It breaks the project down into tasks and milestones for your team.* Depending on the project's complexity, the project plan may include a detailed task list or general milestones.
- *It makes an honest estimate of time.* Although creating a project plan takes time, it can save time by helping you accurately estimate how long a project will take. Thinking through functional and strategic questions ahead of time will save time later.
- *It communicates the expectations of stakeholders and team members.* Getting the project in writing clears up misunderstandings and clarifies roles and responsibilities.
- *It keeps stakeholders abreast of project status.* Whether the project is broken down into discrete tasks or grouped into larger phases, the

project plan can serve as a working document that you and your team can use to keep yourselves and stakeholders informed of the project's status.

What's In It?

Depending on the complexity of the project, you may wish to include all or only some of the following information. The important part is to balance the project complexity with the level of detail in the project plan. There is no need to over-document.

- *Basic information:* The title of the project, a short description (both understandable for lay readers), and a business justification of the project.
- *Requirements:* The goal of the project, including specific requirements for the project to be considered successful.
- *Dependencies:* Any systems, processes, or people who are affected by or affect the project. This is also a good place to enunciate any nonobvious business rules that will impact your project.
- *Timeline:* A rough outline of the project, broken into phases or discrete tasks. Project milestones can be set here. If listing tasks, list due dates and responsible team members. Depending on the size of the project, you can be as specific or as general as you want.
- *Roles:* The tasks to be performed by the person who initiated the project (project owner), the project leader, and any other important stakeholders.

Once you develop your first project plan, you can use it as a template for the next.

PUTTING IT ALL TOGETHER

The following steps describe how to leverage the sharing features in Google Docs to create a comprehensive package of project documents:

1. Create a shared repository. (a) In Google Docs, create a folder named for your department. (b) Place your master project list and all of your project plans in the folder. (c) Give write access to appropriate users for the entire folder by adding e-mail addresses for your supervisor, members of your team, and whoever else should be allowed to edit the documents. (d) Give view access to the folder for anyone who has the link.
2. Add a link to the master project list and/or the entire folder from your team's home page or another place where organizational stakeholders can easily access it.

3. For each project entry on the master project list spreadsheet, add a link to the individual project plan document, if there is one.
4. After your project is complete, move the project to a "completed" sheet on the master project list. Having a list of completed projects will help you in writing up reports or monitoring your team's progress.

Finally, be sure to remain flexible in your approach to this system. This is just a suggested framework for managing project information. As you document more projects using this system, you will begin to understand what type of documentation works best for you and your team. Leave behind the elements that are not proving useful and add others that you find helpful. Each project will have its own unique needs. With this framework, you should be able to tailor your approach to each project and create some order from the chaos.

WORKS CITED

Fagan, Jody C., and Jennifer A. Keach. 2010. *Web Project Management for Academic Libraries*. Cambridge, UK: Chandos.

SEVENTEEN

A Novel Approach to Project Management: Seven Lessons from NaNoWriMo

Karen Munro

In November of each year, thousands of people around the world attempt the nearly impossible. They isolate themselves from loved ones; wipe their social calendars bare; and hole up in attics, coffee shops, and libraries. Some are well prepared; some are flying by the seat of their pants. Some join online communities, where they post about their setbacks and progress or meet up with others doing the same thing in their area. Others go it alone for the whole month. But they all have one thing in common: they are trying to write a novel in just thirty days.

Over the last decade, National Novel Writing Month (NaNoWriMo) has blossomed from a tiny venture involving just a handful of people (including founder Chris Baty) into a major event that brings thousands of people back year after year. Its offshoots include a NaNoWriMo Young Writers category for kids and teenagers and Script Frenzy, a challenge to complete a screenplay of at least one hundred pages in the month of April. The overall aim is to help people write prolifically, without hesitation or self-editing—to force them to get words down on the page and worry about the details later. Sometimes this even produces commercially successful results: Sara Gruen's *Water for Elephants*, Erin Morgenstern's *The Night Circus*, and Gayle Brandeis's *Self Storage* all started out as NaNoWriMo projects.

But real success in NaNoWriMo's terms is reaching the 50,000-word mark—which in turn demands great dedication, self-discipline, and organization. NaNoWriMo and other extreme writing schedules offer something to the busy, under-resourced librarian tasked with a major project. Whether you're working on a website redesign, a grant proposal, a space renovation, or any other multifaceted and time-sensitive project, you face many of the same challenges as writers working under tight deadlines. Just as thousands of people manage to wring 50,000 words out of thirty days of their lives while still accomplishing everything else they need to do, so can librarians find ways to pack more into our workdays when we really need to.

This chapter examines some practical lessons librarians can draw from deadline-driven writing, to help us complete project-based work. Some of these strategies may also improve the efficiency and order of our regular working lives, after we have met our project deadlines and are celebrating a return to our regularly scheduled hectic routines.

LESSON ONE: HAVE A PLAN

This is the foundation for everything else. A plan will help you understand how your daily work feeds into your short- and long-range project goals. It will help keep you on track when budgets are cut and crises occur. The plan will give your work meaning and bolster your morale. And it will help you make the best possible use of your time and energy, so you don't waste either.

Michael Moorcock, legendary author of over fifty sword-and-sorcery novels, claims to have written many of his early works in no more than three days. As a hand-to-mouth author, he had no choice but to write quickly and in volume, sometimes producing up to 15,000 words a day. In *Michael Moorcock: Death Is No Obstacle*, a collection of interviews discussing his career, his first nugget of advice is, "If you're going to do a piece of work in three days, you have to have everything properly prepared" (Greenland 1992, 6).

In Moorcock's terms, that means a basic plot structure, some character concepts, and some thematic elements ready to go. Translated for the busy librarian, it means separating the planning stage of the work from its execution. It can be easy to forget that planning is part of the workload of any project. But it's difficult to do the operational part of the project — the actual data entry, documentation, selection, training, etc. — while simultaneously deciding what to tackle next or how the stages of the project fit together. Moorcock elaborates: "The whole reason you plan everything beforehand is so that when you hit a snag, a desperate moment, you've actually got something there on your desk that tells you what to do" (Greenland 1992, 9). A work plan is what tells a busy librarian what to do when crises happen. It reminds us of what's vital right now, what's due, and what can wait.

Work plans might help with projects with distinct end dates, but what about the ongoing and day-to-day tasks? Can a plan help you with your reference desk hours, your collection development, your outreach to patrons or faculty, or any other work that has no clear timeline or end point? Yes, if you take the right approach.

From one point of view, a novel is a distinct project. It has a first and a last page, and though it may go through many revisions, sooner or later it goes to the publisher and is out of the author's hands. On the other hand, a writer's overall practice—daily word counts, self-discipline, the ability to stay in one's chair and work despite competing demands on one's time—is not a project. Just like a librarian, a writer has a day-to-day job and has to learn to manage its ups and downs. Having a plan helps both writers and librarians manage the daily joys, drudgery, and "desperate moments" of their work.

LESSON TWO: TRACK YOUR DATA

Librarians are used to tracking project outputs and outcomes to measure them against standards—but there's more that data can do for you. Tracking your own work habits can help you figure out when, and under what conditions, you're best at doing certain types of work. It can also help you find the hours in your day to handle an additional workload during a project push.

Novelist Rachel Aaron (2011) posted the following advice on her blog, detailing how she managed to increase her word count from 2,000 to 10,000 words a day:

> If I was going to boost my output. . . . I had to know what I was outputting in the first place. So, I started keeping records. Every day I had a writing session I would note the time I started, the time I stopped, how many words I wrote, and where I was writing on a spreadsheet. I did this for two months, and then I looked for patterns.
> Several things were immediately clear. First, my productivity was at its highest when I was in a place . . . without internet. . . . I also saw that . . . the longer I wrote, the faster I wrote. . . . This corresponding rise of word count and writing hours only worked up to a point, though. There was a definite words per hour drop off around hour 7 when I was simply too brain fried to go on.

Aaron describes how she used her data to reorganize her writing schedule so that she got the most out of her time. In an update to the post, she comments that she subsequently completed a novel in twelve days, writing on average between 800 and 1,600 words per hour.

Although Chris Baty, founder of the NaNoWriMo project, advocates a largely seat-of-the-pants approach to writing, he does suggest that writers prepare for NaNoWriMo by taking a close look at their schedules to find time when they can squeeze writing into their regular lives. By listing their daily activities in half-hour increments, then highlighting essential activities in red and important activities in blue, writers can uncover time spent on what Baty calls "forgo-able" activities. For writers, these may be hours spent watching television or chatting online. For librarians, they may be any tasks that can be delegated or postponed beyond the project deadline without major repercussions. As Baty says, "If, like me, you've found that you're spending between an hour and a half and two hours a day on forgo-able items, you're golden" (Baty 2004, 43). These are the hours that can be devoted to completing the project on deadline.

Although librarians may not need to churn out 50,000 words in a month, we can still benefit from Aaron's and Baty's advice. Recording your work habits and examining them for patterns of productivity can help make your days run more smoothly. For example, you may find it more of a struggle to write e-mails or design promotional materials in the late afternoon, or you may notice that if you open your e-mail first thing in the morning, you get lost in minutiae. And you may think there's no way you can handle another project right now—until you examine your schedule and realize you can clear a few things out of it.

If you know these things about yourself and your schedule, you may be able to lessen the stress of an additional workload and make the work itself go faster. But to know them, you have to track them.

LESSON THREE: DON'T LET THE PERFECT BE THE ENEMY OF THE GOOD

We all want to do a great job at everything, all the time. But doing a great job takes more time and energy than doing an okay job—and sometimes, doing an okay job is just fine. In one of NaNoWriMo's collected pep talks from famous authors, Jasper Fforde writes, "The overriding importance is that the 50,000 words don't have to be good. They don't even have to be spelled properly, punctuated or even tabulated neatly on the page. It's not important. . . . The only way to write is to write" (Fforde n.d.). Chris Baty says, "When your novel first peeks its head into the world, it will look pretty much like every newborn: pasty, hairless, and utterly confused" (Baty 2004, 31).

Fforde's and Baty's points are that if you're going to write 50,000 words in a month, you can't spend time worrying about whether they're all great. To accomplish the larger goal, you have to spend your time writing rather than editing—which means letting go of any idea of perfection. In fact, Baty exhorts writers to embrace what he calls "exuberant imperfection," which, he says, "dictates that the best way to tackle daunting, paralysis-inducing challenges is to give yourself permission to make mistakes, and then go ahead and make them" (Baty 2004, 33.)

This is helpful, if counterintuitive, advice for anyone tackling a big project. It's easy to get stuck in the details, polishing every e-mail to a high gleam. But if the point of the e-mail is just to convey basic information, and your to-do stack is tipping perilously over your desk, it may be wiser to dash off a quick note and hit send. It's not always smart or efficient to insist on perfection. The time we invest in finessing every detail of our online tutorials or research instruction pages may be lost as soon as an interface changes or a tool is superseded.

There are times when perfection matters, and there are times when experimentation, flexibility, and a spirit of "exuberant imperfection" are just what you need to lay the foundations of a great project. Hone your judgment to tell the difference between them, and sally forth accordingly.

LESSON FOUR: TAKE CARE OF YOURSELF

Librarians and speed writers have one big thing in common: burnout. Sooner or later, day after day of hard work or high word counts will start to wilt even the most energetic among us. To succeed over the long run, it's important to balance your workload, to keep your sense of perspective (and even humor), and sometimes, to give yourself a break.

Sometimes a change is as good as a rest. In its annual sets of NaNoWriMo tips, the book industry website Galleycat offers plenty of suggestions for changing up your writing routine. You can work with other NaNoWriMo writers in a common location (the New York Public Librarys host NaNoWriMo write-together events), dictate instead of type, or get help building your imaginary world in the NaNoWriMo forums. Galleycat reminds you to correct your writing posture and eat healthy snacks. If all that fails, take a break with a literary drink—maybe a mojito in honor of Hemingway or a gimlet for Raymond Chandler (Galleycat 2011).

Librarians can benefit from the same advice. If boredom and fatigue are catching up with you, look for ways to change your work around. Switch projects, change your routine, or try a new way of doing something. Add a new dimension to daily tasks by tracking your progress and rewarding yourself for milestones.

If your work is computer-bound, be sure to consider your physical health, too. Baty points out that "if you've spent any amount of time using a computer, you already know the range of sneaky, bloodthirsty ways they have of wrecking your body. Carpal tunnel syndrome, eye strain, back problems, numb-butt . . . the list of computer-inspired woes goes on and on" (2004, 27). Several recent studies (e.g., Reynolds 2012) have shown the benefits of occasionally standing up, and the dangers of long periods of unrelieved sitting. Baty recommends using free software to lock your computer and prompt you to stretch (Workspace.com and

Rsiguard.com offer free trials), try eye exercises, and keep eye drops handy to help combat the dry-eye syndrome of too much fixed attention. Whatever you do, consider building some exercise into your day to help keep you strong, healthy, and mentally energized. It's up to you whether you want to consider adding a library-related cocktail to your regimen.

LESSON FIVE: TRY NEW TOOLS

NaNoWriMo writers are famous for exploiting any tool that might help them reach their 50,000-word goal, and there are plenty of free technologies for them to try. Some of these are also good fits for the busy librarian.

- OmmWriter, a free text processor application, clears your screen of everything except a blank page or a peaceful snowy animation and plays gentle music (which you can turn off), a calming alternative to the button- and text-filled screens we're used to coping with.
- Freedom: Billed as "Internet blocking productivity software," Freedom allows you to disconnect your computer from a wireless network for a specified period of time. If you're prone to online distractions when you need to work, Freedom may be your ticket to getting things done.
- Evernote or Simplenote: Two free applications that help you keep track of notes, thoughts, ideas, pictures, and just about everything else. If you use a smartphone or iPad as well as a workstation, you can sync your account across multiple devices, so your work goes with you and you don't lose track of any valuable ideas.
- Instapaper: The next time you run across an interesting article on copyright or public programming, but can't read it because you're in the middle of three other things, use Instapaper. Simpler and cleaner than bookmarking, Instapaper remembers the web pages you're interested in and preserves them for you to read when you have time.
- Dropbox: Need to store or transfer large files? Dropbox gives you all the storage space you need and allows you to share files and folders with anyone who has an account. No more bounced e-mails!
- Mindjet mind-mapping: Mindjet's free Mind Manager software lets you visualize all the parts of a project in relation to one another. You can then annotate, rearrange, and add relationship indicators like arrows and lines. Also available free for the iPhone and iPad.
- F.lux: This free software automatically changes the quality and brightness of your computer screen's light depending on time of day. If you're using your computer intensively over the course of several days, you may find that this helps decrease your fatigue and helps you rest better when you're away from your work.

LESSON SIX: KEEP GOING

To finish a project on time, you have to keep working until it's done. This may seem so obvious that it's unnecessary to state, but in fact momentum and consistency may be the hardest tools to wield in meeting a project deadline.

Moorcock, arguably the master of meeting the impossible project deadline, says that "[o]nce you've started, you keep it rolling. You can't afford to have anything stop it" (Greenland 1992, 8–9). Baty advises would-be thirty-day novelists that "there is one golden rule you should keep in mind when laying out your writing schedule: Don't take more than two nights off from your novel in a row" (Baty 2004, 45). And April Kihlstrom, author of multiple romance novels and self-proclaimed "Mistress of Book in a Week," repeats multiple variations on this advice in her online guide to fast novel writing:

> Write.
> Keep writing. Do not go back and reread what you've done!
> Take breaks but then go back to writing. . . .
> Even if it seems like total nonsense, write. . . .
> If you have an off morning or day, don't waste time beating yourself
> up, just get back to writing and keep going! . . .
> If you only have 5 minutes at a time, sit down and write for 5 minutes!

These exhortations may seem simplistic and redundant, but they clearly produce results. Once you have invested all the time and energy necessary to get a project off the ground (including planning the stages, scheduling your time, setting priorities, and so forth), you have also given yourself the gift of momentum. It's easier to keep a project running while it's fresh in your mind than it is to bring it back to life after an interruption. If you let a project lapse, you'll probably need to spend time reviewing your plans and ideas before you can start work on it again, which eliminates the efficiency you built into your plans in the first place.

As Kihlstrom points out, you may not always be able to work under ideal conditions. Your schedule will change, you'll be handed new assignments, you'll have to put out brush fires. The hour that you set aside to work on something may shrink to just a few minutes. Train yourself to use whatever time you have, and recognize that even working in small increments is valuable, because it keeps the project fresh in your mind and on top of your to-do list.

LESSON SEVEN: CELEBRATE SUCCESS

Chris Baty concludes his thirty-day novel-writing manual with a letter of congratulations to all NaNoWriMo participants:

No matter how many words you have written, you have done an
amazing thing. Through distractions and demands and family obligations, you forged ahead. Your willingness to go out on a creative limb,
to stand up and reach for an impossible goal, is an inspiring example to
us all. (Baty 2004, 154)

As important as it is to train yourself to work more efficiently, it's just as
key to reward yourself for a job well done. NaNoWriMo offers down-
loadable badges and certificates to all its finishers, as well as plenty of
virtual applause. Baty also suggests that writers remember to thank their
support staff: the family and friends who have stood by them during
their month-long effort.

This is good advice for all of us. No matter what bumps and swerves
we encounter along the way, when the project is finished, we should
celebrate our own efforts and those of our supporters. Recognizing hard
work is a crucial, final piece of the project, and one that's often overlooked. Whether you write a glowing formal letter for a colleague's personnel file or take yourself out for dinner and a movie after the deadline
passes, find a way to mark the event. Giving yourself and others a pat on
the back and a bit of a breather will help you recruit everyone's best
efforts next time you're hit with a project deadline, and just like NaNo-
WriMo, there's always a next time.

WORKS CITED

Aaron, Rachel. 2011. "How I Went from Writing 2,000 Words a Day to 10,000 Words a
     Day." *Pretentious Title: The Writing Blog of Author Rachel Aaron*, June 8 (blog). http://
     thisblogisaploy.blogspot.com/2011/06/how-i-went-from-writing-2000-words-
     day.html.
Baty, Chris. 2004. *No Plot? No Problem! A Low-Stress, High-Velocity Guide to Writing a
     Novel in 30 Days*. San Francisco: Chronicle Books.
Fforde, Jasper. n.d. "Jasper Fforde's Pep Talk." *National Novel Writing Month*. http://
     www.nanowrimo.org/en/pep/jasper-fforde.
Galleycat. 2011. "National Novel Writing Month Writers Produced 3 Billion Words."
     December 1. http://www.mediabistro.com/galleycat/national-novel-writing-month-
     writers-produced-3-billion-words_b43169.
Greenland, Colin. 1992. *Michael Moorcock: Death Is No Obstacle*. Manchester, UK: Savoy.
Kihlstrom, April. n.d. *Book in a Week*. http://www.sff.net/people/april.kihlstrom/
     BIAW.htm.
Reynolds, Gretchen. 2012. "Don't Just Sit There." *New York Times*, April 28. http://
     www.nytimes.com/2012/04/29/sunday-review/stand-up-for-fitness.html.

EIGHTEEN

Time Management for Busy Academic Librarians: Strategies for Success

William H. Weare Jr.

Many academic librarians hold positions that include a variety of regular activities, such as time at the reference desk, instructional obligations, liaison duties, meetings, and service commitments, as well as management or supervisory responsibilities. In addition to these activities, many academic librarians—particularly those with tenure-track appointments—are expected to conduct research and contribute to the profession through presentation and publication. Other librarians, though not burdened with anxieties related to tenure, are interested in sharing their knowledge with peers through presentations at conferences or writing for publication. Given the numerous day-to-day responsibilities expected of a librarian, how does one find time to write an article, book chapter, conference paper, or grant proposal, or to complete any other substantial project?

Finding time to work on a project that lies outside of routine responsibilities has become even more difficult during the current economic downturn. This situation has taken a toll on libraries of all types, in many cases resulting in budget cuts and staff reductions. Consequently, many librarians now have more areas of responsibility than in the past. During this same period, what is expected of tenure-track academic librarians with regard to presentation and publication appears to have increased at many institutions. Academic librarians confront many demands on their time that may adversely impact their ability to get things done, especially their capacity to meet long-term goals.

In this chapter I review several time management practices that have significantly impacted my ability to accomplish long term-goals; these practices are relatively easy to implement and maintain. First, I describe an effective work style in which one writes or works *every day* (albeit briefly) on one or more particular, long-term projects. Such a pattern of small, consistent, daily actions on the part of academics has been shown to improve output (Boice 2000). Second, I suggest taking a time inventory, a process that will help readers see how their time is being used. Third, I describe a series of closely related time management strategies that, when applied together, result in a much more efficient approach to completing long-term projects. These strategies include establishing goals, determining priorities, breaking large tasks into small tasks, and mapping these tasks to a calendar.

WORK IN BRIEF, DAILY SESSIONS

Many academic librarians (and disciplinary faculty) find the writing process painful. For some, their fears and anxieties about the process prevent them from achieving success in their chosen fields. Perhaps you have known librarians who have left tenure-track appointments for nontenure positions because they found the research and writing requirements too demanding, or others who have remained in their positions, but failed to produce enough to be granted tenure. If you find the process of writing painful—or feel overwhelmed when faced with any large project—you are not alone.

A common (and erroneous) belief among academics is that they must have big blocks of time in which to conduct research and write. Busy with teaching and service commitments during the semester, they put off their projects, assuming they will have time to write during long weekends, holidays, semester breaks, and the summer (Boice 2000; Gray 2005; Rockquemore and Laszloffy 2008). Robert Boice, faculty emeritus of psychology at Stony Brook University, studied the experiences of new faculty. He compared the behaviors of faculty who thrive with those who struggle. Boice referred to faculty members who depend on big blocks of time to research and write as *binge writers*. Such writers make little progress during the semester and rarely make a great deal of headway during the much-anticipated big blocks of time reserved for writing (Boice 2000).

There is no need to suffer and struggle using the binge writer's approach. Boice has provided a better way. He wrote several books, including *Advice for New Faculty Members*, in which he advocated that faculty approach teaching, writing, and service with what he called constancy and moderation. This particular approach to teaching, writing, and service—successfully employed by many academics—makes it possible to enjoy academic work while enjoying greater productivity. He found that some new faculty model better ways of working; he usually referred to these people as *quick starters* or *exemplars*. They have learned to work in brief, daily sessions: usually just twenty to thirty minutes per day on a particular project or task. Boice measured the scholarly output of such exemplars as opposed to the output of binge writers and found that the quick starters who worked in brief, daily sessions ultimately were much more productive than those who tried to complete their work in large blocks of time (Boice 2000). Because these work sessions are intentionally brief, they can fit easily into an already busy day. This practice accounts in part for how successful and prolific academics get things done.

The approach Boice advocated—constancy and moderation—is widely practiced among successful academics and endorsed by others, including Tara Gray, author of *Publish & Flourish: Become a Prolific Scholar* (2005); Paul Silvia, author of *How to Write a Lot: A Practical Guide to Productive Academic Writing* (2007); and Kerry Ann Rockquemore, coauthor of *The Black Academic's Guide to Winning Tenure—Without Losing Your Soul* (2008). My own experience over the past several years of working in brief, daily sessions confirms these findings.

TAKE A TIME INVENTORY

Perhaps you think you are too busy to add anything else to your schedule, and you couldn't possibly find twenty to thirty minutes every day to spare to write. Like almost everyone, academic librarians have time in their days that is poorly used. To discover that time, take an inventory of how you spend your time. The time inventory concept appears throughout the time management literature; it is sometimes referred to as a *time log* or an *activity report*. This concept makes good sense: you can manage your time more effectively if you understand how you are using it now. This approach is similar to advice given to those who are trying to lose weight—"Keep track of everything you eat"—or to those who are trying to control their spending: "Keep track of everything you buy." Completing a time inventory is an opportunity to evaluate how much of your workday is spent addressing routine tasks, how much is spent working on projects that will help you realize your long-term goals, and how much is poorly spent—or just plain wasted.

Doing a time inventory is simple. Using a spreadsheet, record start and finish times for everything you do throughout the day. Do this for several days if your schedule varies a great deal from day to day. You should of course record the tasks that require larger portions of time: your shift at the reference desk, instruction, meetings, and so forth. Also record the seemingly less important tasks: time spent reading and responding to e-mail, making and returning phone calls, chatting with your coworkers, and other activities that occur throughout the day. The log should have a high level of granularity. It is important to capture every activity (Luecke 2005).

A variety of time inventory templates are available on the Web. Use one of these, or create your own. A six-column spreadsheet works well. In the first column, enter a short description of the activity. In the second and third columns, record the start and end times for each individual activity. In the fourth, record the number of minutes spent doing each activity. In the fifth, enter a category: e-mail, phone, time spent with staff and colleagues, reference, instruction, and so forth. The last column is for evaluating your activities; I suggest that you postpone this evaluation until you have completed the goal-setting exercise described in the following section.

SET GOALS

What do successful, accomplished people have in common? Many things, of course, but there is one trait that certainly stands out: they set goals and then work to achieve those goals. Goal setting is essential for effective time management. Without a clear vision of your goals, it is difficult to determine which of your activities are truly important and how you should spend your time (Morgenstern 2004; Tracy 2010).

If you have never done any sort of goal-setting exercise, now is the time. This activity need not be a complicated undertaking—it is a paper and pencil exercise. Write down what drives you, what excites you, and what you wish to accomplish. Is it tenure and promotion? Do you want to be a dean or director? Finish another degree? Assume a leadership role in a professional organization? Become a prolific scholar? Write a winning grant proposal? Launch a program that will have a significant impact on your community? Write a book? Dream big. Why have small goals? After all, you are a librarian—smart and capable—you have great skills.

Successful people envision what it is they wish to accomplish and then develop an action plan to achieve those goals. Committing goals to paper will strengthen your resolve to accomplish them (Rockquemore and Laszloffy 2008; Tracy 2010).

THE TIME INVENTORY, REVISITED

Having completed this simple goal-setting exercise, turn back to the time inventory to evaluate your activities. Evaluate those listed in your time inventory, taking into account the goals you identified. Which daily activities support your efforts to achieve your long-term goals? Which activities do not? If you are indeed spending part of your day addressing long-term goals, then congratulations! Conversely, if you see little or no connection between your activities and those long-terms goals, you have some work to do. Now is the time to start aligning how you spend your workday with your long-term goals.

Some of the activities listed in the first column of your inventory are simply not a good use of time. How much of your day is spent checking personal e-mail, chatting online, shopping at Amazon, or checking your Facebook account? These activities do not support your efforts to achieve your long-term goals. Such activities are a waste of time and have to be abandoned. When the concept of working in brief, daily sessions was described previously, perhaps you balked at the idea of writing every day. Perhaps you said you could not possibly fit another thing into your already crowded schedule. However, if you were to abandon activities such as shopping at Amazon or checking your Facebook account, would you then have twenty to thirty minutes per day to make progress on a long-term project?

Consider also the routine activities you engage in, such as checking work e-mail, taking calls, and interacting with colleagues. In a busy work environment, such transactions happen throughout the day and interrupt any sustained work on a particular project. Grouping activities such as reading and responding to e-mail is more efficient than being interrupted throughout the day. Consider, for example, checking e-mail only two or three times a day and closing the e-mail program while working on other activities. Alternatively, you might consider working on your primary long-term project—article, book chapter, or grant proposal—for twenty to thirty minutes in the morning, *before* you check your e-mail (Morgenstern 2004; Silvia 2007).

Although taking a time inventory, completing a goal-setting exercise, and evaluating your time inventory in light of your goals may seem like a lot of work, these exercises can yield valuable information. You will see how much of your time is spent on "real work"—work that produces results and contributes to your long-term goals—and how much time is spent in activities that do not contribute to your career in a meaningful way.

DETERMINE PRIORITIES

To get more things done, you do not necessarily need to work harder, faster, or longer, but you may need to learn how to make better use of your time. Determining priorities will help you address what really counts. Robert J. McKain has been credited with saying, "The reason most major goals are not achieved is that we spend our time doing second things first." Turn back to your list of goals and decide which ones— and the tasks associated with them—are first things and which are second things. Focus on first things. Choose your most important task and begin work on that task (Tracy 2010).

This is another paper and pencil exercise. List the items that must be addressed to meet the expectations of your employer. This list should include all of the tasks or job duties that you are responsible for: time at the reference desk, instruction, liaison duties, meetings, service commitments, and so forth. Then list your professional development goals. Rank these items on your list in a way that will help you see which are more important than the others. Getting this down on paper will help you see your obligations to your employer as well as what you need to do to advance your career.

Next, review the list, identify the items that have time boundaries, and determine what can safely be delayed—or even ignored. Of those with time boundaries, figure out which items need to be completed in the near term and which can be addressed at a later date. Although you need to identify those tasks that have time boundaries (and prioritize accordingly), focus on those goals that will have the most impact on your long-term success.

Finally, it is essential that you determine what is truly important in your work life, and what is merely urgent. If you work in a hectic environment, you know how easy it is to confuse urgent with important. Don't sacrifice the time necessary to address long-term goals by expending all of your energy on the *seemingly* important issues that arise daily.

BREAK LARGE TASKS INTO SMALL TASKS

Your list of long-term goals may include the completion of some very large projects, such as writing a book. Clearly, adding "write my book" to your list of goals won't move it much closer to completion. If the goal is too large or too complex (and thus too daunting), it can be very difficult to get started. Such a project can be put off day to day until the deadline arrives. Putting off work not only increases the chance that yet another day will pass without making any progress on your project, it also clouds your day with guilt. Some of us have behaved as if the only option for completing a large project is to jam the whole thing into several days of frenzied effort just prior to the date the project is due. Sound familiar? Fortunately, there is a better way.

The key to meeting a long-term goal or completing a large project is to break down the goal or project into smaller steps, then identify each component task necessary to complete that step (Rockquemore and Laszloffy 2008). These component tasks are small, doable pieces that can be completed in one or several sittings. For example, completing a large project such as writing an article comprises a series of steps. One is to write the literature review. The tasks include searching various databases, reading relevant articles, and synthesizing the material in a way that provides the rationale for the research question to be explored in the article. The small, doable pieces include a search in a particular database or reading an article and taking notes. Such actions can be completed in one or several sittings.

The crucial concept here is granularity. Breaking up projects, such as articles, book chapters, and essays, into component pieces allows you to complete work in a series of small steps and feel more in control of your time. As each small, doable piece is finished, progress is made by executing the steps that will eventually result in the completion of the entire project.

MAP TASKS TO YOUR CALENDAR

Block out on your calendar time to work on your projects, just as you use it to schedule meetings and other recurring activities (Gray 2005; Rockquemore and Laszloffy 2008; Silvia 2007). Once you have broken large projects into steps and broken those steps into component tasks, the tasks can be mapped to your online calendar. For example, specific tasks—such as drafting a query, gathering images for a presentation, or checking the citation list at the end of a chapter—can be added to your calendar as if they were appointments. In a sense they are; treat these project appointments as if they were meetings with others. Don't miss them.

Alternatively, you could block out the same timeslot every day to work on a particular project, but not specify the task to be completed during that time. Instead, enter the name of the project as a recurring appointment. If you use this approach, consider using a spreadsheet to maintain a project calendar on which you can track your progress. Use one spreadsheet for each project. Include day and date, goal (number of minutes you hope to work), start and end times, actual work time (minutes), whether or not the goal was met, and a comments field. Use the comments field to record what you have completed during each work session; note where you left off or what you plan to accomplish next time. If it is a writing project, consider tracking words written and revised, rather than minutes worked.

When working on a project involving writing, it is important to identify the time of day that you are at your physical and mental peak. Sometimes people think they have to do their "real work" (i.e., routine tasks) first and save time at the end of the day for writing. This doesn't work well for academics; most of us are too tired and are unlikely to get quality work done. For many of us, our most productive time is in the morning. Reserve this peak time for writing. Each day, you should address those things that will help you achieve your long-term goals first and do the routine work later. This concept is sometimes referred to as "paying yourself first" (Rockquemore and Laszloffy 2008).

LET GO

If you have acted on these suggestions, you have identified goals, set priorities, and developed a plan for making progress on substantial, long-term projects. However, like most academic librarians, you probably still have more to do in a day than you are likely to get done. What then? It is time to let go of some of the things you think are so important. This letting go process is very difficult. First, consider routine tasks. Many tasks in librarianship that once seemed particularly important are no longer priorities—or even necessary—because the needs and habits of our users have changed. Although academic librarians have done an admirable job of addressing the needs of current users by implementing new services, many have not let go of the practices associated with what users once needed.

It is also important to acknowledge that there are tasks on your calendar and your to-do list that may never get done. Holding on to all of these must-do items may result in guilt, frustration, and disappointment. Such negativity can impact productivity as well as your attitude about your work. It is important to focus on all you have accomplished and will accomplish, rather than on what has not been completed or is unlikely to be completed. Periodically update your calendar and to-do lists. Examine each item that remains undone to determine if you can delegate the task to someone on your staff, if you can delay the task until a later date, or if you can let go of it (Morgenstern 2004). Not everyone has the option of delegating some of their work to others. However, nearly everyone has some leeway in determining what might be rescheduled for a later time and what might be left undone. Keeping the focus on what really is important—and letting go of what is not—will reduce stress and help keep the focus on achieving long-term goals.

The application of the strategies outlined in this chapter—setting goals, determining priorities, breaking large tasks into small ones, mapping tasks to your calendar, and working with constancy and moderation—will enable you to complete significant long-term projects and achieve your goals.

WORKS CITED

Boice, Robert. 2000. *Advice for New Faculty Members: Nihil Nimus*. Needham Heights, MA: Allyn & Bacon.

Gray, Tara. 2005. *Publish &Flourish: Become a Prolific Scholar*. Teaching Academy. Las Cruces: New Mexico State University.

Luecke, Richard. 2005. *Time Management: Increase Your Personal Productivity and Effectiveness*. Harvard Business Essentials. Boston: Harvard Business School Press.

Morgenstern, Julie. 2004. *Never Check E-Mail in the Morning and Other Unexpected Strategies for Making Your Work Life Work*. New York: Fireside.

Rockquemore, Kerry Ann, and Tracey Laszloffy. 2008. *The Black Academic's Guide to Winning Tenure—Without Losing Your Soul*. Boulder, CO: Lynne Rienner.

Silvia, Paul J. 2007. *How to Write a Lot: A Practical Guide to Productive Academic Writing*. Washington, DC: American Psychological Association.

Tracy, Brian. 2010. *Goals! How to Get Everything You Want—Faster Than You Ever Thought Possible*. 2nd ed. San Francisco: Berrett-Koehler.

V

Getting Organized

NINETEEN

Avoiding Information Overload

Meredith Selfon

We all know that, especially in this time of rapid technological advancements and social and economic change, it is essential to keep apprised of news and developments in the field of librarianship. What sources do you turn to for news and book reviews? Do you have favorite print resources, website, blogs, or e-mail lists that you regularly consult? Maybe you attend conferences and training sessions to keep up to date or follow other librarians on Twitter and Facebook. Chances are good that you use a combination of these in your quest to stay informed. And yet, how many times do you eye with despair the precarious pile of magazines on your desk, your inbox overflowing with e-mail digests, and your bulging files of training handouts? Not to mention all the tweets and blogs you forgot to check in on. It would take you until the end of time to get through it all, at which point the information would be out of date. It's easy to be tempted to cancel your subscriptions and call it a day.

Staying informed without suffering from information overload can be challenging, but I have collected some tips and recommendations for free tools that can help you get organized and start making use of these resources in an efficient way.

IDEAS FOR MANAGING OVERLOAD

The first thing to do is schedule time to keep up with the resources you use. If possible, choose the same time each week, but you can also snag smaller units of time here and there if your schedule allows. The important thing is to make staying informed a priority so it doesn't constantly get pushed to the bottom of your to-do list. Another valuable step in managing information overload is to learn to let go. I had to admit to myself that I wouldn't be able to absorb everything all of the time, and that was okay.

PRINT RESOURCES

I find managing print materials the most challenging of all information resources, perhaps because of their physical bulk. Some magazines that I consult for book reviews and library news are *Publishers Weekly* (about 60 pages per week), *Kirkus Reviews* (around 100 pages twice per month), and *Library Journal* (about 140 pages per month). Quite honestly, I just don't have the time to read through all of this material. Few librarians do! More often than not, a pile of it accumulates on my desk, threatening to obscure my keyboard. I used to find this very stressful, but I have come up with a system that helps me process the pertinent information in these resources as efficiently as possible. I started using several electronic tools to organize the most relevant information from print resources and eliminate some of their physical clutter. I use Good Reads, an online social book cataloging website, to manage my reading lists. Shelfari and Library Thing are similar sites. For print references to online resources I want to keep track of, I use my browser's bookmarks, but you could also use social bookmarking websites such as Delicious, Reddit, Digg, or Stumble Upon.

To maximize efficiency, I decided to identify the parts of journals that were most important to me and to concentrate on reading those. For example, rather than try to read *Publishers Weekly* cover to cover, I skim the table of contents for any interesting articles, then skip to the book reviews in the back. I only read the full reviews for general fiction, and if I am really pressed for time, I limit myself to the starred reviews. Before I begin going through a print resource that includes book reviews, though, I open my Good Reads account online. This way, I can add books to my to-read list as I move through the reviews. If I decide to keep any of the articles, I bookmark them online through the publication's website, if available.

Another source of paper buildup is the material brought back from meetings, conferences, and training sessions. I have learned that it is important to touch these items as few times as possible. For example, let's say that you attend a fantastic lecture at a conference. The speaker gives you a four-page resource list, her business card, and a printout of her PowerPoint presentation slides. In the past, I would have come back to my desk and added these materials to the leaning pile of magazines. Eventually, I would make my way down to them, and, deciding that they had some useful information I might need one day, file them away. When that file became too crammed to handle, I would evaluate the material yet again and decide to recycle the list of resources, which would by then be out of date. At that point I would have interacted with the packet three separate times and never even used the information it contained.

Now, when given printed resources of this kind, I try my best to deal with them as soon as they come to my desk. If it is a list of Web resources, I add the useful ones to my browser's bookmarks. Titles from a reading list get added to Good Reads. Contact information goes straight into Outlook. Often, conference presentations are available after the fact on-line, so I might bookmark the presentation rather than keeping the print-outs around. If I attend an internal training session and am given a guide or other printout, 99 percent of the time it is accessible either through my e-mail or our library's intranet, so I just make sure to file the e-mail or bookmark its location, rather than hold onto yet another piece of paper.

MANAGING YOUR INBOX

Subscribing to e-mail lists is a convenient way to have information de-livered, but they can pile up even more quickly than print resources if you aren't vigilant. I subscribe to three e-mail lists: Fiction_L (a readers' advisory listserv), Library Link of the Day, and LISNews. For each of these I created a separate e-mail folder and a rule directing them auto-matically there, so that they don't crowd my inbox. It's easy to access these messages at my convenience. The downside is that it is also easy to ignore these folders until they are overflowing. Try to schedule time once or twice a week to go through your e-mails. It's also just fine to cut yourself some slack with this, and any, information resource. If you get behind, consider reading the most recent week's worth of material and letting the rest go. Think of it this way: you are still better off taking in some information than none at all.

BLOGS, WEBSITES, AND RSS FEEDS

There are many wonderful blogs and websites written by and for librar-ians and other information professionals. These treasure troves of news and insights into our profession are updated as often as several times per day. I have found that using an RSS reader/aggregator has saved my sanity in trying to keep up with these resources. Like the e-mail folders, an aggregator allows you to control when you access updates to websites and blogs. I use Bloglines, but other solutions are Google Reader and Microsoft Outlook. There are also several smartphone apps that will do feed aggregation. Following are some suggestions for interesting blogs to follow:

Resource Shelf, http://www.resourceshelf.com/
Librarian In Black, http://librarianinblack.net/
Librarian.net, http://librarian.net
Walking Paper, http://www.walkingpaper.org/
The Unquiet Librarian, http://theunquietlibrarian.wordpress.com/
No Shelf Required, http://www.libraries.wright.edu/noshelfrequired/
Tame the Web, http://tametheweb.com/

CUSTOMIZED SEARCH ALERTS

If you want to be alerted when new information on a specific topic becomes available, a useful tool is a customized search alert. These take the
form of e-mail messages that contain search results corresponding to a set
of specific search criteria as they are created. Google Alerts will manage
this for a Google search string. Many electronic journal databases also
have this type of feature. Again, you may wish to create a separate e-mail
folder to collate these messages. Be as specific as possible when creating
the search string for this type of alert, as this will prevent overloading
your folders with new results.

ONLINE SOCIAL NETWORKS

If you use Facebook or Twitter, you know that the information coming
out of these sources is staggering. New posts and tweets gush forth every
second, and it is far too easy to get behind. In fact, I would venture to say
that it's pretty much impossible to interact with every comment, link,
photo, and article that comes along. This is definitely a situation in which
it's best to let go and just do your utmost to keep up. However, there are
tools that can help you round up this information and save you from
visiting several websites several times per day. I use Hoot Suite, a social
media dashboard that allows you to view updates in several accounts at
once. Tweet Deck is a similar tool. Not only do these sites help to consolidate your social media, they also allow you to create and schedule your
own content. This can be a vital time-saving tool if you are responsible
for contributing content to your library's social media presences. Twitter
and Facebook are worth the time it takes to monitor them, because by
their nature they solicit interaction. Merely reading a journal article is of
value, but there is a deeper level of interaction with the content when you
share the article via social media and engage in a conversation with other
professionals. These interactions can be extremely valuable for staying
educated and up to date.

If you are going to attempt to stay informed of developments in the library world, accept the deluge of information, wade through it, and make it work for you by selectively filtering and prioritizing. The important thing is to make the effort to seek out news and information, consume it efficiently, and use it to grow professionally.

TWENTY

For Every Librarian a To-Do List

Sarah Troy

If you work in a public services department, you know that staffing is a revolving door. And if you are alive in the universe, you know that the current economic climate has made that door more of a one-way exit. As the head of user services and resource sharing at the University of California, Santa Cruz, I have been feeling the impact of the economic climate for several years. As a result of staff attrition, I have taken on additional responsibilities, ranging from higher level management, to system-wide and consortia membership, to day-to-day interlibrary loan (ILL) processing and public service desk shifts.

All of these responsibilities come together to create quite a list of competing priorities. What should I work on today? Department projects that will help me get additional staffing and improve services? Library projects that are top priorities for senior management? Operational work that will help our patrons get their items quickly? System-wide commitments that affect multiple campus ILL units? Professional commitments that will help further my career? My priorities on any given day are fluid, changing with the particular needs of that day. To ensure that my overall vision for the department is not subsumed by the urgent tasks that spring up every day, I work on short- and long-term goals regularly. The way I successfully manage that process is through the use of online to-do lists, which help me keep track of all the balls I'm trying to keep in the air.

I began experimenting with online to-do lists several years ago. I used Google Desktop for about a year and found it to be useful for keeping track of daily lists. Unfortunately, it did not play well with my computer, and I had to uninstall it. I tried Google Tasks, which also proved useful for smaller lists, but was not scalable for the kind of long-term planning I needed to do. I attempted to use my campus calendaring system, but the daily task function really only allowed for a few daily commitments, which doesn't work if you have two dozen items to tackle in a day. I required something more. Following are the characteristics of my dream to-do list:

- *Flexible:* My day changes constantly. I may have to attend an unexpected meeting or staff an unanticipated public service desk shift. I need a to-do list that is easily manipulated so I can reprioritize my day quickly and without hassle.
- *Clean:* I do not need distractions on my to-do list. I do not want to see blinking advertisements or wild colors.
- *Delineated:* I want to keep track of the tasks I have completed for the day, and I want those tasks to be easily distinguishable from what remains on my plate. Not only does this give me a sense of accomplishment, it is useful if I need to review when I completed a particular task.
- *User-friendly:* I want something uncomplicated. I want my to-do list to be as intuitive as possible.
- *Accessible:* I work from multiple computers. On any given day, I sit down at seven different machines. I need a list that I can access from any computer, including my iPhone.
- *Scalable:* I maintain multiple to-do lists. I have one for each day of the week, one for short-term goals, one for long-term goals, one for each of the projects I'm working on with colleagues, one for my supervisor, and one for items for my biannual review. I move tasks from one list to another regularly. I need an option that captures all of my to-do lists.
- *Stress free:* I want a to-do list that supports my work. I want a reliable system that does not require workarounds.

I didn't expect to be able to find everything that I wanted in one tool, but I did find a tool that meets my needs. There are many online to-do lists available, and I'm willing to bet that at least one of them will meet your needs, too.

BLA-BLA LIST

Bla-bla list (blablalist.com) is currently free, although additional features may come at a premium in the future. It allows you to share lists publicly or privately. You can invite others to edit lists with you, and you can share lists with people who don't have an account with Bla-Bla List. The site was text heavy for my taste. There is a lot of extraneous text on the home page, so my first response was, "What am I supposed to pay attention to on this page? What information is important?" Creating and editing lists is easy. Once you have created a list, you can identify what work has been completed and what remains, but it is not easy to review previously completed lists. You can create multiple lists, but you can only view one at a time. Bla-Bla List requires Flash, so it won't work on the iPhone, but it is Web-based, so it will be accessible from any computer that can get you online.

CHECKVIST

Checkvist (checkvist.com) has a free version and a pro version. The free version allows you to create lists, share lists, collaborate on lists, create notes, tag your items, create due dates, filter and search for items, import and export items, get e-mail notifications, and integrate with Gmail. The pro subscription includes increased security, automatic daily backups, e-mail reports on changes to tasks, and interface customization, among other features. The site's interface is relatively pared down. Checkvist allows an unlimited number of lists, which can either be useful or self-defeating. Old checklists can be archived, allowing you to refer back to them at a later date. Checkvist has a toolbar widget that allows you to easily access your list, but if you work from multiple stations, it is unlikely that you could have your own Checkvist widget in every toolbar. There is also a mobile version. I found Checkvist to be nonintuitive; it wasn't immediately apparent to me how I should go about creating a new list. I would have liked a demo video for new users. Overall, I found that figuring out the ins and outs of Checkvist requires more time and energy than I am willing to commit.

GOOGLE TASKS

Although I found Google Tasks (mail.google.com/tasks) unsatisfactory for my purposes, I think it is a great tool. It's free, reliable, and user-friendly. Google provides many helpful how-to videos. Google Tasks is extremely accessible; you can access your list through Gmail, Google Calendar, and iGoogle, and on your mobile device. I appreciate how easy it is to integrate Google tasks into your workday. For example, you can move tasks into Google Calendar, and, if you adjust the date in your calendar, the due date will simultaneously be updated in your task list. It's easy to set due dates, add notes, and print your list of tasks. This tool didn't work for my purposes because it doesn't scale up to cover my full suite of to-do items with a single list. It does allow multiple lists, however. It works very well as a simple daily to-do list.

NOW DO THIS

Now Do This (nowdothis.com) is the most straightforward tool I found. It is a one-at-a-time to-do list. It has one purpose, so it's not flexible, but it can be highly motivating. Enter the task that you should be doing right now in a simple text box. The screen stares you in the face, forcing you to work on that task until you can hit the *done* button. This tool is extremely easy to use. It is accessible from computers and mobile devices. I appreciate the simplicity of Now Do This, but it wouldn't work for me. It doesn't allow me to keep a broad overview of my work or a history of tasks completed. This tool could help keep me on track with one or two items that might otherwise fall off my radar.

REMEMBER THE MILK

Remember the Milk (rememberthemilk.com) is a free online tool that offers extensive Google integration. It allows you to create multiple lists, which you can manage in Google Calendar, and you can add tasks from iGoogle or via e-mail. You can send reminders via e-mail, text, or instant message. You can also share your tasks with others. Remember the Milk is very user-friendly. It has an extensive FAQ, user forums, and blog. As for accessibility, Remember the Milk is a model tool. You can manage tasks offline using the Gears browser plug-in, via Blackberry, Android, iPad, iPhone (via Siri), Gmail, Microsoft Outlook, Twitter, Google Calendar, a mobile version, and a bookmarklet on your web browser. The overview lets you see what is due soon (and what is overdue), and the weekly planner lets you print your tasks for the coming week. Overall, Remember the Milk has a very polished look and feel. For my purposes, this tool doesn't give a sufficiently comprehensive overview. I want a single view that shows everything I need to be thinking about on a daily basis.

TA-DA LIST

Ta-da List (tadalist.com) is a free tool accessible via Web and iPhone. You can share lists in two ways, either with people you trust to edit your lists or with the general public via a link that does not allow them to edit. Although the site is fairly text heavy, the lists themselves have a spare look. The list allows you to see easily which items you have completed and which you have left. You can e-mail yourself your to-do list. If you need to reorder your list because your day has taken an unexpected turn, you have to press a few buttons. It's not quite as simple as I would like, but is certainly workable. Lists can be edited, but there are some extra steps involved if you want to organize your list by date instead of subject.

You can only view one list at time; if you want to see all the tasks for your day or week, you have to keep them all on a single list. It is difficult to see a history of all the tasks you have completed, so if you want something to serve as an archive, this is not the best tool available.

TEUXDEUX

TeuxDeux (teuxdeux.com) is different from the other tools I surveyed. It is visually compelling, largely because it was created by designers. Many of these tools were created by programmers, and programmers have a different eye. I enjoyed TeuxDeux's humorous FAQ. The Web version of TeuxDeux is free, but there is a small fee for the iPhone app. TeuxDeux does not offer the application on other platforms at this time. The to-do lists are organized by date, so you can scroll back to see work completed on previous dates, or scroll forward to create future items. There is a *someday* heading for items that aren't pressing. Once you have created a list, it is simple to reorder and edit tasks. How-to videos educate new and experienced users, as well as users who opt to purchase the iPhone app. I found this tool to be a nice change from the other options surveyed, primarily because it has a different look and feel.

TODOIST

Todoist (todoist.com) is a free online tool with helpful integration options. For example, if you have a Gmail message related to a particular task, you can add that item to your list. When you click on the task, you will return to the original Gmail message. If there's a web page you would like to save for later, you can add the URL as a task. When you click on the task, it will take you to the web page. As someone who stores many online articles and blog posts for later reading, I found this feature appealing. There are many other user-friendly features, such as color coding, nesting tasks (for projects that require several smaller tasks), organization by due date, and prioritization. You can have a widget in your browser that allows you to see your tasks at any time. This feature is less useful if you work from several shared workstations. Todoist is accessible from your mobile device, web browser, Outlook, and desktop. As a new user, I appreciated the demo video and the clean design of the welcome page.

TOODLEDO

ToodleDo (toodledo.com) is a free online tool with many useful features. It is very flexible, in that it allows you to select and define the fields you want to use, and to filter items so that you can hide less urgent items and focus on high-priority tasks. You can tags items, assign due dates, and set their priority level. You can use tags, due dates, and priority to sort and search lists. ToodleDo allows you to import tasks and set reminders. It can analyze the work you have already completed and make recommendations for you based on how much time you have to devote to an item. For example, if you have thirty minutes free, you can have ToodleDo show you items on your list that you could complete in that period of time. ToodleDo can give you a broad overview of all the tasks you have to complete. It offers blogs and forums to help guide users. ToodleDo is Web accessible. You can also access it via e-mail or a calendaring system. The interface is a bit busy for my taste, but given its many useful features, it may be worth overlooking the interface in favor of the functionality.

TUDULISTS

Tudulists (tudu.ess.ch) is a free, bare-bones tool. It is accessible only via the Web. It allows you to see your highest priority items, or what's on tap for the day, but not a comprehensive overview of all your work. Once you complete an item, it moves to the bottom of your list, and you can view previous lists if necessary. Although it's easy to edit individual tasks, if you want to reorder your tasks, you have to assign them different priorities. You can share lists and be notified via RSS feed if your lists have been updated. There's no demo video, and it's not completely intuitive. Tudulists is not completely seamless and requires more work than I am willing to put into it. Having said that, there's probably not a very steep learning curve for someone who feels like this is the right tool.

VOO2DO

Voo2do (voo2do.com) offers a free version and a premium version with additional features. The free version includes the abilities to track time spent and time remaining on a task and to organize tasks by project. Voo2do is flexible in allowing you to view tasks either all together or within their specific contexts (such as work, home, or hobby). You can see your highest priority tasks and deadlines. You can share tasks either publicly or with collaborators. Collaborators cannot currently modify tasks. The pages are very busy, which I find distracting. The time-tracking feature would do me more harm than good. I would become obsessed with watching the time, making it hard to focus on the task at hand.

WORKHACK

Workhack (workhack.com) is a free, Web-accessible, whiteboard to-do list. You can change the order of your tasks and hide (or show) tasks once you have completed them. You can organize lists by priority. If tags or due dates are important to you, you will have to add them manually to the text of the task. Once you have created a list, you can't edit the tasks. The interface is somewhat busy, with loud colors and too much text. Workhack is excellent as a simple, daily to-do list. There is an FAQ and an easily accessible feedback link. For those of us who have enough passwords to remember already, this tool might be appealing, because it doesn't require a password—you can just bookmark your list.

AND THE WINNER IS . . .

Clearly there are many options for online to-do lists, including additional tools that I have not covered here. It is likely that there is at least one that will meet your needs. Though several of these tools would have worked well for me, I settled on TeuxDeux, which I have been using for several months. It has made my life simpler. Both the Web version and the iPhone app have clean interfaces. I can see all my work for the week and my long-term projects on a single screen. I can easily move tasks from one day to another. I had to find one minor workaround, which was to create headings within the long-term tasks. Luckily, I only had to do that once. TeuxDeux has made my work life manageable, for which I am grateful.

In addition to helping me prioritize my work, I have found that to-do lists have other significant benefits:

- My to-do list gives me a broad overview of my day and my week. I can prioritize with the big picture in mind. Each morning, the first thing I do is review my to-do list and my calendar to assess the day and make any changes to how I prioritize my work. Over time, this daily review has become a regular part of my routine.
- My to-do list allows me to add items throughout the day. No matter how much I plan and hope for smooth sailing, unexpected things come up. I'm not always in a place where I can make a phone call or send a thoughtful e-mail, but I can usually at least add these tasks to my list so I remember to handle them later.
- I use my to-do list to remind me of future action items. For example, if we agree in a department meeting to revisit a decision in a month, I set a reminder for a month in the future. If I ask someone to work on a project, I set a reminder to check in with that person in a week. I don't have to keep details in my head, where they will surely be lost.

Table 20.1.   Summary of Online To-Do List Features

Tool	Cost	Good for Collaborating?	User Support	Accessibility	Pros and Cons
Bla-Bla List	free	yes	• FAQ	• Web accessible • not iPhone compatible	• create multiple lists • view one list at a time
Check-vist	free and paid versions	yes	• FAQ • reference section • Twitter updates	• Web accessible • browser widget • mobile version	• create multiple lists • archive old lists • creating new lists not intuitive
Google Tasks	free	OK	• how-to videos	• Web accessible • access via Gmail • Google Calendar • iGoogle	• move tasks into Google Calendar • create multiple lists • view one list at a time
Now Do This	free	no	• very simple	• Web accessible	• one at a time to do list
Re-member the Milk	free	yes	• FAQ • user forums • blog	• add tasks via iGoogle or e-mail • manage tasks offline via plug-in in Google Calendar • Gmail • Outlook • Twitter • mobile version • bookmark-let	• create multiple lists • send reminders via e-mail, text, IM • view impending deadlines • weekly planner allows printing tasks for the coming week

Ta-da Lists	free	yes	• FAQ	• Web accessible • iPhone app	• see what you've completed and what remains • view one list at a time • not ideal as an archive • difficult to organize lists by date • difficult to see history of completed tasks
Teux-Deux	free web version, $2.99 iPhone app	no	• how-to videos for Web and for iPhone app	• Web accessible • iPhone app	• create future tasks • scroll forward and backward to view previously completed tasks or create future tasks • easily edit and reorder tasks
Todoist	free	no	• how-to videos	• Web accessible • browser widget • Outlook • desktop	• Gmail integration • color coding • organize by due date or by prioritization
Toodle Do	free	yes	• blogs • forums	• Web accessible • add tasks via e-mail calendaring system	• select the fields you want to use • filtering, tagging, due dates • prioritization, import tasks • set reminders • overview of uncompleted tasks • recommendations for tasks to complete
Tudu-lists	free	yes	• screen shots	• Web accessible	• view by highest priority or daily items • view previous lists • must assign different priorities in order to reorder lists • no comprehensive view
Voo2do	free and premium versions	okay	• FAQ	• Web accessible • add tasks via e-mail	• view all tasks together or within contexts • see highest priority and deadlines

Work-hack	free	no	• FAQ	• Web accessible	• hide or show completed tasks
					• organize lists by priority
					• no password required
					• must add due dates manually
					• cannot edit tasks once created

- My to-do list allows me to break down large projects into manageable bits. I spread out smaller tasks over the course of a week or two. A project that initially feels insurmountable becomes achievable.
- Having a to-do list has helped me to procrastinate less. I have a list in front of me with tasks broken down into manageable pieces, prioritized according to the needs of my day. I even prioritize according to my motivation. I know that I am more productive in the early part of the day, so I work on difficult tasks early and save mind-numbing tasks for later in the day. If I have a predigested list staring me in the face, I have little excuse not to move through the tasks one by one.
- An electronic to-do list is particularly useful, because it keeps everything in one location. I used to be an advocate of paper to-do lists, but it becomes difficult to manage the slips of paper that accumulate throughout the day.
- An electronic to-do list allows me to keep a record of the work I have done and when it was completed.

Librarians are busy. In the current economic situation, many jobs are left unfilled. We have more work to do: operational, administrative, and professional. We juggle many commitments and have to manage unwieldy workloads. Fortunately, there are tools available to help us keep on task. Online to-do lists have a variety of looks and an abundance of features. A wealth of benefits is associated with using to-do lists, including helping us to stay on task. Any tool that can help us support our patrons, coworkers, and profession is worth exploring.

TWENTY-ONE

Optimize Small Library Efficiency with Daily Routines and Organizational Strategies

Stephanie Sweeney

The need to maintain well-organized library catalog records is obvious to all librarians who want the collection to be accessible for their patrons; however, being administratively organized is just as crucial. A great deal of behind-the-scenes work must be accomplished to operate a library successfully. It is important that policies and procedures be spelled out clearly and routines established to ensure the library runs smoothly on a daily basis. All of the procedures and organizational tips that follow can be used by any type of librarian to reduce stress (and clutter) and perform job responsibilities more efficiently and effectively.

THE LIBRARY YEAR

Important library tasks can be broken down by day, month, year, and special events. By establishing routines for accomplishing these tasks, they will become habit. You also won't forget about rare tasks that need to be done only once a year.

Daily

Before closing for the day, take a few minutes to make opening the next day easier on yourself. Little jobs like prestamping date due slips, adding paper to printers, and totaling daily statistics can help you ease into the next day, particularly if your patrons have a tendency to be waiting by the front door when you arrive. Straightening up after a particularly crazy day may be the last thing you want to do before leaving, but it will get the next day off to a better start if you don't have to begin by cleaning up the mess from the day before.

A supply station on or near the reference desk that has frequently requested items, such as art utensils (crayons, markers, colored pencils, etc.), scissors, glue sticks, pens/pencils, a stapler, and a three-hole punch, is very helpful to the patrons and staff. If these items frequently "walk away" from your library, you may want to keep a drawer or box to hold them behind the reference desk, but make it known that these supplies are available for use. Neatly labeling cabinets and drawers with their contents can also assist staff in finding materials quickly, whether in a workroom or behind the circulation desk. Keeping a central "shopping list" for items that frequently need to be replaced is vital.

Monthly

At the end of every month, be certain to run reports that you will need for statistics from your circulation system. Gathering this data can be an overwhelming project if you wait until the end of the year. By completing this task at the end of every month, you will develop a clearer picture of what is happening in your library and notice any trends in areas such as circulation or patron usage.

Designate a time each month to plan ahead. Examine the library calendar through at least the next three months and identify upcoming special events, deadlines for managerial paperwork, staff scheduling issues (vacation, medical or parental leave), and other issues that will need to be addressed. This will give you enough time to order materials, gather data, communicate with staff, send out public relations notices, and complete any other tasks that are necessary in the coming weeks and months. Take advantage of those rare moments of downtime to complete several of these tasks on your to-do list.

Annually

It is important to compile an inventory every year. For a new librarian, this is a good way to get to know your collection because you are forced to handle every item. With the computer-based library management systems, you don't even have to do it all at one time, as you can work on it throughout the year. It is easy to train volunteers or students to scan the collection for you; however, be sure to keep track of where each person started and stopped scanning to avoid duplication of work.

Another collection development practice is to identify one or two areas to weed every year. If you wait a few years, this can become an overwhelming task when you realize that the entire library collection needs to be examined for outdated items. Weeding a few areas every year will allow you to examine the specific section with more than a cursory glance. All new librarians should remember to wait at least one year before initiating any new weeding project. There may be items that you perceive to be disposable based on condition, age, and circulation statistics, but that are in fact used by a teacher or community member. By spending some time observing the usage of the library materials, you can get a more accurate picture of your patrons' needs before throwing out their treasured items. Remember to carefully examine circulation statistics when weeding and make a list of heavily used, but outdated, items that may need to be removed or replaced if the topic is of high interest. If you are going to complete a comprehensive weeding project, do so before taking inventory.

Special Events

Special events are a great public relations tool to bring the community into the library and can be just plain fun. Even if you have the same event every year, it can be difficult to remember all of the details. Document what worked, what didn't, and what you would change if the event is to be held again in the future.

These events often require decorations and supplies. There are simple strategies for keeping supplies organized that can help you avoid wasting time and money by not ordering materials you already have. When you can find the decorations easily, you can complete a quick inventory during your event planning period. This will also allow you to more efficiently direct volunteers to grab a specific box rather than take up your time to find all the materials yourself and then hand them off to someone else to decorate.

Keep holiday and special event decorations together in clearly labeled, large plastic tubs. Copy paper boxes are a cheap option that works just as well, although you may need to reinforce them with tape. Filing cabinets are another option for storage, but they obviously aren't as portable as boxes. Organize your storage by season/event/holiday and be sure to include posters, bookmarks, and bulletin board materials in the boxes rather than keeping those items in a separate location. Save smaller boxes that you received books in for small or fragile items and use manila envelopes to keep bulletin board pieces together.

At the end of each event or holiday season, compile a shopping list of items you need. When you find items you can use on post-holiday clearance (a great money-saving tip), throw them in the designated box to make life easier for next year. As you receive new catalogs, check to see if any reading promotional materials are on sale for a theme you currently use or can adapt for future use. After several years, you will have built up a nice collection of materials. And, most important, because everything is neatly organized, decorating for special events will be stress free.

RECORD ORGANIZATION

It is important to keep accurate records so that important information can be located quickly. Any format of record organization can be used for this: digital files, binders and tabs, filing cabinets; the point is to pick a system and actually use it. If everything is clearly labeled and filed, then a great deal of stress will be avoided when filing reports, filling out grant paperwork, or planning events. The following examples use the binder and tab method because this has been the most successful method for me. Because each topic has its own binder, the pages don't fall out if it is dropped, and they easily fit on a desk or shelf. Many of these files can also be digitized and shared among staff members on the network or through online collaborative tools. If you do go digital, remember to back up your information frequently!

Procedures File

You may believe that everyone understands how the library operates, especially if you are a one-librarian show, but documenting library procedures is a must. The library procedures manual should be the go-to guide for the who, what, where, when, why, and how of processes. This manual is crucial when the reins change hands and will ensure that library procedures are consistent as personnel change. It can serve not only as a reference tool, but also as a training tool. It is also important to have the manual approved by the overseeing board periodically to make the administrative team aware that the library policies and procedures are documented and to ensure that everyone is in agreement on them, should an issue arise. It is more difficult, though not impossible, for a board to oppose a policy it has approved.

Several areas that should be included in the procedures manual are outlined here. You may also wish to include supporting documentation from state and national organizations.

- *Overview:* Include the mission statement, vision statement, goals, and objectives of the individual library or the library district and those of any overseeing bodies.
- *Collection development:* Include the selection policy detailing who is responsible for collection development, criteria for selection and tools to be used, and the procedures for the weeding of outdated materials; a detailed reconsideration policy, outlining each step to be taken, from the initial complaint to the formation of the review committee to the appeals procedure; detailed instructions for the

processing of materials and inventory procedures; and established procedures or programs for the donation of materials.

- *Personnel:* Include anything your human resources department deems appropriate, including job descriptions, professional development day attendance requirements for aides and secretaries, and requirements for professional development for all library staff.
- *Library program:* Subdivide this section into the different areas based on the program offered. A school library may have sections for each level (elementary, middle, high), whereas a public, special, or academic library may have sections for technical services, children and youth services, reference, and special collections. The library program section should clearly outline the services provided to patrons, including, but not limited to meeting space, reference services for walk-in or phone-in requests, archival work done for the sponsoring organization (school, community, university, corporation), library use by nonmembers (e.g., can use materials on-site, but not check out), copyright policy, equipment usage policy (fax machine, copiers, computers, time limits, fees for use, Internet acceptable use policy), and special events and promotions.
- *Evaluation and reports:* Keep a copy of at least the most recent program evaluation in the manual, including short- and long-range plans based on the findings.
- *Interlibrary loan (ILL) procedures:* Include in- and out-of-system lending, fines, patrons served, lending policies, procedures for check in and out, and copies of any laws or regulations pertaining to ILL.
- *Facilities:* Include everything from how to operate special equipment, such as the copier and fax machine, to the procedures for the security alarm, how to enter work orders to get problems fixed, facility usage and space reservation procedures, and how to handle emergencies that require outside assistance (plumber, electrician, etc.).
- *Services:* Include information and policies on lending of materials (consider all possible populations, such as nonstudents for academic libraries, general public for special libraries, and homeschool students for school libraries), teaching of information literacy skills, and continuing education classes.

Master Copies

It is important to keep a file somewhere of master copies of signs, forms, and other paperwork used frequently. You may designate a special binder for this information or keep a digital file on the network.

Special Events File

Some special events will be one-time functions; others will be annual. Certain celebrations, such as Banned Books Week or Read Across America, might be held annually, but the theme may change from year to year. Keeping a file for special events will help you remember all the minute details that went into planning and executing each event. Even if one person is the designated party planner for the library, it can be difficult to remember how many children showed up, how many vegetable trays were ordered, or from which company the promotional materials were ordered a year or more after the event occurred. By keeping detailed records, you can avoid over- or under-ordering supplies the following year, make changes in the promotional materials and strategies, and remember which parts of the event went well and what flopped. This record doesn't have to be a typed, formal report; simply jot down the important details on a sheet of paper shortly after the event, copy any invoices, and file it away.

Budget File

One area of library management that requires careful organization is the library budget. An organized filing system can keep you from misplacing and forgetting to pay bills or overspending because you forgot about standing orders or encumbered funds. A budget binder that has tabs for the following categories can keep all the information you need organized at your fingertips. The tabs can be in any order that makes sense to you, and you may choose to add more depending on the type of library in which you are working.

- *Current-year budget:* Keep a copy of the approved current-year budget handy so you can easily refer to it.
- *Previous-year budget:* This will be needed during budget planning, and you may wish to check what was paid for an item the previous year.
- *Next-year budget:* Keep a copy of your proposed or approved budget for the following year.
- *Closed purchase orders:* Keep copies of all purchase orders for items that have been received and paid for.
- *Open purchase orders:* Keep copies of all purchase orders that are still pending to easily see outstanding bills and items that haven't been received yet.
- *Supplies:* If you work in a school or other type of library that has central purchasing for some basic office supplies, keep the request forms here. You can also use this section to keep track of supplies used to help determine what you are over or under ordering, as

well as vendor contact information, coupons, and discount information.

- *Account information for vendors:* Keep one page per vendor that has on it the account information, website logins, representative contact information, etc.
- *Grant information:* Keep track of any grants that you are currently working with; any grants that have been completed can be filed away elsewhere.
- *Recurring expenses:* Keep a sheet for each item that is a recurring expense, whether it is a science database or electric bill, including the item name, vendor, website, user name and password, and at least a four-column chart listing the start date, end date, price, and annual percent increase
- *Optional tabs:* Utilities, mortgage, petty cash, etc.

If you keep a budget binder on your desk, be certain to have a secure, dedicated location for old financial records. Check with your business office or accountant to determine how long you need to maintain such records for auditing and tax purposes.

It is easy for libraries with smaller budgets to supplement the budget binder with a simple spreadsheet workbook. There are several ways that you can set it up. If you have a large number of accounts, use the first page of the workbook as a chart listing all of the account numbers, names of the accounts, budgeted amount, and current balance. Then use pages to organize each account similar to a basic check register: date, purchase order number, reconciled (post check number), vendor, encumbered, spent, balance.

Technology File

Technology issues can be frustrating, especially when problems appear sporadically. Having a technology binder can make problem solving quick and easy (well, easier). Keeping the binder in a central location will allow all staff members and volunteers easy access to not only solve problems but contribute solutions as well. Create a tab in the binder for each type of technology issue that may arise, add a few sheets of paper to each section, and begin building a custom manual. Following are some sections you may want to include:

- *Forms:* Keep handy a copy of your policies regarding equipment and Internet usage.
- *Logins:* Keep any instructions for logging onto computers by staff or patrons here, as well as a master list of database passwords.
- *General computer problems:* Jot down notes for quick solutions and print out instructions from help menus for longer ones, then file them away in this section.

- *Specific program problems:* Create separate sections for specific programs.
- *Equipment:* It is advisable to keep on hand the numbers of repair services as well as an inventory spreadsheet of the equipment the library possesses, including the equipment type, brand, model number, serial number, date of purchase, and warranty information; keep track of repair histories; create additional sections for equipment, such as telephones, printers, copiers, and fax machines, as needed

Database File

Keep track of database subscriptions in their own binder. Create a tab for each database (rather than by vendor) and file everything you receive, from e-mails with passwords to promotional fliers and instruction sheets. As you drop database subscriptions, pull the paperwork from the binder.

Interlibrary Loan File

Processing interlibrary loans can be time consuming. Having a binder with all of the paperwork in one place can make the process a little quicker.

- *Policies and procedures:* Include the passwords for any ILL systems that your library may belong to, the step-by-step procedures for processing and mailing items, and any local or state policies and regulations.
- *Borrowed:* On the top right corner of clear sheet protector pages, place an item barcode sticker and a label that says "ILL (number)"; enter the pages as items in your circulation system as copies of the "ILL" item or as individual items; file loan paperwork.
- *Borrowed returned:* Keep any paperwork for as long as you feel necessary after statistics are counted and material purchases considered.
- *Loaned:* Keep paperwork on each loan made.
- *Loaned returned:* Keep any paperwork for as long as you feel necessary or toss after statistics are counted.

Statistics File

It is important to keep an ongoing record of library statistics, including circulation, subscription database usage, patron usage, and any other numbers deemed important in your library. This can be done by printing and filing reports from the library management system and compiling daily statistics. It can also be done using online collaborative tools by creating spreadsheets that will organize and total your statistics. Because multiple people can easily access these programs to work on the same documents, the role of record keeper is a team effort, rather than to be left on the shoulders of one person. When the data is needed, you can easily print out an up-to-date report in minutes. Make it a habit to calculate the data monthly, because you may have a limited window of opportunity if you are pulling the data from vendor sites. By keeping your own data, you can ensure the information is available when you need it. Even if you don't run a formal annual report (which is highly suggested for all libraries), keep a tally of important figures, because you may need them to justify a budget request or the amount of staffing you require. At some point, the need for this information will arise. Statistics can be powerful, so be sure to have them readily available and up to date.

FINAL THOUGHTS

It doesn't matter whether you use a filing cabinet or binders, copy paper boxes or plastic tubs; the important thing is that everyone in your library knows his or her role, the established routine, and where to find important documents. By keeping supplies organized and paperwork in order, the day-to-day library routine will be less stressful and planning will be more efficient.

TWENTY-TWO

The Power of Lists

Meredith Selfon

Librarians specialize in the organization of information. It seems natural to assume that we must also be adept at organizing other aspects of our lives, both personal and professional. Unfortunately, with an increasing number of us being asked to do more with less time, staying on top of a multitude of tasks and projects can become overwhelming. As a part-time librarian, I use to-do lists for every project and responsibility. They allow me to prioritize my tasks and manage my time as efficiently as possible. With the right combination of planning, assessment, and maintenance, the humble to-do list can become a powerful tool in the modern librarian's quest to accomplish more with minimal resources.

GETTING STARTED

Start by setting aside some time to create your lists. You can't start prioritizing until you make getting organized a priority! And remember, to-do lists aren't static. You will be adding to, revising, editing, and reorganizing your lists constantly, so it is not necessary to make everything perfect at the start. The more you use your lists, the more refined and streamlined they will become. The important thing at the beginning is to brainstorm as many of your responsibilities and projects as possible. Something that helps me is to move mentally through my typical day, week, and month to identify tasks. You may also want to sift through your e-mail to find more. Don't forget to look at any notes or minutes you may have from recent meetings. I use three types of lists: action lists, recurring checklist templates, and daily to-do lists.

ACTION LISTS

Begin by writing down all of your responsibilities and projects. This in itself becomes an important list that you will want to save. Once you lay out all your areas of work, it's easier to create manageable action lists and to prioritize them. For each area of responsibility or project, write a separate list of tasks. Try to phrase the tasks as specific actions. "Write blog entry for June" is easier to act on than "Blog." You want it to be very clear when you have accomplished a task and can cross it off your list. One of my areas of responsibility is, in fact, to write for and help maintain our library's readers' advisory blog. Therefore, "Blog" would never get crossed off my list, because I will always have another blog entry to write. But I only have to write an entry for June once, and when it's done, I can cross it off and move on to the next task. Here is an example of what my readers' advisory blog to-do list looks like:

1. Write blog entry for July.
2. Check capitalization and spacing for last month of entries.
3. Find two titles that haven't been blogged yet and place holds on them.
4. Write blog entry for August.

Notice how specific number 3 is. This helps me stay on task. If I had written, "Find books to blog," I might have spent too much time on this, because of its unclear goal. This way is straightforward and helps keep me focused: find two titles, cross number 3 off the list, move on. Of course, once I have crossed everything off this list, that doesn't mean that I'm done with the blog. It is important to reevaluate and edit your lists as you move through them. Once I finish writing my blog entry for July, I cross that item off my list, but I then need to add "Write blog entry for August" to the bottom. It is up to you how far into the future you want your to-do lists to run. Perhaps it would work better for you to have all the tasks for the next six months or year on the list at once. I find that to be overwhelming, so I tend to keep my lists to no more than ten items, if I can. The key is to keep maintaining your lists, so they don't become outdated.

RECURRING CHECKLIST TEMPLATES

For certain multipart recurring tasks and projects, I use checklist templates. For example, each month I need to accomplish a series of tasks that relate to publicity. I created a to-do list template that I can print (or copy/paste into an Outlook Task) every month. This way, there is no need to start from scratch each time. If you are regularly assigned projects with similar related tasks, such as planning library programs, you can create a template for that type of project, which may then be easily customized. Here is my template for monthly program publicity:

- Submit Book Page back page.
- _____ Mail copies of Book Page to mailing list.
- E-mail calendar to staff and contact lists.
- Post large calendar in lobby and acrylic.
- Place small photocopies of calendar in lobby.
- _____ Mail small calendars to snail-mail list.
- _____ Mail author event flyers to bookstores.

Note: I use the blank spaces to record the dates on which certain tasks were completed. In this example, they are only needed for the snail mail items. The e-mails will be saved in my sent items folder, so there is no need to track those dates. Depending on the nature of your tasks, you may or may not need to keep a record of their completion dates.

DAILY TO-DO LISTS

The third type of list that I use is a daily to-do list. A good time to create this list is at the end of the previous day. Take a few minutes before you leave your desk to jot down the tasks that you may have left unfinished that day or the projects you need to check up on the next day. Even just a few quick notes on a sticky note left on your monitor can help alleviate a great deal of stress and prevent work from following you home. I always find it easier to relax when my to-do lists are in order.

TIME TO PRIORITIZE

Once you have your lists written out, it is time to prioritize. This is a very helpful, but often overlooked, step in the to-do list process. The first thing to think about is the difference between urgency and importance. It's easy to focus on the urgent tasks on your list, which may or may not be important, because they are by nature time-sensitive. If you only focus on the tasks that have to get done today, you will never get to your important, but less urgent, tasks. This also makes it very hard to get ahead and avoid deadline stress. If you make an effort to give high priority to a few important/low urgency tasks every day, you will find that meeting your deadlines is far more manageable.

TOOLS

Although only pen and paper are necessary to create effective to-do lists, there are also many paperless tools available online and through standard computer software. At work, I use a word processor to create my checklist templates. These are saved in a folder on my computer, and I can easily copy and paste their contents into other applications, or print them out, if necessary. As much as I love pen and paper, a list in a Microsoft Word document is much easier to edit. My work e-mail runs through Microsoft Outlook, which has a Tasks feature that works well for organizing my to-do lists and creating reminders. My daily to-do lists are almost always done on scrap paper or a sticky note. This combination of tools is efficient for me, but there are other tools available that help manage to-do lists. For my personal to-do lists, I use a simple smartphone app. This works for me, because I am usually on the go when working on personal projects, but I find that it is more effective to have my work project lists live where I do most of my work, at my desk. There are several to-do list websites and applications available:

- Remember the Milk (http://www.rememberthemilk.com) is a website and an app for mobile devices. It enables list sharing and reminders, and it works with many other services, such as Gmail and Twitter.
- Todoist (http://todoist.com) can also follow you from your computer to your mobile and includes easy prioritizing and nesting tools for more complex lists.
- Toodledo (http://www.toodeldo.com) has powerful tools for prioritizing and organizing, such as tags, context, and subtasks. You can also import tasks from other managers.
- TeuxDeux (http://teuxdeux.com/) is good for simple lists and boasts automatic task rollover and a someday bucket.

It takes a bit of time and some practice to get in the habit of using and maintaining to-do lists. They are like vegetable gardens: they take some time and effort to establish, but with careful tending, you will reap benefits, including improved efficiency and less stress.

TWENTY-THREE

Tame Your E-mail

Erin White

This chapter introduces some e-mail management techniques to help librarians alleviate clogged inboxes. Tips include inbox task management, filters, message organization systems, dealing with listservs, and smart calendaring. This chapter is brief, but many other authors have offered their e-mail management expertise in books or online. References to some of these works are included at the end of the chapter.

FIRST: GIVE UP

If your inbox is filled with thousands of messages, and you are seeking to clean it out, you have two options: either process all of the messages or archive them all and start fresh. With even more messages arriving every day, processing backlogs of messages can be a Sisyphean task. Thomas Limoncelli, author of *Time Management for System Administrators* (2006), offers a couple of strategies for parsing those messages, including choosing one hundred random messages per day to answer or grouping all messages by person and responding to one person per day. Ultimately, Limoncelli encourages readers to give up on the idea of incrementally emptying a clogged inbox. Instead, it is easier to start fresh by clearing out the inbox and starting at zero. Items that are urgent will reappear in your inbox, while items that are not urgent will make their way back to your attention eventually, if at all.

Declaring E-mail Bankruptcy

An optional component of rebooting your inbox is a public announcement of e-mail bankruptcy. In 2004, Internet guru Lawrence Lessig was one of the first public figures to announce that he would be clearing his inbox and starting from scratch (Fitzgerald 2004). He sent a form e-mail to everyone who had sent him a message, apologized for not writing back in a timely manner, and encouraged people to resend their messages if they really needed a response.

SECOND: WHITTLE IT DOWN WITH FILTERS

Filters are the most powerful tool to help maintain the sanctity of the inbox. Most modern e-mail systems have a feature that will perform actions on e-mail messages that meet set criteria. Filters can be used to automatically sort e-mails into folders, forward the messages to other addresses, mark them as important, or send them to the trash. The following are some filter recipes that will reduce your inbox to only the most important messages.

Filtering Listservs

Many librarians juggle memberships on multiple professional e-mail lists. Luckily, those messages are usually easy to identify, because their subject lines contain a "slug" identifying the listserv, or the to: address is always the listserv's e-mail address. The filter you set up may look like this:

- If message subject contains "[lita-l]"
- Move to folder Listservs\LITA

Or

- If to: address is "lita-l@lists.ala.org"
- Move to folder Listservs\LITA

Clearing listservs from the inbox is a fast way to reduce clutter and allows you to come back to that listserv's folder at your leisure and catch up on the threads.

If you do not see yourself responding to listserv messages regularly, consider switching to a daily digest e-mail for each listserv. Many e-mail lists have a Web interface at which you can manage your subscription and set your delivery options. If you are not sure where that management interface may be, try visiting the address that is after the @ sign in the listserv's e-mail. For example, if the listserv e-mail address is lita-l@lists.ala.org, you can visit the Web management page in your browser at http://lists.ala.org.

After a vacation or a busy time at work, you may find that your listserv e-mail folders are filled up with lots of unread messages. Rather than read them all, you can save your time and sanity by simply marking all the messages in the folder as read. Your time is valuable.

Filtering Other Automated Messages

If you get automated alerts from systems, daily digests, or other messages that do not necessarily require your immediate attention, you can filter them as well. This filter might look like this:

- If message subject contains "Tech forum daily digest"
- Move to folder News\Tech Forum

Filtering Important Messages Back to the Inbox

Sometimes your coworker or supervisor may respond to or forward an e-mail that would otherwise meet the filter criteria to be moved out of your inbox. Most e-mail systems will allow you to layer or prioritize filters. For example, the rule below could be prioritized above a listserv filter.

- If message sender is my.boss@employer.org
- Move to Inbox
- Make this filter more important than other filters

INBOX AS TO-DO LIST

Merlin Mann's concept Inbox Zero (Mann 2006) is one method of e-mail organization aimed at busy information professionals. The central tenet of Inbox Zero is that the inbox is a to-do list, and each message should be seen as an action item to be processed and removed from the inbox. According to Mann, each e-mail should receive one of five actions, outlined in the following discussion.

Delete

Some e-mails can be read or scanned, then sent directly to the trash folder. Examples are generic announcements, product pitches, and daily news updates that are not directly relevant to your work. Delete them. If the messages are junk, use the "mark as spam" feature.

Delegate

If the content of the e-mail can or should be handled by another person in your organization, forward the message to that person and archive the message.

Respond

Respond to the sender's request: briefly, if possible.

Defer

If the e-mail presents a task that you can't perform at the moment, or the task requires more thought, defer action until you are ready. Mann recommends that this action not be used very often.

Do

Perform the action requested in the e-mail, follow up if necessary, then archive the message. Limoncelli (2006) recommends a similar step, "record," in which you add the item to a separate to-do list and file or delete the message.

Mann claims Inbox Zero will help "reclaim your inbox, your attention, and your life."

ORGANIZING MESSAGES

Where do messages go when they leave the inbox? As librarians, we may all have distinct methods for organizing e-mail. Organization methods can range from a very complex foldering system, featuring multiple levels of folders and subfolders, to the simplistic "big bucket," one-folder approach. For some e-mail clients like Gmail, which feature robust search capabilities and encourage users to archive e-mails instead of deleting them, the big-bucket approach can be very easy. For e-mail clients that may be slower to search, a basic foldering system can be a faster approach to managing and retrieving messages. Common folders librarians may find useful include the following:

- *Administrative* work-related, HR, or organizational messages that don't necessarily pertain to your day-to-day projects
- *Committees* committee work at your library
- *Scholarship* papers, presentations, travel plans, external committee work
- *Listservs* subfolders for each listserv
- *Projects* subfolders for each large project you're currently working on

- *Dossier/smile file* any messages that could be added to your promotion and tenure dossier. This folder can also be a place to put "thank-you" or other feel-good messages that you can return to later for motivation.

E-MAIL LIKE A PRO

Learn Shortcuts, Save Time

Advanced software users can shave off a good deal of time by using keyboard shortcuts in lieu of using the mouse. Studying your e-mail client's keyboard shortcuts for a short time can pay dividends in time saved. To find keyboard shortcuts, look at your client's dropdown menus to see if keyboard alternates are listed to the right of each command. For example, some e-mail clients' shortcut for "reply" may be Ctrl+R; reply all, Ctrl+Shift+R. More than likely there are also resources on the Web from the software's vendor or other users who have used keyboard shortcuts to save time.

Keyboard shortcuts are not solely available in stand-alone e-mail clients; some Web-based e-mail clients have keyboard shortcuts, too. If your organization uses Gmail, for example, you can enable keyboard shortcuts in your Gmail account settings. Refresh your memory on shortcuts at any time by typing a question mark (?), which will bring up a dialog listing all available keyboard shortcuts.

Keep It Brief and Write for Scannability

Sending good e-mail is a part of smart inbox management. When composing messages, follow the golden rule of e-mail: write it how you'd like to read it. Though sometimes e-mails cannot always be short, they should be broken into smaller paragraphs where possible, with bulleted lists used wherever they can be for increased readability.

If you find yourself spending a lot of time composing a message, step back for a few minutes and do something else. When you return to the draft, clarify with yourself the main idea that you are trying to impart and go from there. Don't rewrite to death. It doesn't have to be perfect.

Know Your Contacts

Knowing your co-e-mailers' communication habits is part of being an effective e-mail user. For example, if you have a time-sensitive issue to communicate to someone who does not quickly respond to e-mail, you could mention the time constraints in the subject line of the message and follow up with a phone call if necessary. If it's something that can wait, put a reminder on your calendar to send that person a follow-up e-mail on a certain day in the future or keep a reminder e-mail in your inbox as a placeholder until the person responds.

Take a Break

Constant connectivity at work and in our personal lives can take its toll. Sometimes it is healthy and necessary to simply take a break. Internet researcher Danah Boyd (2011) advocates taking e-mail sabbaticals concurrent with vacations and offers tips for successful sabbaticals, including announcing the sabbatical ahead of time and creating an auto-reply message for transmission during the break.

IT'S YOUR INBOX

At the end of the day, these tips may or may not get you closer to a comprehensive e-mail management strategy. It is your inbox, after all, and how you manage it is up to you. There is no wrong way to manage e-mail, but there are ways to make it a little less painful.

WORKS CITED

Boyd, Danah. 2011. "How to Take an Email Sabbatical." http://www.danah.org/Email-Sabbatical.html (last modified July 11, 2011).
Fitzgerald, Michael. 2004. "Call It the Dead E-mail Office." *Wired*, June 7. http://www.wired.com/lifestyle/news/2004/06/63733 (accessed January 25, 2012).
Limoncelli, Thomas. 2006. *Time Management for System Administrators*. Sebastopol, CA: O'Reilly Media.
Mann, Merlin. 2009. "Inbox Zero." http://inboxzero.com.

ADDITIONAL RESOURCES

Allen, David. *Getting Things Done: The Art of Stress-Free Productivity*. New York: Penguin, 2002.
Lagendijk, Ad. *Survival Guide for Scientists*. Amsterdam: Amsterdam University Press, 2008.
Mann, Merlin. *Inbox Zero*. New York: HarperCollins, 2012.
Pash, Adam, and Gina Trapani. *Lifehacker: The Guide to Working Smarter, Faster, and Better*. Hoboken, NJ: Wiley, 2011.

VI

Using Technology

TWENTY-FOUR

Let's Not Meet: Making the Most of Time with Asynchronous Collaboration

Jolanda-Pieta van Arnhem and Jerry M. Spiller

Productivity is achieved by a variety of means. Well-chosen technology can be a big part of the equation. In the past, choosing one technology over others involved making a commitment that was not easily changed later (Lambson 1991). With the plethora of open source, low-cost, and free alternatives abounding today, this is often no longer the case. Further, interoperability among choices is a key component of the standards-based Web and applications that take advantage of it.

The power of these tools is often in their asynchronous nature. In our experience as information professionals, we have found that asynchronous collaboration can be a much more efficient and modular way to use time than calling everyone to the same place at the same time for a meeting. We have come to depend on it.

We all, hopefully, have learned to deal with the maelstrom of potential activities and connections that are now always at our fingertips, making it important to manage the use of our own attention. Rheingold (2009) calls this "infotention," a combination of our own mindfulness and the technological tools we use as filters.

Shirky (2008) has similarly argued that the "shared awareness" created by the Web is exactly what makes our shared efforts more adaptable and effective. In fact, the opportunities for collaboration enabled by the Web are precisely the cure for attention blindness, according to Duke's Cathy Davidson, cofounder of the Humanities, Arts, Science, and Technology Advanced Collaboratory (HASTAC, pronounced "haystack"). In her book *Now You See It: How the Brain Science of Attention Will Transform the Way We Live, Work, and Learn,* Davidson (2011) challenges many of the assumptions that structure our schools and workplaces, concluding that a collaborative and creative future open to the contributions of many voices lies ahead. How can we collaborate, then, without having to meet face to face?

DEVICES, PROGRAMS, AND APPS TOOLS

One of the quickest ways to maximize effective time on collaborative projects is to take stock of all the devices you use on a daily basis and find out how to employ them to your advantage. What devices and programs do you use regularly? Why do you use them? Would you like to do more with them or be more proficient with them? How do all of your devices connect to the Internet? Do all your devices sync the same information?

We use Android phones connected to the Internet by a service provider, iPads with Wi-Fi capability only, Macbooks (ethernet and Wi-Fi), and general computing lab computers, which are often PCs. We have a preference for cloud-based programs and apps that run on multiple operating systems and devices. Consider that if your favorite device isn't working well across platforms anymore, it may be time to update.

All of our devices run the same programs and apps and sync their data in the cloud. The "cloud" just means the data are stored on the Web centrally, then synced to devices. This means that if we change information in programs or applications on our laptops, phones, iPads, or a public computer, the same information is updated on the rest of our devices. Take a thoughtful inventory of your own workflow and do the necessary research on devices, programs, and apps to find the best fit. You can find out more about this in our information guide, available at http://libguides.library.cofc.edu/notmeet.

We have found that customizing your choices to fit your workflow is vital for successful collaboration on projects. The ability to sync informa-

For more information on using these and other technologies visit our information guide:

http://libguides.library.cofc.edu/notmeet

If you need to download a QR code reader, visit

http://goo.gl/eM4RQ

Figure 24.1.

tion from multiple devices allows us to use our time productively, meeting and working where we are, helping us to carve out creative space and reflective time in our busy days, instead of losing time traveling from one location to another to meet. Seamlessly syncing information also helps everyone stay on the same page and work with the same information, a key to being able to work asynchronously. You may find you have other preferences. As they say on the Internet, YMMV ("your mileage may vary").

Once you have taken stock of your own devices, skills, and preferences, the next step is to consider who your collaborators are. Are your collaborators tech savvy? What technologies and platforms are they comfortable using? Are they willing to learn new skills independently or with instruction? Your selection of programs and apps should be tailored to meet the needs of the project and the skills, workflows, and devices of the collaborators.

Many of the recommendations we provide are what we consider "tried and true." They have been selected based on our experiences working collaboratively on projects with a wide variety of individuals over the past five years. We have successfully collaborated with people of varying levels of skill and expertise in different locations. The types of projects we have collaborated on have included coauthoring publications, recording and editing video projects, designing and delivering guest lectures, and making virtual presentations.

MEETINGS AND SCHEDULING TIME

One of the reasons that we started looking into the option of collaborating virtually was the level of frustration we experienced with face-to-face meetings. These meetings tend to be thrown into an already hectic day as a matter of habit rather than out of a real need. They often do not have a clear agenda, run over their allotted time, and accomplish little.

In a library setting, scheduling appointments with colleagues, students, vendors, and others is a normal part of a routine day. Inevitably, everyone uses a different calendaring system: pen and paper planner, Outlook/Exchange, iCal, and Google Calendar, to name a few. Keeping track of everyone's preferences and correlating them is draining and time consuming. Multiply this experience by two to five meetings per day, and the result is an immeasurable loss of quality, productive hours in a typical week.

One way to combat all the confusion, whether meeting in person or trying to schedule a virtual meet up, is to set up a Doodle meeting poll. The Web-hosted scheduler is free, does not require users to register for an account to confirm their availability times, is mobile friendly, and allows the meeting organizer to preconfigure several date and time options for a meeting. Invitations are sent to the participants via e-mail and include a hyperlink for invitees to select their preferred meeting times. If users open the invitation on their mobile device, Doodle automatically detects this and redirects the user to a friendly mobile interface. The process is simple and straightforward.

Registration for a free account offers more functionality, including the ability to integrate Doodle with your calendar interface, allowing the application to automatically tally and sync tentative times from all participants on your calendar. Doodle allows you to respond to a meeting poll, initiate a poll, and see all your polls on your dashboard, so that you can manage scheduling on the go between other meetings and appointments, using whatever device you have at hand. Doodle has Android and iOS apps. It is "platform agnostic," meaning it works on a variety of operating systems, and it gets higher marks than the less well-designed Google Appointment Slots.

SETTING UP COMMUNICATION

Maximizing effective time on collaborative projects requires both asynchronous and synchronous communication. Prior to starting a collaborative online working environment, poll the collaborators to determine which programs and applications they use and are comfortable with. We use Poll Everywhere, which is Web-based, doesn't require software or a login to use, correlates and displays audience responses in real-time, accepts text message responses, and integrates with Twitter. Poll Everywhere also provides a survey layout, which can be set up to answer a single question or a series of polls synchronously or asynchronously on a variety of devices. Google Forms can also be used for polling; however, a downside to using this method is that responses are recorded in a single

Figure 24.2.

spreadsheet, and organizers have to tally the results. Overall, we have found Poll Everywhere to be more effective for this task.

Once you have a sense of the types of users you are planning to collaborate with and their preferences and skill levels, you can define the parameters for working on the project and provide suggestions based on each user's workflow that will help facilitate the process. We cannot stress this step enough. Failing to take the time to plan, advise, and correlate all participants' preferences can lead to frustration and ruin a great collaboration. This is your opportunity to get everyone on the same page; provide tutorials and assistance in areas needed; and exchange all relevant information, such as e-mail addresses, time zones, types of equipment and capabilities, screen names for programs, and phone numbers. Tailor your choice of apps to the project and the people, and make sure that everyone is in agreement.

LESS IS MORE

The tricky thing about e-mail addresses is that most people have too many of them. Ask participants to provide a single e-mail address for communication about the project. A helpful tip is to ask participants to provide the e-mail address that they actually check, and, if possible, an address that they can access from more than one place, such as their phones. If users are not already Google Docs users, encourage them to sign up for an account. Once you have a single e-mail address for all collaborators, you can create a master list of all the participants and share it with them as editors. Put the fields in for the accounts that you have gathered from your poll and ask them to fill in their screen names. This document can serve as the project plan, with links to programs, tutorials, tasks, and notes.

The same problem exists with instant message programs. People generally have multiple IM clients, are still using older clients, or are not instant messaging at all. For those who don't have an account, Google Chat is a good option and will be seamlessly integrated into Google Apps. For the novice chatter, this may be a good starting point. For others who have already invested in an IM client that they use regularly, we recommend using that. For the project organizers, a multinetwork IM client, such as Trillian, allows you to interact with multiple IM clients and social media applications. It supports all major platforms (Windows, Mac, iPhone, iPad, and Android) and provides users with the ability to sign in from multiple locations and devices.

Always find out how savvy users are with their phones. It is important to know if they have cell phones, whether or not they send and receive text messages, and if their phones are smartphones. Some members of your team may only use a land line. If this is the case, don't despair; there are other options, such as Google's phone and video chat plug-ins, available directly from Gmail. Google Voice is another option if you do not want to freely distribute your cell phone number or if you want to forward your calls and voicemail to another line. It is important when collaborating to always have your phone at hand. It is often the first line of defense to ward off confusion or help collaborators get connected.

GETTING TOGETHER

Getting the most out of people requires getting them together, whether virtually or in person. Once you have set up various ways to contact people, consider that each method has strengths and drawbacks. Many of us text or tweet and have adapted to succinctly describing information or getting our message across in 140 characters when that is possible. Some of us may keep an IM client open, obviating the need for calling or walking over. Others send tweets, watch trending hashtags, and monitor other social media accounts using TweetDeck or HootSuite. Voicemail may only be checked once, late in the day. E-mail leaves a record, but overload is quickly making it ineffective. Always consider the best way to send a message.

With communication channels open, how do you keep a project on task? How do you know where everyone else is on a project if everyone is working asynchronously? Every project needs to be kept on task. One way to do this is to use a project management application. We prefer the simple elegance of Scrumy. Collaborators can post status updates to their project task by posting a virtual sticky note on the project wall. The free version of Scrumy is generally fine for most projects; however, it is worth noting that project URLs are public, and inactive projects are deleted. The pro version of the program is inexpensive and provides additional features such as private URLs and multiple projects.

Another way to keep projects on task and share information with each other without meeting is to use specific applications for specific tasks. If researching a topic is a large part of the project, find the best method for organizing and commenting on the material that everyone is contributing. We often use social bookmarking sites like Delicious, Pinboard, or Diigo for collecting general information found on the Web related to a project. Links and resources can be "tagged" with a project tag and shared with others via URL or RSS feed. Diigo provides the opportunity to create groups and allows members to add material, highlight important text, and provide comments.

If a literature review is part of your project and you need to upload documents for review or annotation, Google Docs is a great tool for this purpose. The project organizer can create a project folder and share it with all the team members. Researchers can search independently and upload copies of the documents they find for evaluation and review by others. The comment feature in Google Docs allows everyone to provide their thoughts and get feedback from other members of the team. Each comment generates an e-mail to the team, keeping everyone in the loop.

If looking at images and representations is part of your project, use a specific graphic organizer to collect pictures and other visual resources. For example, designing a learning space or planning a very visual presentation might benefit from Evernote or Pinterest. Evernote is a popular cloud-based space for organizing and sharing information using virtual notebooks. We are fans of Pinterest, a very visual site for "pinning" bookmarks of images, videos, and other content, in the style of a virtual pinboard. Pinterest integrates with many social media sites and works well on mobile devices.

Once you have collected all of your resources and information, you will most likely want to meet and discuss where you are and what you have found. You may need to present your findings to a group or cover questions that are better suited to spoken conversation. Our favorite free application for meeting virtually with audio or video is the popular video chat software Skype. The application can be used on a computer, smartphone, or tablet equipped with a camera on the front. We have used Skype on all of our devices at one time or another to attend or bring people into appointments from other locations, meet one-one-one virtually, bring students and guest presenters into class, and conduct research consultations. The screen-sharing feature allows you to share your own screen while videoconferencing and is great for providing one-on-one guidance or keeping your virtual attendee engaged. This feature simplifies the delivery of virtual professional presentations and allows meeting attendees to share with the rest of the group. In our experience, Skype provides great functionality, has a wide variety of options, and is easy to use. In addition, Skype audio and video calls can be recorded and hosted on the Web for later viewing, or transcribed and archived.

WORKING COLLABORATIVELY

Once a project is up and running, ground rules have been established, and systems have been put in place for collaboration and communication, it is important to be able to work on a project and leverage our "cognitive surplus" (Shirky 2010) by being adaptable, connecting with others, working effectively, and making the most of scattered moments in our day. This can be accomplished by looking at common tasks.

Meetings always generate e-mails, agendas, follow-ups, minutes, and to-dos. Save time and energy by changing your meeting workflow cycle. Decentralize the workflow. Stop sending out an e-mail requests for agenda items, compiling the results, creating an agenda, taking notes, retyping handwritten notes into electronic minutes, and e-mailing minutes to the team. Instead, create the agenda using Google Docs, share it with the team, use the feature in Google Docs to e-mail the collaborators, and in the memo field request that participants add agenda items to the shared document. At the meeting, use the document to keep the meeting on task; assign a note taker; and leave the meeting with minutes complete, archived, and distributed. Virtual participants can also use the document to contribute, using the built-in "Other Viewers" chat feature. Any questions, additions, or status updates for to-do items can easily be added by each participant using the "Insert Comment" feature. Best of all, each comment generates an e-mail to the team. Similar processes can be used for committee and project meetings, allowing committee work to be doled out independently, requiring less face-to-face time with collaborators.

Coauthoring papers with colleagues in different locations is far easier than it once was, no longer requiring keeping up with the multiple versions of e-mailed and downloaded papers or the use of tracked changes in Word. Collaborators can use Google Docs to work synchronously in the same room at different terminals or asynchronously, after they have been given the time to reflect and process information. We suggest that each author select a unique text color for his or her contributions, so that others can quickly see what has been added. This process helps coauthors retain that shared awareness and makes coauthoring more dynamic and adaptable. Once the document is near completion, use the Google Docs "Download File as Word Document" feature to move the document to Dropbox for final revisions and formatting. All revisions can be numbered and kept in a single location, accessible from multiple devices by all collaborators.

There are also a number of options for creating and delivering collaborative professional presentations. Google Presentations features document sharing, chat, as well as a "View Together" feature that allows the presenter to control viewers' progress in the presentation. Prezi Meeting allows collaborators to work together in real time and can be delivered to audiences via Skype using the "Share Screen" feature to give presenters similar control. Both presentation programs allow collaborators to create sharing links that can be e-mailed to participants or embedded on the Web.

These are just some of the methods we use in collaborative projects to make the most effective use of time. Figure 24.3 is a more comprehensive list of productivity and social media sites and applications we find helpful, including those we have discussed in more detail, along with our breakdown of the best uses we have found for them. With mindful infotention, you will find your own.

When it comes to "high-complexity" jobs like those of library and information professionals—true knowledge workers if there ever were any—a happy worker really is a more productive worker (Judge et al. 2001). A happy and effective worker is one who is able to tailor his or her environment, physical or virtual, to suit personal and organizational needs (Cain 2012b). Addressing the administrator's propensity to pile meetings on top of meetings, Susan Cain was clear in her calls to stop the madness in her recent TED Talk, "An Introverted Call to Action" (Cain 2012a). Meetings take up precious time, a very finite resource, and they may very well be sapping the will of many library professionals. As

Service	Document Collaboration	Email	Graphic Organizer	Instant Message/Chat	Phone/Voicemail/Forwarding	Polling	Project Management	Presentation Collaboration	RSS (Site Feed) Aggregator	Scheduling/Tasks	Screencasting: Audio/Video	Screen Sharing: Audio/Video	Social Bookmarking	Twitter	Web Portal	Windows	OSX	Web Browser/Cloud App	iOS (iPhone/iPad)	Android
									Uses									Platforms		
Delicious									✓				✓					✓	✓	✓
Diigo									✓				✓					✓	✓	✓
Dropbox																✓	✓	✓	✓	✓
Doodle										✓								✓		
Gmail		✓		✓					✓									✓	✓	✓
Evernote			✓													✓	✓	✓	✓	✓
Google Calendar										✓								✓	✓	✓
GoogleDocs	✓			✓				✓										✓	✓	✓
GoogleTalk				✓														✓	✓	✓
Google Reader									✓									✓	✓	✓
GoogleVoice					✓													✓	✓	✓
HootSuite														✓				✓	✓	✓
iGoogle															✓			✓		
Pinboard									✓				✓					✓		
Pinterest			✓															✓		
Prezi								✓										✓	✓	
Poll Everywhere						✓												✓		
Skype				✓	✓						✓	✓				✓	✓	✓	✓	✓
Scrumy							✓											✓		
Trillian				✓												✓	✓	✓	✓	✓
TweetDeck														✓		✓	✓		✓	✓

Figure 24.3.

many of us are asked to do more with less in current budget and staffing cut trends, perhaps our energy is better spent using other methods to collaborate.

WORKS CITED

Cain, Susan. 2012a. "An Introverted Call to Action: Susan Cain at TED2012." *TED Ideas Worth Spreading* (blog), February 28. http://blog.ted.com/2012/02/28/an-introverted-call-to-action-susan-cain-at-ted2012/ (accessed March 5, 2012).

Cain, Susan. 2012b. *Quiet: The Power of Introverts in a World That Can't Stop Talking.* New York: Crown Publishing Group.

Cain, Susan. 2012c. "The Rise of the New Groupthink." *New York Times*, January 13. http://www.nytimes.com/2012/01/15/opinion/sunday/the-rise-of-the-new-group-think.html?_r=1&pagewanted=all (accessed February 21, 2012).

Davidson, Cathy. 2011. *Now You See It: How the Brain Science of Attention Will Transform the Way We Live, Work, and Learn.* New York: Viking Adult.

Judge, T., C. Thoreson, J. Bono, and G. Patton. 2001. "The Job Satisfaction-Job Performance Relationship: A Qualitative and Quantitative Review." *Psychological Bulletin* 127, no. 3: 376–407.

Lambson, Val. 1991. "Industry Evolution with Sunk Costs and Uncertain Market Conditions." *International Journal of Industrial Organization* 9, no. 2: 171–196.

Rheingold, Howard. 2009. "Infotention." *Smart Mobs | The Next Social Revolution* (blog), August 20. http://www.smartmobs.com/2009/08/20/infotention/ (accessed April 14, 2012).

Shirky, Clay. 2008. *Here Comes Everybody: The Power of Organizing without Organizations.* New York: Penguin Press.

Shirky, Clay. 2010. *Cognitive Surplus: Creativity and Generosity in a Connected Age.* New York: Penguin Press.

TWENTY-FIVE

Making Memory Portable

Sanjeet Mann

Librarians seeking to organize their thoughts and remember important information can now supplement time-tested tools such as paper, pens, and file folders with freely available note-taking programs such as Evernote, Springpad, and Catch. These programs use cloud computing, keyword searching, and the abundance of mobile devices to externalize your memory and make it portable. Online discussions testify to their usefulness not only for sharing personal interests, but also for professional flexibility and enhanced collaboration. In this chapter I discuss some considerations in deciding whether and how to adopt one of these "portable memory systems," and share how I have integrated one of them into my daily work routines.

IS A PORTABLE MEMORY SYSTEM RIGHT FOR YOU?

The professional benefit you are likely to receive from a cloud-based note-taking program depends on the nature of your position, your comfort level with using new technology at work, and the kind of balance you seek between your work and personal life. In particular, you may want to try one of these systems if the following apply:

- You already use or are considering getting a mobile device.
- You need to get work done from multiple locations (e.g., your home computer, your office computer, and the reference desk).
- Your responsibilities include planning and brainstorming.
- You frequently collaborate on group research or problem-solving endeavors.

- You enjoy learning about new technologies and sharing lessons learned with library users or colleagues.
- You would like to minimize your use of paper.

BENEFITS OF A PORTABLE MEMORY SYSTEM

Once you have entered a note into a program like Evernote, Springpad, or Catch, it is synchronized and available from any computer or device you use to connect to the service. This kind of flexibility offers significant opportunities for library workers.

Mobility

At the university where I work, librarians have faculty status and are salaried exempt. Our schedules are irregular to accommodate evening and weekend reference shifts and instruction sessions, as well as time dedicated to research or service on faculty governance committees. As our systems/electronic resources librarian, I also like to monitor the status of our ILS or e-resource systems from home if needed. This requires access not only to e-mail but also to login information and documentation of settings.

Storing some of this information in Evernote gives me access to the information I need to troubleshoot access problems if an emergency occurs while I am out of the office. Although I work predictable hours for much of the year (so that I can attend meetings and troubleshoot problems reported by colleagues during their workday and be on call for the reference desk), I appreciate having options of when and where to accomplish work on a given day and to be able to keep up with what is happening in the library when I am away attending a conference.

I have also been able to take advantage of "found time" to write notes to myself while waiting for a meeting to begin or between appointments. If I have a good idea while I am away from the computer, I can write it on scratch paper and then scan or type it into a note later.

Multiple Content Types

During a typical workday, I can add content to Evernote as it arrives from e-mail, blogs, or web pages that I read. I can also type up notes based on phone calls I received or meetings or informal conversations I had regarding a problem, and attach related Microsoft Office documents or PDF files to any note. I can read my notes from home on my iPad or at the reference desk in a web browser and keep them organized using a combination of folders and tags.

Collaboration

Much of the work in our library involves working collaboratively to solve problems without clear parameters or a self-evident solution. Projects proceed in spurts, with cycles of individual research followed by group meetings for brainstorming and consensus forming, then implementation by individuals or smaller teams. My portable memory system helps with each stage of the process. As I have time to research a problem, I can add what I am learning to a note dedicated to that issue. In a meeting, I can call up the note to contribute a piece of information needed to keep the discussion moving forward, or I can pass my iPad around the table as a visual display if the conversation centers on a particular document or web page.

When I work with an individual collaborator (e.g., to teach a workshop or give a research presentation), we will usually hold an initial meeting to clarify the project parameters, then divide up responsibilities and schedule a follow-up meeting to share our progress. I can share brainstorming notes before the meeting or a summary of my meeting notes afterward for confirmation.

One area of collaboration I have not yet explored is sharing notes with library users I work with as part of a research appointment or as follow-up to an instruction session. Buffy Hamilton (2010) has documented her use of Evernote as a library instruction tool at Creekside Elementary School, suggesting the potential of these services to build library users' research skills.

CHOOSING A MEMORY SYSTEM

Just as we use collection development guidelines to select items for our collections, it makes sense to apply selection criteria to your choice of a portable memory system.

Interface

Cloud note-taking programs may be similar in their use of the note metaphor and the way they synchronize information through a central server, but they have strikingly different interfaces and methods for adding, managing, and exporting information that can take some getting used to. For example, you can add notes to Springpad about a thing or place by typing into a search box, and the service will use semantic technology to classify results as books, movies, mapped locations, etc.

When you evaluate a note-taking system, consider how you can add different types of information (e-mail, web pages, documents) and whether you can export the information out of a note as easily as you imported it. Complications can arise with mobile devices; for example, if

I want to add a document directly to Evernote on my iPad, the app that created the document needs to have Evernote listed on its "Open In" menu. (If it is not, I can still e-mail the document to my Evernote account with an additional step.) Look for the program that gives you the most efficient way to accomplish what you need to do. Extra clicks, menus, and scrolling add up, particularly if you write dozens of notes to yourself each day.

Findability

A computerized note system is only convenient insofar as you can search for information faster than browsing through paper files. When you start using a system, you will be able to see everything at a glance, but if you use it regularly it will eventually grow too big to browse. Before that point, make sure that not only the title but also the full text of content and attachments are indexed and keyword searchable. A good search interface will also allow you to filter search results and save searches for reuse.

Confidentiality

Librarianship's core value of confidentiality is increasingly valuable as more and more companies approach personal information as a commodity to be traded. Before adopting a portable memory system, scrutinize its website and terms of use. What protections are used to ensure that notes are not associated with the identities of their authors, and that a minimal number of employees have access to the data? Are intellectual property rights of users respected? Does the service employ up-to-date encryption protocols to protect content while it is synchronized with and stored on the central server? Can you easily configure whether notes are shared or private? When someone stops using the service, what happens to his or her notes?

Sustainability

The value of a portable memory system increases as you add information to it over time, so you want to be able to depend on it for years to come. Companies cannot always deliver on this promise, so it is important to evaluate a provider's business model before committing to use its product. Like many Internet start-ups, Springpad, Catch, and Evernote have all begun with venture capital investments; this funding eventually must be translated into a steady revenue stream through advertising, affiliate programs, or incentives to upgrade to a paid version (Darlin 2009; Boehret 2010). Other considerations include whether there are monthly or lifetime caps on content uploads, whether you can back up your own data in commonly readable formats, and whether you can easily transfer notes from one service to another in case you decide to switch to a competitor.

Support Community

Working in libraries has probably given you experience distinguishing well- from poorly supported products, particularly if your job involves interaction with vendors. Ideally, software companies stand behind their products, offering multiple avenues to technical support, frequent updates, and timely notice of downtimes and new features. Usually their customer support and product management staff maintain an online discussion board linked from their company website. Browse the forum to see what kind of problems are being reported, evaluate users' attitudes toward the product, and gauge the quality of communication between support staff and users. Product release notes can tell you how often updates are released and what kind of issues have been fixed. An engaged user community that shares advice and user stories is always a good sign.

SUMMARY

Cloud-based portable memory systems have the potential to add flexibility to your work routines, refresh your memory, enhance collaborative work, and even support research and creative activity. (I used a note system actively in writing this chapter.) If you're now ready to experiment with a portable memory system, take a moment to consider your work habits and how you envision electronic note taking fitting in to your existing system, then test drive the products and make an informed choice.

WORKS CITED

"About Springpad." n.d. *Springpad* http://www.springpad.com/about (accessed April 11, 2012).

Boehret, Katherine. 2010. "A Service That Says 'Yes, We Have Bananas on Sale'." *Wall Street Journal*, September 15, D3.

Catch.com. n.d. http://www.catch.com (accessed April 7, 2012).

Darlin, Davin. 2009. "Using 'Free' to Turn a Profit." *New York Times*, August 30, BU4.

Evernote. n.d. http://www.evernote.com (accessed February 18).

Hamilton, Buffy. 2010. "Supporting Transliteracy with Evernote: Evernote for Every Literacy." *The Unquiet Librarian* (blog), March 23. http://theunquietlibrarian.wordpress.com/2010/03/23/supporting-transliteracy-with-evernote-evernote-for-every-literacy/.

TWENTY-SIX

Social Media as Time Drain: The Myth of Efficiency

Jennifer Nardine

By 2012, participation in the most popular social media outlets—sites like Facebook, Twitter, and Flickr—had become an all-but-mandatory task for academic librarians. As leaders at the nexus of education, information, and technology, university libraries have embraced the social media phenomenon as an effective medium to disseminate information, gain new patrons, and communicate with subscribers. In turn, the immediacy of being "plugged in" to a constantly updating stream of information helps keep these libraries fully current with their campuses, academia, and the world in general. However, effectiveness is not the same thing as efficiency. Social media effectiveness, as we will see, comes with some significant hidden costs. Managing social media efficiently requires a realistic analysis of costs versus benefits.

BEING SOCIAL TAKES TIME AND MONEY

Fan and Follower Expectations

For all of the inherent benefits of social media participation, the primary cost is the time required to keep feeds current and to respond to incoming comments and inquiries. Postings must be updated frequently enough to maintain followers' interest, but not so frequently that they tune out or unsubscribe from the feeds (Lowenthal 2009, 16). Most Facebook audience members expect at least one update per day, while Twitter followers appear to lose interest in a stream that updates less frequently than three to five times daily ("How to . . . Wrangle" 2011). In addition, all streams must convey information of pertinent interest to a target audience comprised mostly of undergraduates (Bumgarner 2007). And of course, any subscriber who tweets or messages an inquiry to a library expects a nearly instantaneous response. Academic libraries that wish to maintain a large social media following must keep the information relevant to their readers and flowing forth at a steady clip.

Academic Library Resources

Some libraries actually have the personnel and budget to employ faculty or staff whose primary responsibility is managing their social media presence, but these lucky institutions are few and far between. Most libraries do not have the resources necessary to support a full-time social media specialist. This duty often falls to the library's webmaster, whose skills may be more IT than IS in nature. Most likely, though, the library has one or more faculty or staff members who have been reactively tasked with maintaining the library's social media presence and perform this duty in addition to their other responsibilities.

The Thrill—and Peril—of the Hunt

Due to the nature of social media—and of librarians—there exists a secondary peril. The temptation to research background information on an article or to follow a "thread" that comes through Facebook or Twitter, and the ease with which it can be done in an electronic environment, is strong for those people who have chosen research and information tracking as their vocation. Library people, especially the bright, inquisitive ones, can easily spend the vast majority of their workdays researching, updating, and visiting social media sites, to the obvious detriment of the balance of their work. Maintaining a library's social media presence is a temporal balancing act at best. At Virginia Tech University Libraries (VTL), we found it to be much more of a "time suck" than a modern model of efficiency in interactive communication.

VIRGINIA TECH LIBRARIES' FIRST FORAY INTO SOCIAL MEDIA

Although VTL created its first Facebook and Flickr profiles in 2007 and 2008, respectively, in the years following their debut the sites were underutilized and rarely updated, and thus virtually invisible to the Virginia Tech community at large. VTL's webmaster created our social media accounts, using his e-mail and password for the access points. He and the rest of the reference and instruction (RIS) department were tasked with updating the sites, but without any concrete action plan in place with regard to content or frequency of posts. RIS librarians and staff agreed to feed interesting "copy" and accompanying illustrations or links to the webmaster, who would then post these items to Flickr or Facebook. The webmaster was also responsible for either responding to incoming messages or redirecting those conversations to the individuals best equipped to respond to them. Despite good intentions, the flow of posting material from the RIS department to the webmaster rapidly fell off as other tasks and priorities pushed to the fore, and the webmaster's own workload did not allow him sufficient time to research and create new material on a regular basis. As most of the posts at that time were expository rather than conversational in nature, there was virtually no feedback from either Facebook or Flickr subscribers.

IF AT FIRST YOU DON'T SUCCEED

VTL's Social Media Working Group

In 2010, we formed a VTL social media working group and initiated a project to revive and raise campus-wide awareness of VTL's Facebook presence. The group consisted of the webmaster, two representatives from the science and technology reference team, and two from the business, humanities and social sciences reference team, including myself as chair. At the same time that we were reinvigorating the original VTL social media accounts, we created two new profiles: a new Twitter account for general use and a new secondary Facebook page that focused on the science and technology (SciTech) area of VTL, managed and updated by the SciTech librarians. It should be noted that since then, the SciTech-specific feeds have been reabsorbed into the main VTL social media stream, because the librarians responsible for maintaining it encountered the same time and workload challenges that befell the original VTL social media streams.

Concurrent with the new launches in July 2010, the working group discussed methods for maintaining social media feeds at an activity level that would attract and retain reader interest. An important goal for this social media revival was our unanimous desire to make our media truly interactive, with our patrons taking an active role in shaping its scope and services, as well as influencing the services and resources provided by VTL in general.

Past Practices and Future Goals

As outreach and instruction librarian, I had primary responsibility for keeping all feeds except the SciTech topics current. Up until that point, I had done this by keeping Facebook open in a background window whenever I was at work and periodically clicking over to the VTL profile to add a new post. Aside from creating three or more posts daily, I also spent a significant amount of time searching for items of interest to our readers and creating new VTL promotional messages. Depending on the day and the topic, this took from five to thirty minutes per post. Even though much of the material I posted on Facebook could also be sent out through our new Twitter feed, actually posting to Twitter—after making sure each "tweet" conformed to its 140-character limit—would involve even more time than I was already spending on social media. We needed a tool that would enable us to increase our social media activity without additional demands on our time.

In addition to a more efficient method of maintaining our online presence, VTL librarians also wanted a secondary administrator in place for the times I wasn't available, so that the stream of posts would remain uninterrupted. Further, we needed an avenue for other librarians to post interesting, time-sensitive items without having to filter everything through a single administrator. This complicated matters somewhat, because each Twitter and Facebook account is associated with a unique login and password, and a Facebook group page links to the e-mail account of a primary creator. Because we didn't want to share e-mails and passwords, we decided that a social media "dashboard" would facilitate access to the various VTL social media streams without creating security issues.

SOCIAL MEDIA DASHBOARDS

In terms of social media, a dashboard is a software tool that allows an administrator to manipulate feeds to and from multiple social media outlets through a single control panel (SocialBrite 2010). Entries in a dashboard can be sent to multiple platforms at once, eliminating the need to copy and paste or to type information multiple times. Posts can also be created and then scheduled to appear at a particular time in the future. Incoming messages are organized on a single window for easy tracking. The social media working group decided to "test drive" the best dashboards on the market. After some initial research, we focused on the two most popular dashboards available: Tweetdeck and HootSuite.

Tweetdeck versus HootSuite

Tweetdeck was designed with Twitter as its focal point while also allowing users to receive status updates from other sites. The 2009 version accommodated both Twitter and Facebook feeds, allowing them to be read on a single page. In 2010, when our working group was reviewing its options, Tweetdeck also supported inclusion of Google Buzz, LinkedIn, MySpace, and FourSquare. Following Twitter's purchase of Tweetdeck in 2011, they have streamlined their services to include only Twitter and Facebook accounts (see table 26.1).

HootSuite, Tweetdeck's main competitor in 2010, was designed to optimize marketing via social media (HootSuite 2012). It, too, started as a Twitter-only dashboard in 2008, and by 2010 it had expanded to include Facebook, LinkedIn, FourSquare, and several other sites. HootSuite continues to expand its list of compatible inputs.

THE DECISION PROCESS

I started our test process by setting up a free basic account on each platform. Both systems require only a user name, e-mail address, and password to get started. Tweetdeck immediately opens to a window in which to link to a Twitter account. In contrast, HootSuite provides a short menu of profiles from which to choose. The process for establishing a link in each dashboard is essentially identical:

1. Follow the link within the dashboard to a social media site login page.
2. Log in to the social media account.
3. Give permission for the dashboard to access and use various subparts of the social media account.

At first glance, Tweetdeck's interface seems very straightforward. The controls for the system extend across the top of the window in icon or abbreviated text form. All tweets feed into a single, continuous column as they arrive. There are separate columns for Facebook posts, Twitter interactions (notifications of new followers), and Twitter messages exchanged. However, its provisions for shifting column order and accessing different tools are not intuitively labeled, and even those with text descriptions, such as "Lists," give little context for situations in which one might use that particular tool.

HootSuite's dashboard seems to have been created with higher usability standards driving its design. The menu of icons with pop-out descriptive text extends down the left side of the page, while the main text entry box is located at the top left of the window, next to a magnifying glass—the universal icon for "search"—and a dropdown box for choosing the desired profile. The main part of the window is divided into columns, the content of which the user controls. Users may further sort incoming and outgoing information by creating tabbed sections that include various "streams" or subsets of information from social media sources.

After reviewing each platform, we chose to start with a free HootSuite account. We based our decision on these observations and concerns:

Table 26.1. Side-by-Side Comparison of Tweetdeck and HootSuite

	Tweetdeck	**HootSuite**
Purpose	To enhance Twitter use	To efficiently manage brands via social media
Website quote	Tweetdeck is an app that brings more flexibility and insight to power users (Tweetdeck 2012).	HootSuite is a social media management system for businesses and organizations to collaboratively execute campaigns across multiple social networks from one secure, web-based dashboard (HootSuite 2012).
Interface with	Twitter, Facebook	Facebook, Twitter, Google+, LinkedIn, Foursquare, Mixi, MySpace, Ping.fm, WordPress, Tumblr, Trendspottr, Constant Contact, Digg, Flickr, Get Satisfaction, InboxQ, YouTube
Function-ality	• Filter for important items. • Schedule tweets ahead of time. • Monitor and manage unlimited number of accounts. • Stay current with notifications of new tweets. • Display incoming and outgoing messages in one stream.	• Allow users to manage multiple social profiles. • Schedule messages and tweets. • Track brand mentions. • Analyze social media traffic. • Display incoming and outgoing traffic in easy-to-read columns in one window.
2011 plans & pricing	• Free.	• Free: 1 social profile, message scheduling, 2 RSS/Atom Feeds • $5.99/month: 1 team member, unlimited twitter accounts • $15/month: each additional team member • $1,500/month: unlimited

2012 plans & pricing	Tweetdeck has been purchased by and absorbed into Twitter. It is still free, but very focused on Twitter, with other social media given less attention.	• Free: 1 social profile, message scheduling, 2 RSS/Atom Feeds • PRO ($9.99/month): 5 profiles, message scheduling, 2 free users, 1 free enhanced analytics report, Google analytics integration, Facebook insights integration, unlimited RSS feeds • Enterprise (price unlisted): unlimited profiles, 10 free reports, unlimited users, unlimited RSS feeds, enhanced analytics, Vanity URL, tier 1 support, VIP setup, opt out of ads, archive tweets, 10 seats at HootSuite certification program

- While our dashboard use was in pilot mode, we had no start-up funding for paid accounts.
- The ability to create and schedule posts in one interface and send them to multiple networks appeared to be a great time-saver.
- The HootSuite dashboard display was, in our opinion, both better organized and easier to read than Tweetdeck's interface.
- HootSuite was designed to work with multiple social media platforms equally, rather than being primarily optimized for Twitter.
- HootSuite's original purpose was closer to our goals than was Tweetdeck's.
- We liked the potential ability to "buy up" our account, with the option to include multiple users and added analytical capacity in the future.
- One librarian had already done her own dashboard comparison and found HootSuite to be more user-friendly, so we could make use of her significant experience with it and thus reduce the initial steep grade of our dashboard learning curve.

IMPLEMENTATION

Establishing Best Practices

Once we chose HootSuite as our dashboard and linked all of VTL's social media feeds to its system, we established a few guidelines. We created the HootSuite account with a password shared among the administrators, which eliminated the need to share any university or personal passwords, thereby minimizing security issues. We also decided that, at the outset, we would post at least five times per day between 7:00 AM and 6:00 PM, which we felt would be frequently enough to retain reader interest, but not so often that users would delete our feed out of sheer overexposure.

Next, we created a standard set of message categories that could be researched, created, and scheduled ahead of time to post at set intervals. Based on an analysis of our previous posting habits, the task force had seen several broad categories emerge. Some posts were service-oriented, and others focused on available resources. We saw that campus-wide notices were distributed sporadically, but were concentrated at the beginning and end of semesters, whereas general interest posts were much more frequent and regular. Based on these observations and several conversations with other librarians, library staff, students, and faculty, I developed a protocol for regular post categories and frequencies:

Resources

- A weekly post on a new acquisition
- A weekly post about an already-available item or database of interest

Services

- A weekly post about a service offered by VTL, such as the availability of online reference sessions or off-campus sign-in to databases
- Intermittent posts about changes in hours of operation, the library's exam week coffee service, and other end-of-semester events
- Welcome messages to groups coming to Newman Library for tours or instruction

Campus-Level Announcements

- A "go team" post before major sporting events
- Information about holidays, vacations, and closures

General Interest

- A weekly post wishing a notable person from the past or present a happy birthday
- At least one post per week from the *Chronicle of Higher Education*
- Links from the campus calendar and the student newspaper, at least once per week

I also left space in the schedule for just-in-time posts to ensure that our feeds didn't become too stale or predictable. Although I spent more time than I had previously done in each prep session, the total time I spent working on and logged into social media decreased from almost constantly to about five hours a week.

Refining the Process Based on Performance

With our newfound flexibility in creating and managing our postings, I further improved my post creation strategy. With the introduction of the dashboard, I had shifted from inefficient continuous updating to writing a week's worth of posts in one sitting. Shifting again to writing sets of one category of post per session—two or three months of "Happy Birthdays," for example—streamlined the process further. This illustrates one of the transformative powers of HootSuite: it converts time from an adversary to an ally. Users create and schedule postings at any desired time and interval and propagate messages from a single entry to multiple platforms. In my case, this freed me to focus on other tasks without having to repeatedly return to Facebook and Twitter to create updates. I can create just-in-time posts at the beginning of each day, knowing that if something important arises that should be included in our stream, I can simply insert another note "on the fly."

VTL saw an increase in the number of "likes" and followers on Facebook and Twitter in the first several months after our dashboard deployment, but interactions remained discouragingly low. After further discussion, the social media working group decided that we would include more interrogative posts that would actively prompt reader input. Accordingly, I added another regular posting category to the weekly distribution schedule: an opinion poll or request for materials suggestions, once per week.

The next few months saw a slight uptick in the number of interactions on our social media feeds, but these mostly consisted of conversations with graduate students, faculty, and staff, rather than the much larger undergraduate population. Surprisingly, we received the most feedback on our "new items" entries, so I have increased the frequency of those posts to twice a week. We continue to seek new ways to engage our undergraduate patrons.

CONCLUSION

By experimenting with social media dashboards and implementing regular posting categories and schedules, VTL librarians have drastically reduced the time necessary to maintain our social media presence. Demands on my own time decreased from an almost-constant secondary task to a handful of two-hour sessions each week, leaving my remaining hours completely free for me to attend to the myriad other responsibilities in the life of an academic librarian. This has increased my efficiency and effectiveness with social media, as posting remains a distinct and thus fresh and interesting activity. I have eliminated a major distraction from my other work activities, processes, and tasks, and changed my social media focus to policy and strategy from the "nuts and bolts" of production.

The social media phenomenon now occupies an increasingly important and still-growing role in academic libraries' communication priorities and practices. Unfortunately, few libraries can muster the additional resources required to keep pace with this growth. Acknowledging these realities by leveraging a social media management dashboard like Hoot-Suite minimizes distractions and maximizes librarians' time—and provides a significant productivity solution to shrinking budgets and increasing demands on personnel.

WORKS CITED

Barrett, Joan. 2011. "How Much Do Pro Social Media Management Tools Cost?" *The Content Factory* (blog), May 20. http://contentfac.com/blog/how-much-do-social-media-management-programs-really-cost/#ixzz1uJJX2pwc.

Bumgarner, Brett. 2007. "You Have Been Poked: Exploring the Uses and Gratifications of Facebook Among Emerging Adults." First Monday 12, no. 11. http://firstmonday.org/htbin/cgiwrap/bin/ojs/index.php/fm/article/viewArticle/2026/1897

HootSuite. 2012. http://hootsuite.com/ (accessed May 8).

"How to . . . Wrangle Your Reputation Online." 2011. *PR News*, August 1. ProQuest (2412995411).

Lowenthal, B. 2009. "Optimal Posting Rate." *Brandweek*, October 19, 16. ProQuest (1900305431).

SocialBrite. 2010. "Top 10 Social Media Dashboard Tools." November 9. http://www.socialbrite.org/2010/11/09/top-10-social-media-dashboard-tools/.

Tweetdeck. 2012. http://www.tweetdeck.com/ (accessed May 8).

Wikipedia. 2012a. "HootSuite." http://en.wikipedia.org/wiki/HootSuite (last modified May 4).

Wikipedia. 2012b. "Tweetdeck." http://en.wikipedia.org/wiki/Tweetdeck (last modified April 28).

VII

Work–Life Balance

TWENTY-SEVEN

Managing Professional and Family Commitments

Libby Gorman

Librarianship, though increasing in diversity, is still an overwhelmingly female-dominated profession: of the 4,790 LIS graduates counted in *Library Journal*'s 2011 Placements and Salaries survey, 3,743 are women (Maatta 2011, 22). These women form a large percentage of a generation of workers as interested in work–life balance as in promotion opportunities and compensation. Despite this historical and current trend, most libraries have no special policies or benefits to accommodate maternity leave and families.

Although there are few accommodations in the library world directly aimed at new parents, knowing how to make use of the leave that is available and how to be flexible with work and day-care options can put the balance of work and family within closer reach. This chapter discusses how to make the most of family leave, how to seek out flexible work options, and how to find a career–life balance that works best for your family.

MATERNITY LEAVE/FAMILY AND MEDICAL LEAVE

Your library may or may not have maternity leave available for its employees. Even if there is no maternity leave per se, you will most likely be able to take advantage of the federal Family and Medical Leave Act (FMLA). The FMLA entitles employees of covered employers to take up to twelve weeks of unpaid leave for the birth or adoption/placement of a child, among other possible reasons. All public employers are covered by

FMLA, and any private-sector employers that have fifty or more employees who work at least twenty weeks in a year are also covered, so most library workers have access to FMLA leave (U.S. Department of Labor 2010).

To make use of the FMLA, contact your library's human resources department to request the necessary forms. FMLA leave for the birth of a new child requires your doctor to fill out a form that certifies your pregnancy and expected due date. FMLA leave can also be used if you need time off during pregnancy due to complications, and you would need your doctor to certify that as well. If you do not need to take leave unexpectedly (i.e., for pregnancy complications or premature birth), you are generally required to give thirty days' notice of taking FMLA leave (U.S. Department of Labor 2009) for a birth. An important fact to be aware of is that employers can, and usually do, require you to use any accrued paid vacation and sick leave while on FMLA leave. You must use the unpaid FMLA leave and your paid leave "concurrently" (U.S. Department of Labor 2009, 10), which means that you can't extend your total time off: twelve weeks is generally the maximum that you can take off (full-time) when making use of FMLA. On the other hand, you may be able to use some of your FMLA allowance to return to work with a part-time schedule for a few weeks, and fathers are also eligible to take FMLA leave for the birth of a child (U.S. Department of Labor 2010). If both parents work for the same organization, however, there is only one twelve-week allowance for both parents.

Although the FMLA provides valuable job protection, it has obvious limitations, and the support of your supervisor or human resources representative is probably your greatest tool in securing alternate leave arrangements for maternity or paternity leave. I was able to take a six-month leave of absence following the birth of my second child because I requested the extended time off and my supervisor advocated for my request with human resources. The use of FMLA leave to return to work part time, mentioned previously, is another possible variant. If you are unsure of leave procedures and precedents at your employer, you may wish to talk to coworkers who are recent parents themselves or arrange a confidential meeting with your human resources representative.

Requesting family leave can be stressful, because it's never fun to tell your boss that you won't be at work for an extended period of time. Despite this, remember your value as an employee as you decide how much leave you plan to request. Difficult as it is to cover someone's job duties during a period of leave, it is even more difficult to hire excellent workers. Your employer may not be able to fulfill your ideal scenario regarding parental leave, but may surprise you in how accommodating it is willing to be. If you do your homework, it won't hurt you to ask for the amount of leave that best meets the needs of your family.

CHILD CARE

One of the greatest hurdles working parents face is finding child care that both suits your schedule needs and fits in with how you wish to raise your children. There are a wide variety of child-care options: individual babysitters, home day care, larger day-care centers. Some information professionals may be able to take advantage of child-care resources within their institutions; many universities have child-care centers on campus, for example. There are other options in addition to traditional child-care venues. Some parents participate in child-care co-ops, in which time is traded or expenses are shared. This option most likely works best for short-term needs, but I had one colleague whose church organized a co-op for the entire summer to help parents of school-aged children.

Whichever form of child care you decide to use, conducting research as early as possible is important. Day-care centers often have long waiting lists for spots, and you want to give yourself time to visit several child-care providers to find the best fit. When getting started on your child-care search, referrals from friends and colleagues are indispensable. You can also make use of community organizations, such as North Carolina's Triangle area Childcare Services Association (2006), to help find and rate child-care providers. I had success with using both a list of available babysitters from my husband's graduate school and the student listserv from my library school to find sitters.

In the case of my family, however, we chose to rely as little as possible on outside child-care by staggering our working hours. The next section discusses options for creating a nonstandard work schedule.

FLEXIBLE WORK ARRANGEMENTS

One advantage that library workers have in the workforce is the variety of libraries and schedules that are available. Although there are certainly a large number of Monday through Friday, 9-to-5 jobs, many libraries are open evenings and weekends. If you are flexible about the hours you are willing to work and the type of library you are willing to work in, you may be able to find a job arrangement that better works with your family's schedule. There are two ways to think about flexible job scheduling: one is to arrange an existing job so that its hours better fit your ideal schedule; the other is to actively seek positions that are already suited to job flexibility. My own experience mostly fits the latter, so I discuss this option first.

During library school, I focused on school library and children's services. Despite my professional interest in these areas, I began my job search looking for any and every position that was part time or had a nontraditional schedule, because my son was born just as I graduated.

Because I knew I wanted to spend some time at home, and we could not relocate because of my husband's job and education responsibilities, I found myself being flexible in both the hours I was willing to work and the area in which I was willing to work. The position I eventually obtained was a full-time evening reference and instruction position in a medium-sized university library. My schedule allowed me to be at work afternoons and evenings, while my husband worked mostly mornings and early afternoons. This schedule was just the right fit for our family for several years.

To seek jobs with built-in flexibility, you first need to decide on which points you are willing to be flexible. Can you work late nights or a greater percentage of weekends? Will relocating be an option? Will a part-time job work for you? Are you willing to work in several different kinds of libraries or information fields? You don't need to be willing to negotiate every single detail of your career, but the fewer non-negotiable items you hang onto, the easier it will be to find a job that works. The next step is to determine how you can use the experience and background you do have when you apply for those "off-the-radar" jobs. I had not concentrated in academic libraries, but I had taken an advanced reference course, and my background in teaching gave me a foundation for my instruction duties. Between these experiences and the fact that fewer people actively seek jobs with regular night hours, I was able to fit my professional life into the existing fabric of my family life.

If you are already established in a satisfying job, it may make more sense to investigate ways to increase that job's flexibility. As with asking for time off, enlisting the support of a supervisor can be your best strategy, nerve-racking as it may be. In a 2009 interview with work–life consultant Pat Katepoo, the *New York Times*' Lisa Belkin tackled the issue of asking for greater flexibility at work during difficult economic circumstances. Katepoo's central point was that, although not every position is equally flexible, flexibility is possible if you can demonstrate that it makes sense for both your employer and you. As with parental leave, it is a good idea to first determine the current environment at your employer by talking with a human resources representative or any other employees who have negotiated flexibility in their positions, but don't let the current environment be the absolute boundary.

You know your position better than anyone, so you are best equipped to analyze if and how you might complete your job duties in a different structure. First, consider how a change in your job's current structure might make sense. You need to be realistic: a reference librarian probably doesn't have a good chance of telecommuting, for example. However, there are many ways that a job can be flexible: telecommuting/working from home, sharing the position with another employee to create two part-time positions, or changing a schedule to work a greater percentage of off-hours are all possibilities. Once you determine a mode of flexibility that makes sense, create a detailed plan that includes how you will implement the changes, how the new schedule will work, and how its success will be evaluated. Keep in mind that this plan needs to make as much sense to your employer as to you, so think about how the change will affect the organization. If you are proposing a job-sharing arrangement, how will the breakdown of hours and provision of benefits (if any are provided) be determined? If you are interested in working more off-hours, what hours can you work that will benefit the organization as a whole and your colleagues who may currently cover those shifts? Whatever you choose to propose, make sure that your plan is detailed and sensible.

When fitting your work schedule to better match your family's needs, a little bit of flexibility can make a big difference. Either through changing the way you search for a job or changing the structure of your current position, you can often find an arrangement that differs from a traditional 9-to-5 work schedule both to your benefit and your library's. Even if a flexible job schedule is not available or desirable in your current circumstances, you can still strike a balance between work life and family life.

WORK–FAMILY BALANCE

Besides the large issues of leave, work schedule, and child care, hundreds of smaller decisions and responsibilities crop up every day. Everyone's individual mix of daily concerns is different, but no matter what yours is, setting priorities and boundaries will help you manage it.

Some priorities seem to set themselves—after all, we all have to eat, we need clothes to wear, etc. However, even within the absolute necessities of life, there are some choices to be made about how to get things done. Do you want to save money by cooking at home most of the time, or do you want to save time by eating out more often? Or, in between these two extremes, do you want to cook at home, but rely on the ready-made convenience options that many grocery stores now offer? Another factor to consider is whether you or your spouse enjoy cooking for its own sake—if so, then it might become a higher priority than it would otherwise. Similarly, are you willing to live with pulling clean clothes out of the clothes basket, or will it drive you nuts if they aren't put away in a drawer? There's no way to do everything, so deciding what is most important to you is a key step in taking care of those essentials. For items that are priorities, share the work with your spouse or partner as much as is practicable and in a way that matches your family style. It may work best to take turns preparing dinner, or you may prefer to have one of you always cook and the other always wash dishes. Make sure that your priorities also include time for relaxing—for everyone!—and sleep. Despite the "supermom" (or superdad!) images that seem to have captivated American society, sleep is not optional, and taking time to get the rest you need does not make you weak.

Equally important to setting priorities is establishing boundaries between work life and home life. Again, the exact boundaries that you set depend on your personal preferences, but choosing some boundaries to set is absolutely necessary. Maintaining work–life balance does not mean that you allow your work and your personal life to bleed together, but that you find a way to give the necessary time and attention to each. With current technology, we can be available to our jobs even when not physically present, but this can be both an advantage and a disadvantage. Mobile technology may allow you to leave work early to attend a child's sports event, but it doesn't do much good if you can't concentrate on the game because you are answering texts or e-mails. There are many ways to set boundaries on your job availability. Some people choose not to check e-mail except at designated hours (only between nine and five, only once first thing in the morning, only for one hour in the evenings, not on weekends, etc.); others check their messages but only respond to items with a given importance the next day. Even if you rely on the ability to take work home for creating the schedule you need, you must still set a clear limit on how much time you are spending on work and stick to the boundaries you set. It is easier to maintain borders when you are not the only one patrolling them, so let others help you. Make sure your supervisors and colleagues know when they can and can't expect you to receive and respond to messages, and enlist your family members to remind you when you need to stop work for the day. You can help your colleagues and friends maintain their boundaries in the same way and improve work–life balance throughout your organization.

STAYING CONNECTED PROFESSIONALLY

At the other end of the work–life choice spectrum from the full-time librarian is the full-time parent. With the birth of our third child in August 2011, my husband and I decided that I would take a few years off to parent full-time. In our case, this decision arose from several different factors: my enjoyment of spending time at home with the kids, my husband's entry into a doctoral program that requires him to spend more time at school, and difficulty with both finding and paying for the amount of child care we would now need for me to continue working. I don't know exactly how long I will be out of the workforce, but I do know that I want to be ready to go once I decide to reenter. With that in mind, I spend the last section of this chapter discussing options for staying connected with the library and information profession while stepping away from the workforce.

Two of the best ways to stay connected are the same as those for continuing professional development while employed: reading professional literature and maintaining professional organization membership. I have found it easy to read at least a few blog entries and *American Libraries'* AL Direct e-mail each week. In addition, I read children's and YA books and book reviews to continue developing my interest in this area of librarianship. Although this hardly counts as in-depth professional reading, it does allow me to keep an eye on news in the field. I also hold membership in the American Library Association (ALA) and the North Carolina Library Association (NCLA), which is easier to do because ALA offers a "non-salaried or unemployed member" dues category, significantly less expensive than the regular member category. Aside from providing a great deal of professional reading, news, and educational opportunities, professional membership also helps if you are interested in volunteering.

Taking on a volunteer opportunity is a great way to keep a foot in the door of library work, and there are a number of options for doing so. If you are a member of a professional organization, you may want to volunteer for a committee or task group. In the case of ALA, committee membership used to require attendance at Annual Conference and Midwinter, an expensive proposition, but now at least some committee work is being done virtually. Professional organizations aren't the only venues for volunteering, of course. Your local library (or perhaps your former workplace) may have need of volunteers who are willing to donate an hour or two a week. In my case, I am volunteering one hour a week with NC Knows, a North Carolina statewide consortium for virtual reference that allows me to keep my reference skills up-to-date without leaving the house. If you choose to volunteer, just remember that you need to be as reliable as a volunteer as you are when getting paid; organizations that use volunteers need to be able to count on their presence and competence.

CONCLUSION

Building a fulfilling library or information career while raising a family is a very attainable goal. Knowing the leave, child-care, and schedule options that are available can allow you to best determine the shape you want your career to take. If you are starting to investigate this topic because of an expected child, then take the time to talk with your colleagues and friends to learn what you can about your organization, support systems in your area, and their own experiences as you set out on this new path. If you are simply at a point when you are rethinking your work–life balance, then take stock of your current situation and what changes would bring you closer to your ideal situation. No matter your situation, a little flexibility and planning can help a great deal in achieving both an exciting career and a satisfying family life.

WORKS CITED

Belkin, Lisa. 2009. "Telecommuting During Tough Times." *New York Times, Motherlode* (blog). http://parenting.blogs.nytimes.com (accessed January 1, 2012).

Childcare Services Association. 2006. http://www.childcareservices.org/index.html (accessed January 2, 2012).

Maatta, Stephanie L. 2011. "The Long Wait. (Cover Story)." *Library Journal* 136, no. 17: 20–27. Academic Search Premier, EBSCOhost (accessed December 7, 2011).

U.S. Department of Labor. Wage and Hour Division. 2009. *Frequently Asked Questions and Answers About the Revisions to the Family and Medical Leave Act.* http://www.dol.gov/whd/fmla/finalrule/NonMilitaryFAQs.pdf (accessed December 7, 2011).

U.S. Department of Labor. Wage and Hour Division. 2010. *Fact Sheet #28: The Family and Medical Leave Act of 1993.* http://www.dol.gov/whd/regs/compliance/whdfs28.pdf (accessed December 7, 2011).

TWENTY-EIGHT

Time Management, Reducing Stress, and Getting Organized

Linda Burkey Wade

Overworked, overbooked, and stressed out with not enough time to get work done? Your desk is cluttered and your family is screaming for some extra time with you. Worried about your job? Don't know when to say "no"? Then most likely you are stressed and looking for more hours in the day. Librarians tend to be overscheduled, which leads to a lack of focus and balance. Learn to get organized, say "no," and reduce stress while you figure out strategies that are right for you. This chapter explores techniques that take a few minutes out of your hectic schedule.

WHAT DO YOU MEAN, I AM STRESSED OUT?

Constant stress has effects on your health, mind, attitude, and performance. According to an American Psychological Association report (2010), the physical symptoms of stress are headaches, joint or muscle pain, fatigue, upset stomach, muscle tension, and sleeping problems. Furthermore, continuous stress may affect your emotional health, resulting in anxiety, irritability, lack of energy, and being restless or sad. Stress may also materialize as bad eating habits, drug abuse, and being antisocial. Knowing that you are experiencing stress and not another illness is the first step to managing your stress.

Librarians tend to be stressed out by numerous events that occur in libraries. "Anticipatory stress" usually occurs with a huge project, a performance review, or layoffs, whereas "situational stress" is caused when interacting with the outside world. These events occur when dealing with a problem or irate patron, an unhappy colleague, or the boss. Additional mental stressors can be feelings of regret, losing an employee, or wishing you had more time (Siess 2002, 96). In the realm of the new digital aspect of libraries, librarians have technology-related stressors deriving from applying, troubleshooting, and developing new technologies for staff and patron use (Ajala 2011, 3). In addition, not having functional tools to perform a task is considered technology-related stress.

Stress becomes chronic when the causes are ongoing over a period of time, such as when librarians are asked to do more with less, whistling heating/cooling systems never get fixed, or there is a lack of respect from management. Another leading cause of stress is multitasking, focusing on more than one thing and not giving your full attention to one project, person, or task (Horstman 2009, 59). Librarians regularly multitask by talking to patrons while typing an e-mail and have multiple projects ongoing at the same time.

Librarians struggle to fulfill customer information needs, professional activities, and education all at once. In addition, the librarian's perfection-ism in customer service and giving 100 percent to all patrons leads to an unattainable goal. Now more than ever, changes in the library lead to job ambiguity and ultimately stress, because no one librarian does the same job, especially with new roles in the digital library setting. The best way to manage stress is to reduce the influence of stressors in the workplace.

MANAGE THAT STRESS: STRESS-REDUCING TECHNIQUES

When you cannot change jobs and are feeling stuck, there is a solution. You can control your time and spend it doing the things you love! Stress is caused by being disorganized, having clutter, not having enough time, and not refusing to embark upon new projects. The following are strate-gies to reduce your stress triggers by getting organized, reducing clutter, promoting time management, and just saying "no."

Some positive ways to react to stress are by eating right, exercising, practicing relaxation, having a sense of humor, and seeking professional help when needed (Mayo Clinic Staff 2010a). One technique is to practice the Four "A"s when dealing with stress: avoid, alter, adapt, and accept (Smith and Segal 2011, 2). Avoiding or altering the stressor may not al-ways be possible, especially if it is a situation that involves confrontation with a coworker or your boss.

Avoid the stressor whenever possible and learn to say "no." Know your limits and communicate to your supervisor the responsibilities you can handle professionally. Avoid coworkers or acquaintances who cause frustration and stress by limiting the amount of time you spend with them. Another simple way to reduce stress is to avoid topics that upset you (Smith and Segal 2011, 2).

Alter the stressful situation by expressing your feelings and doing what you can to change it. Adapt to the stressor by viewing the situation with a positive attitude and adjusting expectations to accept less than perfection. Acknowledge the things you cannot change, such as a co-worker's or boss's behavior; focus on the things you can control. Finally, make time for fun and relaxation (Smith and Segal 2011, 4). Reduce stress in your life by taking care of yourself. Build fun into your stressful life by calling friends, listening to music, working in the garden, reading, taking a long bath, or getting a massage. Take care of yourself and give yourself permission to nurture yourself and have fun.

TIME MANAGEMENT: FINDING A STRATEGY THAT WORKS IN YOUR LIFE

Organizing your time goes a long way to managing stress and creating time for you to enjoy work and leisure. Time wasters include being disorganized, not saying "no," overscheduling, answering e-mails, returning calls, having a bad attitude, and procrastinating. Much of time and stress management involves controlling the same aspects of the workplace and home. Judith Siess states in *Time Management, Planning, and Prioritization for Librarians* that time wasters are mostly internal and under your control. Only a few are external; they include miscommunication, lack of information, disorganization, and emergent situations. Simply put, librarians have control over most of the things they waste time doing. Siess emphasizes that librarians should streamline and figure out strategies that will work in individual situations by setting goals and priorities and adjusting attitudes for a positive outcome. Librarians can better utilize time at work by analyzing workflow and streamlining various tasks that make demands on their time (Spencer 2012, 4). In addition, setting boundaries for work and personal time will go a long way in helping you to better manage time and reduce stress (Emmet 2009, 115).

Rita Emmet writes about setting boundaries for work and personal time, but do not expect others to respect them. Know when to give up volunteer and nonpriority projects. Learn to work at work, not at home during family time. However, when work cannot be avoided during family time, try blending them together and being creative (2009, 118, 119). Do not forget to "just say no" to new commitments because you already have a full schedule. When others do not respect your boundaries, put time limits on those who drop by or phone. Create realistic goals, and place a limit on interruptions and family traditions (2009, 126, 128). Because supervisors rarely know how much work you do, inaugurate boundaries and ask for their help to get your taxing work done. Have them suggest who could help with the project, or send them a list of tasks and ask them to tell you which one is the highest priority. Be forewarned that some supervisors may not listen when they are first approached, but you may notice a difference in behavior at a later date (2009, 129, 130).

HOW TO SAY NO WITHOUT SAYING NO: NOPE, NAH, NADA

My mother said the word "no" was one of the hardest words to teach me. But once I understood the concept of "no," it was all I would say. I would say "no" when I disagreed with my mother about going to bed or taking a nap. My response was "no" whenever I was having fun and did not want to stop playing. The word "no" became a staple as I grew older when there were jobs I did not want to do. There are tasks we all hate to do, but I took a lesson from my assistants this past year: do the job you hate to do first. This way it is done and over with, and there is no dreading it. Somewhere along the line, adults lose that concept of self-happiness and stop saying "no." Soon you are over scheduled and overworked, and there is never any time to do the things you enjoy.

It's tough to say "no" when you are in a service-oriented profession specifically to help people find their information needs. A Mayo Clinic Staff article on stress relief advocates learning to focus on your priorities and responsibilities (2010b, 1). It also suggests asking yourself, "Is the new commitment important to me?" If it is not something you feel passionate about or committed to, then say "no." Find out if the new activity is a long- or short-term commitment while seeking projects that will allow you to help without taking up much of your time. Never agree to a task because of guilt or to one with which you disagree. When tempted by a friend's request, sleep on it. Take time to consider how the new activity will impact your current commitments and how it fits into your priorities. If it is something you do not feel passionate about, decline.

You can refuse without elaborating, being rude, or even using the word no. Be sure to avoid vague phrases such as "I'm not sure" or "I don't think I can" (Mayo Clinic Staff 2010c, 2). There are ways of saying no to keep yourself on track with your priorities without burning bridges or feeling guilty. Be brief and respectful. At times people will not respect your boundaries, so be prepared to answer them again. However, I have found that most people understand the first time you say "no" and accept it when you do not participate in their project. The following are direct and to-the-point ways to say "no," from or based on a blog by Belinda Munoz (2010):

I can't do that.	I'll be out of town.	I'm unavailable.
I'm not interested.	It's not a priority for me.	I have a conflict.

These are additional ways of saying no without saying no:

- I'm focusing on other things right now.
- Listen, I've got to get going, but thanks for asking.
- You go ahead and let me know how it goes.
- It's my policy to be discriminating about what I commit to.
- Let me check my calendar.
- I need to see if I can get a babysitter/dogsitter.

These are even more ways to "just say no":

- It's not up to me, I need to check with my spouse/boss.
- I bet you'll find someone else who can do a better job than I can.
- Sounds tempting, but I'll have to pass.
- I would love to, but I don't want to make anyone sick.
- This doesn't meet my needs right now, but I'll be sure to keep you in mind.
- I'd love to help, but unfortunately I am already overextended.

Now that you know how to say no, it is time to get organized.

HARD TO MUDDLE: DECLUTTERING THE MIND AND SPACE

Whether it is clutter in your mind, on your desk, in a spare room, or on your dining room table, that clutter is wasting time and producing stress. Today clutter is not just on the desk; it is also electronic. It comes in the form of computer files, contact lists, and e-mails. If you cannot find what you are looking for when it is needed, then clutter is costing you precious time to locate that item. For example, having been shopping for a pair of slip-on tennis shoes, I decided to clean out my closet. After removing full and empty shoe boxes, I found five pairs. Much to my surprise, I already had the shoes I was looking for in the store. You cannot use what you do not know you have.

According to Dictionary.com, *declutter* means "to simplify or get rid of mess, disorder, [or] complications." Clearing out my office started before the university's homecoming because my staff and I wanted to win the "Dec the Office" contest. I removed anything that was not vital to make the office vibrant with the school colors and homecoming theme. Furthermore, I decided I could be inconvenienced for a couple of weeks by moving all nonessential items off my desk and into storage. The result was an uncluttered desk and nice clean working areas. What I discovered is that I could live without my tower of ten file trays and spiral rack, leaving only absolute essentials on my desk. The phone books were one of the last items to return to my office, because most telephone numbers I need are online. The manuals are back, along with five file trays, two

staplers, a few decorative items, and one functional box. The rest I re-
trieve as needed, use, and return to storage.

Uncluttering the Mind: Worries, Thoughts, and Overload

Most stress comes from thinking and begins in the head. The following strategies are from Donna Smallin's, *One Minute Tips: Unclutter Your
Mind*. The book is from a few years ago, but the information is timeless.
Smallin believes in putting a handle on thoughts to get your thinking
clearer. Spend time in the present and stop thinking about what might
happen tomorrow or years from now (2006, 7). Concentrating on today
will keep you focused on those activities that you have made a priority.
Paying attention to what you are doing will help you make sensible
decisions about the activities you do and how you spend your time.

Getting Your Office Organized

I used to think having numerous organizing tools would make me
well organized. One might think putting out ten file boxes would do the
trick. I soon realized that using items did not bring order to my office. All
I was doing was adding clutter. Now, with only two clusters of file boxes
on my desk, I work more efficiently and effectively. I stopped saving
everything just in case I was going to need it, and I found out I did not
need those materials. Smallin's advice in *One-Minute Organizer* is to
change your attitude and behaviors. Begin by thinking and acting organized so that you will achieve your goal and become a tidy person (2004,
7). You are never going to have the time to organize everything at once,
so just start organizing something small (2004, 1). Smallin points out that
simply working for five minutes a day on a clutter project will become
thirty-five minutes weekly and two hours and twenty minutes monthly
(2004, 4). Start small, and you will be amazed at how much progress can
be made in a short amount of time.

Clear the muddle and start with things that will not require much
decision making (e.g., garbage, broken or expired items). Put, throw, or
give unwanted things away. Keep only the items you value or actually
use. Create an "umbrella rule" by setting a time frame. For objects, and
possessions that have not been used for one year, ask these questions:
"Do I need it?" "Do I need it for legal or tax purposes?" "Can I get
another one easily when I need it?" If you answer "no" to these questions, then get rid of it. Put the items you cannot part with in a box to get
them out of your office/living space. Move things out of your office and
house quickly once you have made the decision to get rid of them. Do not
think of this as discarding your precious things, but as recycling or sharing with others who could use them.

Paper, Pens, and Staples, Oh My!

Donna Smallin points out ways to clear the muddle in your office. Unclutter your workspace by placing supplies in the same place and putting out only what is needed or used daily. Place all other things in a drawer, on a shelf, or in your supply cabinet (2004, 63, 138). Throw away promotional materials and freebies that are not being used. Establish a plan for dealing with paper requests just as with e-mails. Decide what you need, what needs to be filed, and what to discard into the recycling bin (Siess 2002, 36, 46). Create an inbox, and never return papers to the box once they have been taken out. Sort your mail as soon as it is received, throwing away junk mail. Remember to delegate, forward, file, toss, read, or respond to everything (Siess 2002, 47). Do not forget to schedule filing time for those materials that need to be filed, and avoid placing files and folders on your desk unless you are working on them (Smallin 2004, 188, 194). Do not keep quickly outdated articles or information that is easily accessed on the Internet or in the library's main collection. File articles and put "reading material in a place that you are most likely to read it" (Smallin 2004, 101). Smallin advocates using binders to house reference material and file clippings (2004, 102–103).

Schedule time for materials you have not read. Make sure everything has a place and is put back after every use. A time-saving idea that I practice regularly is to record business and personal commitments on the same calendar, using different colors to tell them apart. Do your best to keep a sense of humor, and work at removing clutter daily for short periods of time.

How to Have 20 or Fewer E-mails in Your Inbox

Clutter is no longer just physical; it is digital. E-mail accounts are notorious for needing the contents to be organized and purged. A technique I learned at a presentation by Molly Baker, "Organizing Your Digital Life," has reduced the amount of time I waste and my stress when opening up the e-mail account. First, turn off notifications, and only check the account every two hours or two times a day. Set rules to presort incoming electronic magazines or mailing lists to be read on a weekly basis. Configure listservs to receive digests so your inbox is not so muddled with e-mails. Create an autoreply for inquiries that are repeated frequently (e.g., office hours, library hours). Delete the junk mail when first opening your e-mail. Read messages only once and convert each reading into an action such as deleting the e-mail, delegating the request, doing it now, or responding quickly. The main rule is to not let any e-mail remain without acting on it and to delete the e-mail once you complete the request (Siess 2002, 15; Baker 2010, 5). Baker proposes saving attachments to designated folders and emptying the trash contents weekly in order to meet the goal of zero messages in the inbox; however, I found that I needed to have twenty left in the inbox. She also suggests creating consistent file names for storing e-mails and attachments. Following her advice, I have created folders and filters for listservs, my boss's and students' e-mails, board/committee messages, and various subject folders. I still act on new e-mails in those folders and only have fifteen to twenty e-mails in my inbox at any time. I review my subject folders annually to see what can be deleted.

CONCLUSION

By adhering to a few simple rules, you will find time and ways of coping with unavoidable external stressors in your life. Librarians need to start by saying "yes" to those things they love and for which they have a passion. Respond to stress by eating right, exercising, and keeping a sense of humor.

- Set priorities in your professional and personal life.
- Get organized and clear the clutter out of your workspace, home, and mind.
- Just say "no"; be brief and respectful.
- Evaluate new opportunities and how they will impact your priorities.
- Decline the projects that are not in sync with your life.
- Establish protocol for organizing and purging e-mails and papers.
- First do tasks you dread or do not like.
- Worry less and laugh more.
- Start small: with a drawer for ten minutes.
- Set boundaries for home, work, and play; stick to them and enforce them.

Remember that nothing is perfect, and ask for help when necessary so you can find time to get back to the things you love doing.

WORKS CITED

Ajala, E. B. 2011. "Work-Related Stress Among Librarians and Information Professionals in a Nigerian University." *Library Philosophy and Practice* (January 1): [1–13].

American Psychological Association. 2010. *Stress in America Findings*, November 9. http://www.apa.org/news/press/releases/stress/national-report.pdf (accessed January 24, 2012).

Baker, Molly. 2010. "Organizing Your Digital Life." Macomb, IL: Western Illinois University, Malpass Library, November 17.

Emmet, Rita. 2009. *Managing Your Time to Reduce Your Stress*. New York: Walker.

Harp, David. 2011. *Mindfulness to Go: How to Meditate While You're on the Move*. Oakland, CA: New Harbinger.

Horstman, Judith. 2009. *The Scientific American: Day in the Life of Your Brain*. San Francisco: Jossey-Bass.

Mayo Clinic Staff. 2010a. "Stress: Constant Stress Puts Your Health at Risk." September 11. http://www.mayoclinic.com/health/stress/SR00001 (accessed January 22, 2012).

Mayo Clinic Staff. 2010b. "Stress Management: Identify Your Sources of Stress." July 23. http://www.mayoclinic.com/health/stress-management/SR00031 (accessed January 22, 2012).

Mayo Clinic Staff. 2010c. "Stress Relief: When and How to Say No." July 23. http://www.mayoclinic.com/health/stress-relief/SR00039 (accessed January 22, 2012).

Munoz, Belinda. 2010. "The Halfway Point." http://thehalfwaypoint.net/2010/02/fifty-ways-to-say-no/.

Siess, Judith. 2002. *Time Management Planning and Prioritization for Librarians*. Lanham, MD: Scarecrow Press.

Smallin, Donna. 2004. *The One-Minute Organizer Plain & Simple*. North Adams, MA: Storey.

Smallin, Donna. 2006. *One-Minute Tips: Unclutter Your Mind*. North Adams, MA: Storey.

Smith, Melinda, and Robert Segal. 2011. "Stress Management: How to Reduce, Prevent, and Cope with Stress." http://helpguide.org/mental/stress_management_relief_coping.htm (last modified December 2011).

Spencer, Roxanne. 2012. "Solo Librarians as Jugglers." In *How to Thrive as a Solo Librarian*, edited by Carol Smallwood and Melissa Clapp, 4. Lanham, MD: Scarecrow Press.

TWENTY-NINE

Working from Home, or How to Get It All Done without Going Crazy

Elizabeth Nelson

Having the opportunity to telecommute, or work from home, can be a fantastic experience, but it also comes with a great deal of responsibility. Working from home has become easier and more accepted in recent years. Advances in technology, including social networking and messaging, e-mail, phone and videoconferencing, and online meeting software have made working from home sometimes just as good as being in the office. One drawback to working from home is the same thing that can make it so appealing: having some time away from coworkers. Although a collaborative work environment makes the workday go faster and can be very productive, at times there are projects that require some time alone to work uninterrupted. Working from home can be an outlet for working on specific projects or tasks to manage time a little better and get work done by the deadline.

TYPES OF TELECOMMUTING

Telecommuting is a general term for many different types of work outside the office. There are three typical scenarios of how working at home is constructed. Each has its own drawbacks and benefits, and each is conducive to certain types of job responsibilities, so there is no right or wrong way to telecommute.

- *Working remotely full time:* Some positions are constructed independent of location and allow for working at home on a full-time basis.

This arrangement requires a specific personality, as communication with supervisors and coworkers has to be more deliberate than when working in close proximity. Those working on their own time must be focused and motivated to accomplish tasks independently.

- *Working at home on a scheduled basis:* Some employers allow for working at home on a particular schedule, such as one or two times a week. This can be a good option for those who have responsibilities requiring focused work time as well as responsibilities that are customer focused or need to be done in collaboration with other team members.

- *Working at home as needed:* Everyone has days when they have appointments or family emergencies that require them to be out of the office, but they are still able to work. The opportunity to work from home instead of taking a vacation or sick day is a benefit that some employers are able to provide.

Just as there are different schedules for telecommuting, there are also different ways to work from home. Some people work the same hours as those who are in the office, just from another location, whereas others work the hours that are most convenient for them, such as at night or early in the morning. Either arrangement can be beneficial to both employer and employee, as long as there is proper communication and expectations are clear.

BENEFITS TO TELECOMMUTING

When libraries have less money for raises and may have a hiring and/or promotion freeze, it isn't always possible to offer many new benefits to top performers. Providing opportunities for telecommuting can be a no-cost solution to this problem. While employees enjoy the benefits of working from home, it also benefits employers, as they have employees who are able to enjoy a greater work–life balance while still devoting time and energy to all of those important projects.

- *Uninterrupted work time is something everyone needs.* Even the most social people or those working on the most collaborative projects need time when they can focus solely on the task at hand. Being in the office can be challenging during these times, as there are always coworkers dropping by, phones ringing, and e-mail to answer. Working from home can provide time "off the grid" when that focused work can be done. In addition, time can be better managed when there is time both in and out of the office for tasks requiring different levels of focus.

- *Work–life balance has been discussed frequently in recent years.* As technology improves, the line between work and home has blurred. If e-mail is always accessible, how is it possible to turn off that flow of information and stop working? It is a fact that more people do work from home after hours, checking and responding to e-mails, writing reports, and any other number of things that they weren't able to finish during the busy workday. Providing opportunities for working at home can help achieve better balance.
- *Many library tasks can be done remotely.* With all the electronic resources and computer-related tasks, there is not always the same need to be physically present in the library as there was in the past. Libraries are fairly traditional institutions, and many processes revolve around what was done in the past. Employees who work from home may be able to look at these processes in a new way and develop more efficient ways of doing work.

THE DOWNSIDE

- *Although there are many benefits to working from home, there are also some challenges.* The biggest one is getting used to working independently, without face-to-face time with coworkers. Working in a collaborative, fairly local, work environment like a library allows for many interactions during the day with coworkers in the department and in other parts of the library. When it is easy to "drop by" and ask a question of your coworkers or supervisor, it can be a difficult adjustment to put that question aside or to compose an e-mail. Working remotely also limits interactions with library patrons. As much of the literature now talks about being where the patrons are, which may include virtual spaces, it may seem counterintuitive to limit those interactions.
- *Not all tasks can be done from home.* Some positions may involve tasks that are better suited for working remotely than others. Those that require advanced preparation, like instruction, or involve report or grant writing, may be ideal for this kind of arrangement. Other positions, especially those that are customer focused or include a supervisory role, may require that those employees be in the office or library. Problems can arise when some employees are able to telecommute and others are not. There may be issues with union contracts as well as feelings about favoritism among the staff. Any policy that is created regarding working remotely needs to be clear and well-communicated to avoid problems down the line.
- *Although working from home can be a boon to both employer and employee, it comes with a lot of responsibility.* There are many distractions at

home that can make work difficult if it is not possible to "turn them off."

TIPS AND TRICKS

When working from home, there are some dos and don'ts for managing time effectively and making the arrangement beneficial to all:

- Do take short breaks during the day to stretch, get a bite to eat, and take care of small tasks.
- Do handle appointments with your supervisor's prior approval and make up the time earlier or later in the day.
- Do have a separate work area set up away from distractions. This serves as a reminder to family members that you are "at work" even if you are technically at home. It also creates a workspace that allows you to be efficient at your job.
- Do track time spent working. Just because work is being done from home does not mean that you have to work a twenty-hour day. Know when to sign off your computer and enjoy the other half of the work–life balance.
- Don't spend the day cleaning the house. Although it may be tempting to quickly vacuum or take care of a load of laundry, don't get distracted from the task at hand.
- Don't attempt to work from home while caring for a small child. Both tasks will suffer for it. If child care is the challenge you are seeking to address, it may be worth discussing part-time work options or having a sitter stay with your child (either at your home or at another location) during your work time. Spending time with your child before and after work when you can give him or her your full attention will be better for both of you.
- Don't try to work from home without the proper accommodations: a laptop, an Internet connection, and any specific programs and access to network folders needed to do the work. This should be productive work time, not a time for you to be frustrated because you can't access the information you need.

At the end of the day, working from home can provide immense benefits for an organization and its employees. The key to a successful telecommuting arrangement is effective communication, both about the policy itself, including who will be allowed to work from home and on what schedule, and between the supervisor and the employee who is working remotely. Even though they don't see the work as it is being completed, supervisors will see the end result of work completed at home, and that result should be a positive one. If handled properly, working at home should help employees get more done in the same or less time, while achieving a good life–work balance and preventing burnout, leading to loyal and productive library employees.

THIRTY

What Personal Life?

Pamela O'Sullivan

It was a typical Monday morning. Jo was up at 5:00 AM, threw a load of clothes in the washing machine, checked e-mail and her daily schedules (both work and home) while on the treadmill, and emptied the dishwasher after getting her son's breakfast and feeding the dog. She was also running over in her head a presentation that she had to give to the faculty-library committee, wondering where they would hold that year's holiday party, and mentally preparing for a confrontation with an employee whose attendance had been spotty over the last couple of months. While driving her son to school, she listened to her voicemail on speaker phone while her son told her about the project he needed to complete and gave her the list of items to be purchased. By the time she got to work, her e-mail was again overflowing, and two staff members had called in sick. There was also a professor at the desk wanting to bring his class in for a library instruction session that day. By 8:05 AM, Jo felt like she had worked a full day, and she had already put aside some work that she would have to complete at home that night.

In today's work environment, it is easy to feel that you are tied to your job 24/7. Developing a healthy work–personal life balance may seem to be an impossible challenge, but it is necessary for the health both of the employee and the organization. A willingness to embrace new technologies where appropriate, as well as a commitment to stop multitasking, can play a key role in helping to regain and retain some time for yourself.

Although at times it may seem that technology has taken over and even added to the amount of work we have, the reality is that ineffective use of the technology is more often to blame. Coupled with a much greater tendency to multitask, the results are higher levels of stress and lower levels of productivity.

How do you turn this situation around and make it work for you? There is no single "right" way, but the two strategies I outline in this chapter have helped me or other librarians bring some control to ever-expanding work schedules.

STOP MULTITASKING, OR AT LEAST REDUCE YOUR DEPENDENCE ON IT

This may seem counterintuitive, especially to those of us who are used to juggling several projects at once. The reality is that what we are doing is not truly multitasking, but rather dividing our attention into constantly shifting perspectives, sometimes to the detriment of all our work. Although the effects aren't always seen or felt immediately, studies have shown that multitasking causes a drop in productivity.

Dave Crenshaw (2008) illustrates the reality of this, demonstrating that the typical office worker, who thinks he or she is multitasking effectively, is in reality losing thirty minutes of every hour by constantly shifting from task to task (13–27).

The implications are more serious for higher-level tasks, as demonstrated by Adler and Benbunan-Fich (2012) in their study on multitasking. There are times when you should be concentrating on one task at hand; budgets, personnel matters, and grant applications are some examples.

Another difficulty in trying to stop multitasking is that perception of it as a positive quality is so pervasive that many supervisors and managers consider it de rigueur for their employees and don't always look at the negative consequences of being unable to concentrate on one task at a time. In addition to reducing your own reliance on multitasking, a mind-set shift for the entire organization may be needed, or at least cooperation from your supervisor if, on the surface, you seem less busy.

LET THE TECHNOLOGY WORK FOR YOU

It is tempting to check your e-mail, Twitter feed, and Facebook profile frequently to keep up with what's going on in the world around you. We all know people who send constant updates and forwards of information that often duplicate what we have already seen. However, it's up to the individual receiving the e-mail to put the brakes on.

E-mail programs can be incredibly helpful in managing the flow of information. Set up rules to divert e-mail to folders so that less comes directly to your inbox. This can be especially helpful if you subscribe to a number of listservs. A folder for each one and a rule that routes posts for each directly into its own folder puts those out of sight until you have the leisure to deal with them.

If you regularly deal with vendors, a folder for each vendor or each type of equipment will further reduce the number of messages you see when you first log in.

Use your out-of-office message for more than just a vacation. If you set up a message stating when you are not available (now) and when you will be (e.g., after 2:00 PM), those who are trying to contact you know not to expect an immediate response. This can work for both your e-mail and your voicemail; callers are less likely to try you every fifteen minutes if they know not to expect you for several hours.

Of course, you could just close out your e-mail rather than bombard listservs with out-of-office messages. That reduces your tendency to flip into e-mail and check it every time you get a notification of a new message.

While you're at it, turn off everything you can when you have a major project to work on. Set a time to work on it without distraction and try to hold to that as firmly as you can. With e-mail and voicemail taken care of, you may be able to close your office door (or retreat to your cubicle with a "Do Not Disturb" sign) more easily than you could when you allowed these distractions to give you the appearance rather than the reality of productivity.

What are some other ways that technology can help you to work more efficiently? Depending on your position in the organization and which forms of technology you use, the following suggestions can benefit almost anyone.

Consolidate your technology. For example, use a single calendar. Google provides user-friendly, free calendars that you can share with others who need access to your schedule. Save all your documents and research, meeting notes, and agendas in Internet-accessible locations, whether provided by your institution or in a free application such as Google Docs.

Take advantage of all that a software program offers. When my library began keeping online statistics a couple of years ago, we used LibStats, which is a free, open source application. It is very customizable, and by putting in the categories about which we were interested, we are now able to arrange reference coverage not just for the busiest slots, but by the types of questions. We have walk-up computer assistance for the times of day that saw the greatest need for it, and our statistics were able to demonstrate the need to add another two-hour shift this academic year. I can generate reports that tell me the busiest times of day, the quietest days of the week, and the most and least frequently asked questions.

Many other widely used software programs have features that allow you to automate routine functions. By trusting these to the software, you can free up time both for you and other staff to work on those tasks that cannot be automated, like grant writing, annual reports, or whatever special projects you currently try to cram in with a dozen other things. Take a look at the software you and your library use, and you may well find a number of things that can help you save time.

Make lists that contain blocks of time for single tasks, and stick to those lists. This can be particularly difficult for those of us who spend a lot of time "putting out fires," but if you regularly block out time to work on the major projects and practice dealing with interruptions by putting them off whenever possible until the end of your current task, it can eventually become a habit that will both raise your productivity and reduce your stress.

All of this is to a single end, of course: allowing you to make a sharper divide between work time and personal time. Although we all have times when we must work longer days or take some work home with us, this should not be the norm. The best employee is not necessarily the one who spends the most time working, but the one who does the most with the time he or she spends working. If you can work smarter, it can increase your productivity. This can in turn lead to greater job satisfaction and more clearly defined "time off" for you to develop your personal life.

WORKS CITED

Adler, Rachel F., and Raquel Benbunan-Fich. 2012. "Juggling on a High Wire: Multi-tasking Effects on Performance." *International Journal of Human-Computer Studies* 70, no. 2: 156–168. DOI: 10.1016/j.ijhcs.2011.10.003

Crenshaw, Dave. 2008. *The Myth of Multitasking: How "Doing It All" Gets Nothing Done.* San Francisco: Jossey-Bass.

VIII

Professional Development

THIRTY-ONE

Getting Things Done in the Library

Sanjeet Mann

According to David Allen, author of the best seller *Getting Things Done* (2001), information professionals have a hard time accomplishing tasks because our work is inherently ambiguous, we take on too many commitments, and we cannot prioritize the best thing to do from the many choices before us. J. Wesley Cochran (1992), Judith Siess (2002), Samantha Hines (2010), and other authors of time management treatises for librarians concur that libraries have been difficult places to work for years, especially given our complex work processes and often intangible products. Nevertheless, we have the ability as individuals to adopt better strategies to manage the everyday chaos.

The most common criticism of Allen's "Getting Things Done" (GTD) system is that it is too complicated to implement in real life. However, I argue that the value of his system is precisely that it is not one integral whole. The value in trying out a productivity system comes as much from the new ideas sparked in your mind by your encounter with the system as from actually making its rules habit. Many readers, like Hines (2010), have had success implementing GTD selectively; others, such as Leo Babauta (2007), have been inspired to create their own unique systems. Regardless of how rigorously you adhere to the literal description of a system, such as GTD, implementing it forces you to examine your professional values and your attitudes toward your work. GTD reminds you to evaluate your steady progress toward your goals and has the potential not only to transform your individual workload, but also to empower you to pursue organizational change.

GTD AS MENTAL HABIT

Allen's productivity system is premised on the idea that information work is rife with "open loops," defined as "anything pulling at your attention that doesn't belong where it is, the way it is" (2001, 12). E-mail, blog posts, meetings, and requests for help from library users all compete for our attention, insisting on some sort of follow-up action. According to Allen, even if we tell ourselves certain items are a lower priority, our unconscious mind will persist in seeking a solution until each "loop" is closed. Furthermore, the decision to admit each piece of information into our consciousness represents a commitment, even if only to ourselves, to define and understand its value. From this perspective, items left unresolved become tiny broken agreements with ourselves, with a cumulative emotional impact. "Your negative feelings [about work] are simply the result of breaking those agreements," writes Allen. "They're the symptoms of a disintegrated self-trust" (2001, 227).

Unconscious mental processing and "open loops" distract our attention and drain energy we need to focus on the task at hand. GTD addresses these problems through an exhaustive initial review of one's responsibilities at system setup and an ongoing habit of externalizing thinking about projects and actions. The idea is to thoroughly document commitments in writing, in a system that ensures information will be recorded at the proper time in a known location. Allen claims this will allow us to relax and free our minds for productive action.

GTD AS INFORMATION CONTAINERS AND PROCESSING WORKFLOW

The most tangible aspects of GTD are the containers in which documents live and the workflow for deciding how to route information entering the system. Allen emphasizes processing everything through the system in the same way, to build trust that we will be able to find that information later. This emphasis on organization and routine processes follows from the principle that disorder creates "open loops" and saps efficiency.

Allen's system defines no less than eight different information locations, but the central principle is that actionable items are kept separate from nonactionable information. Actionable items are projects, which contain action items; nonactionable items are project reference materials and "someday/maybe" items. When embarking on a new task, say, implementing a new circulation rule, we first consider the overall goal and define that as the "project." The individual steps taken to achieve the goal (researching integrated library system settings, discussing the policy with colleagues, getting administrative approval, etc.) are all "next actions," to be completed in a linear sequence. Allen claims that the shift from per-

ceiving the project as a whole to focusing on the single "next step" clarifies the nature of our work and keeps us and our colleagues accountable
to one another.

Of course, no one is perfect, and there are times when this action-by-
action momentum breaks down. A weekly review draws our attention to
"clogs" in the system where items have accumulated during the course of
a busy day and helps us "catch up" to where we want to be.

GTD AS ASSESSMENT SYSTEM

Allen describes GTD as a bottom-up productivity system, in which people first gain a sense of stability about their immediate work environment, then prioritize how to further shape that environment to meet their
goals. He asserts that most information workers are stuck responding to
day-to-day issues arriving by phone, by e-mail, and in meetings. These
issues may be important, but may not necessarily reflect longer-term individual or organizational priorities.

GTD addresses this problem by having one reflect on long-term goals
and values as part of the initial system setup and by building evaluation
directly into the regular functioning of the system through the weekly
review. During the weekly review, one examines projects looking for
items that need resolution and considers how the importance of tasks and
projects may have changed with the arrival of new information. This
review keeps the system responsive and generates a real sense of success
and preparedness. A built-in evaluation cycle should make sense to librarians, given our profession's growing emphasis on assessment and
communicating value. The weekly review is the linchpin that ensures
that GTD actually achieves the results it promises.

GTD AND PROJECT MANAGEMENT

Toward the end of his book, Allen reflects on how the cumulative impact
of GTD adherents working together can bring about organizational
change. Allen claims that GTD empowers workers with confidence that
they can manage and fulfill their commitments. This sense of empowerment is a crucial prerequisite for what John Lubans (2010) has termed
"leading from the middle": a strategy of effecting organizational change
by holding oneself accountable and taking initiative for improvement in
one's own area of responsibility.

People who habitually divide tasks into discrete, actionable units and
act out of a sense of empowerment and mutual responsibility are well
equipped for project work, perhaps the primary vehicle by which things
get done in libraries. Adopting these traits allows us to clarify some of the
inherent ambiguity in projects. When we work collaboratively, we benefit

from hearing others' viewpoints, but we must also negotiate expectations and goals at an elementary level. Projects change radically along the way, under the influence of external stakeholders or simply because the team reached a different understanding of what they were doing.

Groups can be more than the sum of their parts by adopting and implementing GTD strategies. When a team meets to begin a new project, everyone can "process the group's inbox," sharing what they know about the problem and clarifying the goals and actions required to resolve it. Teams can adopt a "next action" mindset, in which action items are delegated at each meeting and individuals are accountable to report back on their progress at the next meeting. And each meeting could include time set aside for a "weekly review," in which members reflect on the group's progress toward goals and discuss what priorities need to be readjusted. Building regular reflection time into projects encourages our teams to develop metacognitive skills, the same type of process we encourage users to develop when we teach information literacy. Teams that understand their own thinking and are comfortable with the way they make decisions are better able to respond to changing situations.

ESSENTIAL GTD

In summary, the minimal elements of a functional GTD system for librarians include

- a thorough assessment of responsibilities and values at system setup;
- consistently documenting the value of incoming information items;
- making distinctions between actionable (project and action) items and nonactionable (reference and someday) items, with a consistent emphasis on doing the "next action"; and
- a weekly review.

Individual preferences will determine how much more of Allen's original system you want to implement; for example, do you want to keep track of items that may be relevant "someday" using one list, or file them in a forty-three-folder tickler system?

MY GTD SYSTEM

I wanted to close by describing the system I created after reading *Getting Things Done*. I conducted my initial scan during the summer when my workload was lighter, and it took several months to reach a stable workflow. I value interacting with my system from multiple locations, so I use a combination of Evernote for lists; Remember the Milk for immediate actions; and Outlook for my Inbox, calendar, and project reference material. I can access all of these information sources whether I am at home, in my office, or at the reference desk.

I try to keep the number of projects I am involved in to a minimum. When I first processed my inbox, I was surprised to find I was trying to sustain more than forty projects! Over the following months, I reduced this by shifting lower priority projects to my someday list and working with my director to reassign some of my responsibilities to other staff so they could be completed more effectively. I have found about ten projects to be a realistic maximum for the amount of work I can juggle at one time, in addition to the daily flood of calls, e-mails, and other requests too small to be projects, which I track on my to-do list. I regularly add new ideas to my "someday" list and swap them into active projects during a review. I usually conduct my review on Friday afternoons, so I can leave for the weekend knowing I am ready for the following week.

My encounter with *Getting Things Done* caused me to rethink fundamental assumptions about my work habits and reconsider how I could contribute to organizational change at my library. I believe I have achieved a better balance between work and personal time and gained confidence that I am accomplishing meaningful tasks when I am working. I encourage you to learn more about GTD and implement it on whatever scale works for you, so you can receive these benefits as well.

WORKS CITED

Allen, David. 2001. *Getting Things Done: The Art of Stress-Free Productivity.* New York: Viking Penguin.

Babauta, Leo. 2007. "Zen to Done (ZTD): The Ultimate Simple Productivity System." *Zenhabits.net* (blog), April 17. http://zenhabits.net/zen-to-done-ztd-the-ultimate-simple-productivity-system/.

Cochran, J. Wesley. 1992. *Time Management Handbook for Librarians.* New York: Greenwood.

Hines, Samantha. 2010. *Productivity for Librarians: How to Get More Done in Less Time.* Oxford: Chandos.

Lubans, John. 2010. *"Leading from the Middle," and Other Contrarian Essays on Librarianship.* Santa Barbara, CA: Libraries Unlimited.

Siess, Judith. 2002. *Time Management, Planning and Prioritization for Librarians.* Lanham, MD: Scarecrow Press.

THIRTY-TWO

The High Road or Easy Street? Saving Time by Picking Your Battles

Kelli Hines and Deborah Farber

As a new librarian, it is easy to fall into the trap of sacrificing reality to ideals. You have a vision of the way a library is "supposed" to look (or perhaps several conflicting, but equally exciting, visions), and when you see that your library falls short, you hasten to mold it to your wishes. But you're not the only person with a vision. There are other interested parties with different concerns and approaches. How can you best balance your ideals with the realities of the situation? When is it worthwhile to take the high road and stick to your vision, and when is it better to follow the path of least resistance and yield to others?

One of the easiest ways to waste time is to devote it to projects that won't get off the ground or advocate for changes that aren't going to happen. This chapter outlines several principles for picking your battles. Choosing your projects carefully is one of the best ways to save time, because no matter how efficient you might be, any time you spend on a project that won't be implemented is ultimately wasted. Furthermore, constantly fighting losing battles leads to frustration and low morale, which sucks even more time and energy away from other necessary tasks.

To understand our perspective on time management, it is helpful to know something about the organization we work for. Casa Loma College is a private nursing and allied health college. Until recently, the libraries were considered computer labs or tech rooms at each campus. In addition, the college did not have any professional librarians on staff, because the school did not offer any degree programs that required library support. Now, however, the college is offering three associate's degree programs and must develop library collections and services to meet accreditation standards. Because of our role in accreditation, the library is considered part of the compliance department. The library is still very much in the process of being defined, so there is a lot of room for growth—and differing visions.

QUESTIONS TO ASK WHEN PICKING YOUR BATTLES

When you are dealing with different visions, you have to choose which concepts and tasks are most important. Following are some questions to ask when setting your priorities.

What Do I Have Time For?

This depends not only on the number of hours you work, but also on your energy levels and the number of other tasks you have to do. We work thirty-five and twenty-five hours a week, respectively, so many projects have been delayed until a more pressing project was finished. Often we will do a little research to get a feel for the scope of a project and schedule time for it accordingly.

Other people's time is also a factor. We might have time to design a full information literacy course, but with some programs as short as nine months, the students don't have time to take it—and the instructors don't have time to excise material from their courses to make room for it.

Because a time frame may not be immediately evident, it is a good idea to establish a flexible timeline. For example, we initially budgeted for an automation system this year. However, when we realized that funds were not available, we scaled back our timeline and looked at what we could purchase this year.

What Do I Have the Budget For?

This may seem obvious, but it can be easy to forget, and it's more complicated than it first appears. The budget includes not just numbers, but priorities and attitudes toward spending. The numbers may say you have $5,000, but if you try to spend $300 on something the administration doesn't value, you will face resistance. On the other hand, most organizations have things they will invest in, even when money is tight. Consider what the administration tends to be willing—and not willing—to spend money on. In our case, we actually got more money than we requested for professional development, because the college values continuing education. The trade-off was difficulty securing funds for books and databases.

It is also important to consider the organization's overall fiscal health. Although the administration may not be willing to share specific numbers with you, you may be able to get a picture of the financial health of the organization and therefore prioritize projects and purchases better. If there have been recent budget cuts, layoffs, or restructuring, any request for money will be a tough sell. Keep this in mind when making a request for a large purchase, hiring of additional staff, or expanding hours to support a new program. You may also want to consider seeking outside grants to support projects or purchases for your library. But do not rely on outside sources for funding. Not only does grant writing take significant time, effort, and some expertise, it is not guaranteed money. Therefore, only pursue this path if you have support from the administration and other staff—you will need their assistance to succeed. Ultimately, you may have to wait, or at least ask delicately and show you can save money in other areas. Even then, be prepared to hear, "We don't have the money right now."

While developing our first budget, we did not seek this broader financial information from the beginning. We made the mistake of drafting an ambitious budget proposal, which included everything from personnel to equipment expenditures. If we had known that our budget was going to be very limited and devoted exclusively to purchasing books, we would have focused our efforts differently.

What Do I Have Support For?

It is important to be aware of outside forces and politics affecting the organization. Often, these issues can impact support for particular projects or change the timeline for implementation. Perhaps enrollment has changed because of shifts in community needs, new laws are affecting how your organization does business, accreditation visits are pending, or restructuring is under way. If so, the administration may not consider your library projects high priority. You may need to scale back your requests, expand your timeline, or look for ways to align your needs with the organization's larger goals. In our case, the college is seeking reaccreditation for two of its degree programs. Therefore, we were able to secure a small budget to expand the book collection for the general education and program curricula.

What Can I Justify the Need For?

It is important to consider not only what you need, but what you can *prove* you need. Use available data to support your case. Recent institutional surveys and state, local, or nationwide statistics or standards can go a long way in providing support for your project or purchase. You may want to conduct a campus- or organization-wide survey to gather evidence of support for the services or resources you would like to implement. If the administration sees that employees, students, or customers need a service or resource, they may be more willing to approve your request.

When we were creating our budget request, we conducted campus-wide surveys to identify needed materials and services. We used the survey data and accreditation standards to justify funding for additional books.

What Do I Have the Passion For?

Everyone brings special talents to the table and enjoys different aspects of working in a library. Think about what parts of your job intrigue or energize you. If you are genuinely excited about something, it will almost always be worth your efforts to pursue it, because enthusiasm is infectious and any time you spend on the project will be time you enjoy. You will also be more creative at finding ways to make things work. If your first thought when you are told you can't have something is, "challenge accepted," you have just found something worth fighting for.

What Is the Worst (or Best) That Can Happen?

Sometimes it helps to visualize what might happen if your project or purchase is approved. What are the risks and rewards? Do they significantly outweigh each other? For example, suppose you advocate for an expensive database that is never used. Not only have you wasted money that could have been used for other things, but the administration may be more reluctant to approve electronic purchases in the future. On the other hand, simple screencast tutorials are cheap or free, take little time, and have a high chance of being engaging and useful.

Where Do I Begin?

When starting any project, big or small, it is a good idea to have goals. If the project is small, perhaps these goals can be informal and for your own use. For example, maybe your project is to catalog all the books in your library. Depending on the size of your collection, this might be quite a large project. In our case, there are fewer than a thousand books at all three campuses, but because we don't have an integrated library system available, this otherwise straightforward project has taken quite a bit longer than anticipated. As a result, we have had to break this project into phases: create an inventory of materials on the shelves, create catalog records, and create a shelf list of books by subject and title. The project is still in progress, but we are confident that creating specific goals will help us reach completion.

TACTICAL ADVICE FOR THE TRENCHES

What do you do once you have picked your battles? Engage! Here are some tips for keeping your sanity while you fight for what you want.

Do Your Homework

You should begin any proposal or request with thorough research to see what has and has not worked, both in your organization and in the field overall. Review the literature to see what programs and initiatives have been successful and how they were implemented. Pore over old budgets to see how the library has spent money in the past. Analyze library statistics to see how resources are being used and what needs are not being met. If you are making a purchase request, ask other professionals for recommendations to get a sense of what you can afford and what makes sense for your organization. The last phase of research is learning what the proposal and approval process looks like where you work. It could be anything from an informal request to a labyrinthine system of committees, written proposals, and formal presentations.

Document Everything

From start to finish, keep notes, drafts, and documents organized. Keep track of your projects, your wish lists, any major issues that arise, communication with higher-ups, and any statistics that may support a project you want to undertake. This saves time, shows the progression of the project, and helps with implementation and future planning. There is no right way to keep project files organized. Do what works for you. We keep outlines for projects in folders separate from final drafts. We also date our drafts so we can see when the file was last updated. We are then able to go back and revise an older version if the latest file accidentally gets corrupted or deleted.

Build Bridges, Don't Burn Them

Look at people as partners, not adversaries. Listen to their concerns and try to address them. You will generate a lot of goodwill by making concessions instead of demanding everything you want. This also makes people take the issues you do advocate for more seriously. Be straightforward and gracious. Thank people when they help you and look for ways to help them back. Although it makes sense to address your efforts toward the people who have the power to approve your project, don't focus exclusively on higher-level administration. By gaining support from your immediate supervisor and colleagues, you are more likely to garner top-level support and get the project or purchase approved.

Find Your Cheerleaders

Work closely with people who are enthusiastic about the possibilities you offer. Not everyone will immediately share your vision, so take advantage of the opportunity when someone does. It makes no sense to waste energy on people who are indifferent or resistant to what you're trying to accomplish. Instead, reward your supporters with your best efforts. This builds their loyalty and enthusiasm, and their word of mouth can wear down resistance from others. In our case, the online education coordinator, career services coordinator, and DMS program coordinator were the first to see the library's potential, so they were the first to get programs and resources geared to their concerns. Once other instructors and program coordinators saw what we could do, they became more communicative and more receptive to our ideas.

Start Small and Build Momentum

It's wise to consider Thomas Jefferson's dictum: "No more good must be attempted than the people can bear." If support is not forthcoming for large projects, it may be best to start small, with something that is easier to say "yes" to. At first, we wanted to completely overhaul our e-library website to make it more organized, intuitive, and interactive. When it became clear that this wasn't feasible, we shifted our focus. Our main concern was making sure students had easy access to resources and tutorials, so we had the online education coordinator set up a library resources section on Moodle, the school's course management system. This gave us a place to post relevant links and any tutorials we designed. Although we still want to improve the website, this solution alleviated our main concerns.

Take Your Time

It sounds paradoxical, but waiting can save time in the long run. If you try to take on too much too quickly, you will run yourself into the ground. Not every minute of your day is, or can be, purely "productive." Be kind to yourself. It is okay to take a break occasionally, especially when there is no immediate deadline. Recently, we found ourselves struggling to conceptualize a Web-based tutorial for a particular assignment. We tried adapting a tutorial created for a different class, but the results were less than satisfactory. We spent almost half a day struggling before we decided it was okay to put it aside and work on other tasks that needed to be done more immediately. Giving yourself a break not only relieves stress; it also frees you up to accomplish more timely projects and allows you to approach the original project with fresh eyes later.

Avoid Procrastination

This is the counterbalance to our previous advice. When a deadline is not immediate, it is easy to avoid a project for as long as possible. One root cause of procrastination is being overwhelmed by a project's size and scope. The best remedy here is to break the project into smaller goals. Returning to an earlier example, the process of inventorying, organizing, and cataloging has been a time-consuming task for us. To make the process easier, we set small goals, tackling one shelf at a time, or even one classification number at a time. Eventually, we completed the project.

Accept Imperfection

This is the hardest lesson we have had to learn on the job. Too often, we have put off trying new things or making necessary changes because the initial results were not as good as we wanted. We also wasted time being frustrated about things we couldn't control. Now we realize that our campus libraries are works in progress. Because we are an allied health school, the curriculum is very structured, and students are often in class during open hours. Although some students visit the library to study, use the Internet, or complete an assignment, they do not regularly use the electronic resources available to them. We have presented a series of workshops on the electronic resources available, with modest increases in usage of the library website and resources. However, we recognize that students are not going to regularly use these resources unless they become a required part of the curriculum. In the meantime, we are focusing our efforts on reaching out to students where they are—in the online classroom.

Go with the Flow

Unexpected obstacles crop up. Perhaps a power outage occurs in your workplace, the network goes down, or you get sick and have to miss a day. The best thing to do is accept the situation and use the change of routine to your benefit. A power outage could be an opportunity to connect with coworkers you never see or a chance to take a short walk. If the network goes down, this could be a chance to catch up on some professional reading you have got piled on your desk. A sick day is time to just relax and give your body a chance to rest and recharge. Of course, other changes may be more difficult to accept. If layoffs or restructurings have left you with more work or less support, you may be under stress. Still, any time spent resisting or lamenting the changes is time not spent doing your job. Accept that this is your new reality and find constructive ways of coping.

Seek Help and Advice

When you are feeling overwhelmed at work or stuck on a particular aspect of a project, reach out to colleagues. They may have some suggestions for moving forward or even be willing to assist you. Maybe you need to partner with another department or outside organization to get the needed funding or support. If the project or purchase supports another department's curricular objectives or your institution's accreditation, you might have a better chance of gaining support from administration. If you are a solo librarian in your organization, you may not have the benefit of colleagues in your department to rely on. If this is the case, reaching out to colleagues in your professional network, particularly individuals in similar roles, can be a big morale boost when you are truly unsure of how to proceed. And if you are feeling completely overburdened, speak to your supervisor. He or she may be completely unaware of your stress and offer suggestions for managing your time better or reducing your workload.

Celebrate Progress

It's easy to look at everything that still needs to be done, but that's a shortcut to Crazy Town. Instead, try to think of something positive that would not have happened without your hard work. This might be something small ("This person is finally responding to my e-mails!") or large ("All the books are finally cataloged, labeled, and on the shelf!"). Keep the focus on what you have accomplished, and you will feel much more empowered to make change.

FINAL THOUGHTS

Being a good librarian involves setting priorities, collaborating with others, and making compromises. Not every battle is worth fighting, but it is important to engage sometimes—even if only for the sake of your principles. You will not get everything you want, but if you are shrewd, you can get enough of what you want to make your efforts worthwhile.

THIRTY-THREE

When Do I Have Time to Be Professionally Active?

Robin Fay

In these days of "doing more with less" with fewer staff and reduced budgets combined with increases in travel costs, professional activities and development may seem like a distant dream. However, librarians need to be professionally active, not only for the good of the profession and our own hopes for future growth and advancement, but also to keep current with the changes in technology. How do we find the time and financial support to be professionally active?

There are tools and tips to maximize your professional time, getting more bang for the proverbial buck. Professional networks have gone digital: many offer webinars, often at low cost or for free; professional or industry discussion groups abound on social media sites like Facebook (http://www.facebook.com) and LinkedIn (http://www.linkedin.com/); and many groups also keep Web space at their own domains or on content building sites like Google sites or Ning (http://www.ning.com). Twitter (http://www.twitter.com), too, can be an excellent tool to build professional networks.

SOCIAL MEDIA: CREATING A NETWORK

Social media can be one tool in creating a free and time-efficient professional network. However, as with all networking, regardless of whether it is face to face or via a website, a little planning will maximize time and ensure the greatest return on your time investment, especially with social media, which can often turn into a time waster! The key to making social

271

media work for you is to use the tools appropriately, schedule time for social media, and use them effectively. Getting started with social media begins with setting up an account and a profile. Make sure your profile and bio reflect the audience you want to connect with; if you are a reference librarian, by all means include that information. Also include information about your research interests, your skills, your experience, the type of library you work in—whatever will help connect you with other like-minded professionals.

Your biographical section (sometimes called "bio" or "about") is where you include information about yourself—your interests, experience, and more. The content that you put in your bio is searchable in many search engines, working as keywords and phrases: searchable, indexable keywords that will help people find you. On Twitter, the biographical information is limited, so make your words count and carefully craft your bio to reflect you and your professional interests. On many social media sites, the bio will also have a place to include a profile photo or image, links to your websites, and more. Make sure that the profile photo or image you choose represents you; photos of children, pets, cartoon characters, and so forth do not really communicate anything about you as a professional. If possible, reuse your biographical information from other social media sites, but expand upon it for sites that do not limit the amount of text. Using the same profile photo across social media sites can save time in image editing, but it will also help provide a consistent look to your social media presences and help your network more easily identify you in the sea of information.

Once you have your profile set up, search for colleagues you know and add them to your network. Some social media sites will search your e-mail contacts (with your permission) to let you know which are on a particular site. You can also manually search a social media site for colleagues by searching for particular names, interests, conferences, libraries, or library types. Your colleagues who have added matching information in their profiles will come up in your search. It is good netiquette to drop a message to colleagues you wish to network with on social media to let them know what you are doing. It can also be a way to get yourself back on their radar, if you do not have regular interactions. Do not be offended if your colleagues do not reciprocate; social media for professional networking is about networking but some of your colleagues may only use social media for personal use, not networking. It may also be acceptable to network with them in one space, such as LinkedIn, whereas Facebook may be reserved for personal use. Always be collegial and professional in your interactions with colleagues. Once you begin networking with colleagues, you can take a look at their network to see if there are other colleagues who would be good for your network. Again, make sure to introduce yourself if you are trying to network with someone you do not know.

In addition to finding people you would like to network with, you need to start participating in social media. Social media are about sharing and conversation; make time consistently to check for and answer messages from your network. You may find once a week is enough time, or it may take several times a week, depending on the activity in your network. Consider your social media messages an extension of e-mail, because in many ways, they are. Depending on your settings, you can choose to be notified via text or e-mail when someone messages you on a social media site.

Take some time to explore the community resources available for discussion for particular social media sites. Facebook has groups and pages; LinkedIn has discussion groups; and Twitter has twitter chats, memes, conferences, and trending topics, distinguished by a *hashtag*, a keyword or tag that is set off by #. Examples of hashtags are #Code4Lib, which distinguishes tweets about the Code4Lib group and conference; #webdesign, which tags posts about web design; #blogchat, which tags posts that occur within the scheduled blogchat discussion group; and #tsunami, which was used during the Japanese tsunami. Hashtags are searchable and indexable; tools like Twitter Advanced Search, Trendmap (http://trendsmap.com/), and What the Trend (http://whatthetrend.com/) can help you see hashtags and trending topics, which can identify interesting colleagues for your network. Attending conferences, workshops, and other library-related events can also be a great way to expand your network online. Many conference presenters, writers, and other colleagues will tell you their twitter *handle* (their user name) so that you can find them online. Conversely, you should do the same: tell your colleagues how to find and connect with you online. You may want to add your networking information on your business cards or as an e-mail signature file; at conferences it is helpful to put your twitter handle on your name badge. Requests for networking have different terminologies and functionalities depending on the site: *friending* is the term used by Facebook for a connection that is reciprocal (you see their content; they see yours). However, Facebook also has Pages, on which the connection terminology is *Like*; in Pages, the connection is not necessarily reciprocal, as it is more like a subscribable blog or website. At LinkedIn, the terminology for connecting is *network* and is reciprocal; in Twitter, the term is *follow*, but it is not reciprocal unless you initiate a follow back; in Google+, the term is *add* a person (circles are used to group people), and it is not necessarily reciprocal.

Choosing the Social Media Website for Your Professional Networking Needs

There are many social media websites out there, but you do not need to participate in all of them. It's entirely possible that you will find Facebook a good fit for your professional networking, or perhaps you will find Twitter more useful. How should you choose which social media site to use for networking? There are tools out there to *aggregate* (post and read to multiple sites through one interface) social media, but choosing one site to focus on is often more time efficient, rather than taking a scattershot approach across the whole Web. All social media sites provide some sort of networking component, but each has its own distinct features.

Facebook requires an individual login and a profile (a bio), which can include quite extensive information. Facebook can often end up a mix of personal, professional, and cultural content, but much of sharing across your network can be controlled through privacy settings. Advantages of Facebook for networking include the variety of discussion groups and pages, the ability to easily see interactions with you, as well as the sheer volume of users. It is very likely that the majority of your peers and colleagues have a Facebook account. Facebook also provides tools, such as Timeline, to build a display of information; posts do not have character limits and can contain photos, videos, and other media. Facebook also supports messaging and instant messaging. Some of the major criticisms of Facebook are about interface enhancements, which roll out sometimes without warning; privacy; and the separation of personal and professional life.

Twitter in many ways is simple; unlike Facebook and Google+, which both have customizable and personalized privacy settings, Twitter does not. Twitter is either public (everyone sees your posts) or private (only your approved network sees your posts). The Twitter profile is limited to 160 characters, and posts are limited to 140 characters (the number of characters available in a standard SMS non-smartphone text). Twitter provides some design customization through a choice of backgrounds and colors. It even has its own vocabulary for actions on the site: *tweet* (post), *RT* (re-tweet: repost what someone else has posted), *MT* (mention: use the @the users handle to mention, highlight, or thank a Twitter user; mentions directed to you are found under the @ connect button); # or *hashtag* (assign keyword; found under the # discover button); and *DM* (direct message: send a private message to another Twitter user). In addition, Twitter posts are primarily read chronologically, which can sometimes feel like walking into the middle of a conversation (and you very well could be). One of the most useful features of Twitter is the ability to search a topic and save the search, so that you can easily see the latest tweets (posts) that meet particular criteria. Twitter searches the entire network; you do not have to be in the network (i.e., follow a particular user to see his or her Tweets) unless that person's account is private. For example, searching in the advanced Twitter search (https://twitter.com/search-advanced) for library webinars will return the latest news posted at Twitter about library webinars. Twitter is an excellent place to find out about webinars, workshops, e-books and resources, events, trending topics, breaking news, and more.

LinkedIn has discussion groups, the ability to message and share content from other websites. Its power comes from its focus on professional networking. The site itself is designed to support professional networking; the bio information is structured to highlight work experience, education, and skills. Although LinkedIn can serve as a CV or an online resume of sorts, it does continue to grow its community and networking aspects. In terms of job searching and career advancement, LinkedIn provides the ability to include traditional résumé information and support job postings. Other digital presence sites, such as about.me, flavors.me, and VisualCV (http://www.visualcv.com/), focus almost exclusively on housing a resume or CV, rather than on supporting network interactions. LibGig (www.libgig.com/) specifically supports career growth and employment in the library field. Other sites that provide similar services are LisJobs, (http://www.lisjobs.com/) and local regional job sites.

MAXIMIZING YOUR TIME ON SOCIAL MEDIA

To make the best use of your time on social media sites, you need to focus on what you are doing there; in other words, networking! Social media have many distractions; it can be difficult to ignore the silly post of the day, political news, or family photos. Just be aware of your time, especially if you are on work time. Professional development is part of librarianship; we are expected to continue growing. Social media can be an excellent tool when used properly. Do what you need to with an eye toward efficiency and being professional: professional reading, networking, learning, connecting with others. Remember why you are there and focus on your goals. If you network with someone and discover he or she only posts foursquare updates (e.g., the "I'm at _____"; geographical updates about where a particular person is), you can certainly un-network (unfollow, unfriend—whatever the particular term is for the site) that person. Depending on the website, you may also be able to keep the person in your network but just hide his or her posts. Facebook has this functionality, but not all do yet. Another option is to use social media management tools or aggregators.

Social media management tools provide a variety of functionalities depending on which websites they work with. Common features of social media management tools are the ability to schedule posts, to easily see and respond to messages, and to manage multiple accounts at one single user interface. HootSuite (http://hootsuite.com/), Buffer (http://bufferapp.com/), and Yoono (http://www.yoono.com/) work with Facebook, Twitter, and LinkedIn. Their features differ slightly and are dependent on the site. Contact management tools like contaxio (http://contax.io/)

and ManageFlitter (http://manageflitter.com/) can help you evaluate your network in terms of whom you follow, evaluating how often they post and when they last posted, among other information. In terms of managing your time on social media, do use tools to help manage your content and network.

KEEPING UP WITH PROFESSIONAL READING

Considering how much information comes across each of our desks these days, professional reading may stack up quickly. Social media can be a tool for professional reading, serving as a filtering and reference agent. Once you develop a network within social media, you will undoubtedly see blog posts, links to books and articles, library-related news, and more coming across your stream. Using social media as a tool for professional reading can be useful because, most likely, you will see the hot topics and breaking news about libraries and library-related issues.

Using an RSS reader, such as Google Reader, can also be extremely valuable and time saving. Many library organizations, institutions, and libraries will blog or post information on a website that updates using an RSS feed. Any website that utilizes RSS technology can be subscribed to in an RSS reader. Not only can an RSS reader help you organize your readings, but it can also be searched. For example, when the first iPad launched, many websites, social media, and discussion groups covered it. In an RSS reader, it was easy to quickly skim the posts about iPad and even skip through those that did not offer any new information. RSS readers also offer the ability to tag or categorize feeds, so that you can sort out what is most important to read, or whatever criteria you want to use to organize your readings. New posts are highlighted in some way, so you do not waste time digging around for what is new. Content comes to you and is organized by the reader according to your criteria. RSS feeds can also provide a means to download and read something later, either on a mobile device or using web browsers. Such tools as Pocket, formerly called Read It Later (http://getpocket.com/) do this; when you find something you want to read, you just add it for later.

Although social media can provide a means of filtering and sharing news, network members can also help by sharing and recommending resources, as well as articles, books, and tools. Stumbleupon (http://www.stumbleupon.com/) is specifically designed as a recommendation service for websites in general; Pinterest (http://www.pinterest.com/) and Delicious (http://delicious.com/) are bookmarking services that can be used to organize, share, and save readings.

LEARNING OPPORTUNITIES AND EXPANDING KNOWLEDGE

Not only can you discover learning opportunities via social media, but there is a wealth of free or low-cost learning opportunities. Unconferences are unstructured, face-to-face meetings at which participants drive discussion, workshops, presentations, and more. They are developed around a central theme, area of interest, or community. Examples of unconferences are CurateCamp (digital curation), ThatCamp (technology and digital humanities), and InfoCamp (information). Many unconferences are free or very inexpensive, as attendees are expected to actively participate and shoulder some responsibility for programming. Camps are similar to unconferences, but they are more structured, with a heavy emphasis on learning, and are frequently workshop focused. Camps have been around for many years in the technology sector and continue to have a strong technology emphasis, but other areas also have used the camp format. Boot camps are structured workshops, frequently several hours in length, and with a hands-on technology component: programming, coding, installing and configuring software, creating content, and so forth. Examples of camps are DrupalCamp (Drupal software, a CMS) and Wordpress Camp (Wordpress software). Regional library conferences can also provide a low-cost opportunity for training and professional networking.

Online conferences are not only inexpensive, they can provide a way to participate in the larger conference. In 2012, the American Library Association (ALA) offered a virtual one-day conference as a companion to the larger annual meeting of its members. The Handheld Online Librarian Conference (http://www.handheldlibrarian.org/) is meant to be primarily online, addressing information needs, technology, mobile and new devices, and more. Other tools for learning and networking are discussion groups online, through social media, such as Facebook or a website. Social media are a great place to discover new training and learning opportunities, especially workshops and classes. MIT's OpenCoursework (http://ocw.mit.edu/index.htm) of free lecture notes, lecture video, and exams; Code Academy's free coding classes (http://www.codecademy.com); O'Reilly's webinars (on a variety of topics; http://oreilly.com/webcasts/); and the Georgia Public Library's Carterette Series of webinars (http://gla.georgialibraries.org/mediawiki/index.php/Professional_and_Continuing_Education_Interest_Group) are all free resources that have been promoted through social media. Other library-related workshops and classes that are generally inexpensive are those offered through ALA (http://www.classes.ala.org/), Lyrasis (http://www.lyrasis.org), Webjunction (http://www.webjunction.org), and TechSoup (http://home.techsoup.org/pages/default.aspx), among many others. ITunes and podcasts can be another tool in the professional development bag, as more and more libraries and organizations are capturing their workshops and programming for archiving later.

Opportunities for professional networking and development abound; finding the time to participate can be the challenging part. Utilizing social media and technology tools can help maximize your professional time by providing mechanisms to effectively network and create professional opportunities, as well alert you to learning opportunities: new resources, alternate conference choices such as unconferences, webinars, and boot camps. Professional development is not only an investment in a librarian's career, but positively impacts the library through new ideas, new methods, opportunities for collaboration, and training. Get linked in to social media; connect with others to share and grow.

Index

Aaron, Rachel, 143
accuracy, 55
actionable items, 258
action lists, 188
activity reports, 151–152, 152–153
Adler, Rachel F., 252
Advice for New Faculty Members (Boice), 150–151
Allen, David, 257–260
American Library Association (ALA), 18, 233, 277
annual tasks, 178
anticipatory stress, 235
Apple, 34
"as-is" process, 5
assessment: GTD as, 259; of processes, 24, 26–27, 55–56; of volunteer programs, 87
assignment of tasks, 98, 99, 108
asynchronous collaboration: advantages, 199; communication, 204–205; planning issues, 200–203; working on common tasks, 205–207
attitudes, 95–96

Babauta, Leo, 257
Baker, Molly, 241
bankruptcy, e-mail, 192
Baty, Chris, 143, 144, 147, 147–148
behavior in the workplace, 84
Belkin, Lisa, 230
Benbunan-Fich, Raquel, 252
best practices, 25–26
"Big, Hairy, Audacious Goals" (BHAGs), 117
binge writers, 150–151
biographical section of profiles, 272
Bla-bla list, 168
blogs, 67, 163–164, 233
board members, 47–48

Boice, Robert, 150–151
book approval plans, 20
bookmarking sites, 162, 163, 276
book reviews, 162
boot camps, 277
boredom, 145
boundaries between work and home, 232, 237–239. *See also* work–personal life balance
boyd, danah, 196
budgets: costs of services, 27; feudal society comparison, 14; organizing, 182–183; priorities/limitations, 14, 34, 89–90, 264–265; savings in, 76; for volunteer programs, 85
Buffer (website), 275
Built to Last (Collins and Porras), 117
burnout, 145
buy-in, 99, 106–107

Cain, Susan, 207
calendars: blocking project time, 155; feudal society comparison, 16; online, 131–132; reducing clutter with, 241. *See also* schedules
camps, 277
Casa Loma College, 263
Catch, 209, 212
celebrations, 30, 101, 147–148, 270
change: accepting, 269; communicating, 29, 53, 54; managing, 11–12, 12, 29–30, 30–31, 68; productivity affected by, 24; resistance to, 101
chat reference, 21
checklist templates, 188–189
Checkvist, 169
cheerleaders, 268
child care, 229
Circa agendas, 128

circulation staff/services: alternatives to full-time employees, 56; evaluating procedures for, 55–56; interlibrary loans (ILLs), 23–31, 181, 184; scheduling changes, 54; skill sets, 53, 74; technology upgrades for, 58–59; in tiered reference system, 74–78

cloud computing, 200, 209–213

clutter, 239

coauthoring process, 206

Cochran, J. Wesley, 257

collaboration: advantages, 259–260; portable memory systems, 211; team building, 78, 94–96, 123. *See also* asynchronous collaboration; professional connections

collection development, 178

Collins, Jim C., 117

communication: in asynchronous collaboration, 202–203; blogs, 67; change and, 29, 53, 54; face-to-face with patrons, 28; feudal society comparison, 19; during staff shortages, 68; transparency in, 112; with volunteers, 85. *See also* e-mail; meetings

community service programs, 44, 57

conferences, 162–163, 277

confidentiality, 212

constancy and moderation, 150–151

contaxio, 275

cooperative chat reference, 21

core competencies: applied to librarians, 36–39; background, 33–34; theory of, 34–35; workload management and, 39–40

core service focus, 67

costs. *See* budgets

Coutts Information Services, 20

Crenshaw, Dave, 252

cross-training, 66, 68

curriculum vitae (CV), 275

customer service innovation, 36

daily digest e-mail, 192

daily operations: changing, 9–12; feudal society comparison, 16; routines, 177–178; to-do lists, 189

Dale, Jenny, 33–40

dashboards, 218–224. *See also* Hoot Suite; Tweet Deck

data: collecting, 17, 18; NaNoWriMo analysis, 143–144. *See also* spreadsheet programs; statistics

database file, 184

Davidson, Cathy, 199

deadlines, 107, 111, 129. *See also* NaNoWriMo

decision making, 99

Decker, Emy Nelson, 89–96

decorations, organizing, 179

delegation, 93, 94, 194

Delicious, 204, 276

Dickson, Gail, 86

Diigo, 204

distractions, 133

documentation: of change, 30; of projects, 139–140, 267; retaining, 55, 180–184

Dolnick, Sandy, 85

Doodle meeting poll, 201–202

dossier/smile file, 195

Dropbox, 146

Drucker, Peter, 115

due dates for tasks, 129

Dworak, Ellie, 125–134

Edison, Thomas, 120

egalitarianism, sacrificing, 26

electronic clutter, 239. *See also* e-mail

e-mail: alerts, 164, 193; backlogs, 191–192; boundaries, 232; as clutter, 241; as distraction, 121, 131, 153; filters, 192–193; organizing, 194–195; taking a break from, 196; tips for managing, 163, 193–194, 195–196, 252–253

emergencies and staffing shortages, 68

Emmet, Rita, 237

employers' expectations, 154

empowerment of student workers, 99–100, 259

environments for work, 121

equipment evaluations, 58–59

The Essential Friends of Libraries (Dolnick), 85

evaluation. *See* assessment
Evernote, 146, 205, 209–213, 260
exemplars, 150
expert advisors, 119
exuberant imperfection, 144–145

Facebook: community resources on, 273; managing information overload from, 164; as professional network, 274; as time drain, 215–216. *See also* dashboards
facilities, 181
faculty members' needs, 93
Fagan, Jody C., 135
failure modes and effects analysis (FMEA), 4–6
Family and Medical Leave Act, 227–228
family leave, 227–228
Farber, Deborah, 263–270
fatigue, 145
Fay, Robin, 271–278
feudal society comparison: background, 13; budgets, 14; cycles, 15–16; health and relationships, 21; innovations, 15; positions/responsibilities, 14; staff positions, 13–14; statistics, 16–18
Fforde, Jasper, 144
filters, 192–193
flexible work schedules, 229–231
F.lux, 146
FMEA (failure modes and effects analysis), 4–6
foreign students as employees, 91
Four As, 236–237
Franklin Planners, 128
"Free Companies," 20–21
Freedom (software), 146

Galleycat, 145
Getting Things Done (GTD), 257–261
Gmail, 194
goals: breaking down, 154–155, 269; evaluating time spent on, 152–153; letting go process, 156; personal, 117; planning for, 116–120; reflecting on, 259; setting, 152, 153–154, 266; student workers'

contributions to, 100–101
Good Reads, 162
Google tools: Google+, 273; GoogleAnalytics, 18; Google Calendar, 62, 120; Google Chat, 203; Google Docs, 136, 139–140, 203, 204, 205–206; Google Forms, 202; Google Presentations, 206; Google Reader, 276; for phone calls, 203; to-do lists, 167, 169
Gorman, Libby, 227–234
Gottfried, John C., 115–124
grant information, 183
granularity of tasks, 155
GTD (Getting Things Done), 257–261
GTE Corporation, 35

Hamel, Gary, 34–35
Hamilton, Buffy, 211
handbooks for volunteers, 83, 84, 85
Handheld Online Librarian Conference, 277
hashtags, 273
HASTAC (Humanities, Arts, Science, and Technology Advanced Collaboratory), 199
health, 21. *See also* work–personal life balance
heralds in feudal systems, 19
Hines, Kelli, 263–270
Hines, Samantha, 257
Hoffman, Roald, 35
Holder, Sara, 61–69
honesty about services, 28
HootSuite, 164, 218–224, 275
hosting computing, 20
Humanities, Arts, Science, and Technology Advanced Collaboratory (HASTAC), 199

ILLs (interlibrary loans), 23–31, 181, 184
images, 272
imperfection, 144–145, 269
Inbox Zero, 193–194
incentives, 95–96
individual core competencies, 37–40
individual project plans, 138–139
information overload, 161–165

innovations, 15, 94. *See also* change
instant messaging, 10, 203
Instapaper, 146
Institute of Museum and Library
    Services, 18
interlibrary loans (ILLs), 23–31, 181,
    184
Internet blocking software, 146
interns: assessing, 87; benefits of, 48,
    57, 83; logistics, 45–47, 83–86;
    recruiting, 86; supervising and
    training, 86; thanking, 87
interviews of student workers, 98
intranet, 19
inventory compilation, 178
iteration of project charts, 108

job descriptions, 99, 127
"just-in-time" approach to tasks, 93

Kapraun, Portia, 83–87, 97–101
Katepoo, Pat, 230
Keach, Jennifer A., 135
Kellam, Lynda M., 33–40
keyboard shortcuts, 195
Kibbe, Andre, 128
Kihlstrom, April, 147
knowledge worker traits, 115

Lamar Dodd School of Art, 89–96
Lannon, Amber, 61–69
leaders (project), 112
learning opportunities, 277–278
learning outcomes, 63–64
Lessig, Lawrence, 192
letting go process, 156
Levenger systems, 128
library instruction, 19
library-specific knowledge, 74
Library Thing, 162
LibStats, 10, 18, 253
Limoncelli, Thomas, 191–192, 194
LinkedIn, 273, 275
lists: action lists, 188; beginning, 187;
    checklist templates, 188–189; tools,
    189–190. *See also* to-do lists
listservs, 192–193, 252–253
literature reviews, 204, 233
Lubans, John, 259

3M, 34

mail, 241. *See also* e-mail
ManageFlitter, 275
management strategies. *See*
    organizational strategies; project
    management; self-management
Mann, Merlin, 193–194
Mann, Sanjeet, 209–213, 257–261
manors/fiefs, 14
Masoka, Jan, 86
master copies, 181
master projects list, 136–138
material selection, 20
maternity/family leave, 227–228
McIntyre, Michelle A., 41–49
McKain, Robert J., 153
meetings: asynchronous collaboration,
    205; managing materials from,
    162–163; during staff shortages, 67;
    student workers' suitability for, 92;
    virtual collaboration, 201–202
mentoring programs, 65
Microsoft Outlook, 189
Middle Ages. *See* feudal society
    comparison
Mindjet, 146
Mind Manager, 146
mission importance, 94
moderation and constancy, 150–151
momentum, 147, 268
monetary transactions, 27
monthly tasks, 178
Moorcock, Michael, 142, 147
multitasking, 122, 236, 252
Munoz, Belinda, 238
Munro, Karen, 141–148

NaNoWriMo, 141–148
Nardine, Jennifer, 215–224
National Center for Education, 18
Nelson, Elizabeth, 3–6, 245–248
networking, 271–275
nonactionable items, 258
nonlibrarian staff. *See* circulation staff/
    services; interns; student workers;
    volunteers/volunteering
nonmanagement tasks, 69

The Nonprofit's Guide to Human Resources (Masoka), 86

non-value added (NVA) steps, 5–6
North Carolina State University, 36
Northern Kentucky University, 71–79
"no," saying, 122, 236, 237–239
note taking, 132, 211, 212
Now Do This tool, 170
Now You. See It (Davidson), 199
NVA (non-value added) steps, 5–6

OmmWriter, 146
168 Hours (Vanderkam), 35
One Minute Tips (Smallin), 240
online calendars, 131–132
open loops, 258
organizational core competencies, 36
organizational strategies: annual tasks, 178; daily tasks, 177–178; importance of, 177; monthly tasks, 178; recordkeeping, 180–184; in small/rural libraries, 41; for special events, 179; tools, 240–241
organizational structure. *See* feudal society comparison; services
O'Sullivan, Pamela, 9–12, 251–254
Outlook, 260
out-of-office messages, 253
outsourcing, 20–21, 38–39

paraprofessional training, 64
partnerships, 267, 270
passion for the job, 266
peak times, 121
perfection, 144–145, 269
perks for volunteers, 84. *See also* celebrations
personal goals, 117
photos, 272
pilot projects, 11
Pinboard, 204
Pinterest, 205, 276
planning process: for asynchronous collaboration, 200–203; exceptions, 25; monthly tasks, 178; NaNoWriMo example, 142–143; staff involvement in, 30; tools for, 116–120

politics, 265
Poll Everywhere, 202
Porras, Jerry I., 117
positivity, 30
Prahalad, C. K., 34–35
preparation time, 129, 131
Prezi Meeting, 206
printing quotas, 12
print resource management, 162–163
priorities: fluidity of, 167, 173; importance of, 263; in project management, 107–111; setting, 107, 107, 109, 130, 153–154, 264–266; for student workers, 93–94; to-do lists, 189; work–family balance, 231
procedures, 55–56, 180–181
process improvement, 30–31
process mapping, 5–6
procrastination, 269
productivity, 24, 257–261. *See also* priorities; project management; self-management; time management
professional connections: during family leaves, 232–233; learning opportunities, 277–278; networking, 271–275; organizations for, 233. *See also* social media
professional reading, 276
professional services by volunteers, 44
profiles, 271–272
program records, 181
progress reports, 109, 110
project management: asynchronous collaboration, 204; breaking down tasks, 130; disclaimer about, 135; focus tools, 132–133; GTD and, 259–260; individual project plan, 138–139; master projects list, 136–138; NaNoWriMo example, 141–148; online calendars, 131–132; sharing documents, 139–140. *See also* priorities; project management charts; self-management; time management
project management charts: assessing, 110–111; benefits, 106, 113; challenges, 111–112; components, 108–110; process, 106–108
purchase orders, 182

quality control, 24–25, 91
QuestionPoint, 21
quick starters, 150

recordkeeping, 131–132, 180–184
recruitment of volunteers, 86
recurring expenses, 183
redundant procedures, 55
reference desk staffing, 36, 71–79
referral performance, 73, 74, 75
registers, 58
relationships (personal). *See*
    work–personal life balance
relationships (professional). *See*
    collaboration
Remember the Milk, 128, 170, 190, 260
reporting lines, 109
reports. *See* data; statistics
reputations, 28
research guides, 19, 77
resumes, 275
reviews of technology, 120
RFID system, 59
Rheingold, Howard, 199
Roaring Spring Community Library,
    45–46
RSS feeds, 163, 276
rural libraries, 41–49

sacrifices, 23–31
safety nets, 25
schedules: changes in, 54; collaborating
    virtually, 201–202; flexibility in
    work arrangements, 229–231; one-
    and-done, 62–63; of volunteers, 84.
    See also time management;
    work–personal life balance
Schmidt, LeEtta, 23–31
scouting troops as volunteers, 43
Scrumy, 204
search alerts, 164
seasonal employees, 56
security personnel, 67
segregation of knowledge, 9–10
self-check technology, 59
self-management: accomplishing tasks,
    120–123; natural rhythms of, 116;
    need for, 115; planning for, 116–120;
    respecting yourself, 123

Selfon, Meredith, 161–165, 187–190
services: desk models, 10–11;
    documenting, 181; matching staff
    to, 98; public awareness of, 78;
    reference, 36, 71–79; restrictions on,
    26. *See also* circulation staff/services
Shelfari, 162
Sheppard, Beth M., 83–87, 97–101
Shirky, 199
Shomberg, Jessica, 105–113
"should be" process, 5
Siess, Judith, 237, 257
silent auctions, 46
Simplenote, 146
single-service desk models, 10–11
situational stress, 235
Six Sigma tools, 3–6
Sizemore, Daardi, 105–113
Skype, 205, 206
Smalllin, Donna, 240, 241
SMART goals, 108, 119
social bookmarking sites, 204
social media: challenges, 121, 164,
    215–216, 217–218; choosing,
    273–275; dashboards, 218–224;
    networking on, 271–275. *See also*
    Facebook; Twitter
special events, 179, 182
Spiller, Jerry M., 199–208
spreadsheet programs: LibStats, 10, 18,
    253; time inventories, 151–152;
    types, 17
Springpad, 209, 211, 212
staff: budget cuts, 15, 66–68; feudal
    society comparison, 13–14;
    paraprofessionals, 64; at reference
    desk, 36, 71–79; reintegrating, 68.
    See also circulation staff/services;
    training
stakeholders, 137
Stanford University, 36
statistics: feudal society comparison,
    16–18; ILL fulfillment, 28; monthly
    need for, 178; organizing, 184;
    proving needs with, 265–266, 267;
    schedules based on, 54. *See also*
    spreadsheet programs
status of projects, 109, 110, 138
Steely Library, 71–79

stress: causes of, 235–236; clutter as, 239–240; reducing, 236–237, 242. *See also* time management; work–personal life balance

strikes (union), 67

student workers: advantages, 91, 92; buy-in of, 94–96, 99; disadvantages, 92–93; empowering, 99–100, 259; hiring, 90; motivating, 97; prioritizing tasks for, 93–94; tasks matched with talents of, 97–98; tiered reference service and, 72–73, 74–78; working with, 90–93. *See also* interns

Stumbleupon, 276

supervision of volunteers, 86

supplies, 178, 179, 182, 241

surveys, 3–5, 266

sustainability of portable memory, 212

Sweeney, Stephanie, 177–185

Ta-da List, 170

talents, 266

team building, 78, 94–96, 123

technical services, 98. *See also* project management charts

technology: core competencies and, 36; customizing, 200–201; distractions from, 251–254; file organization and, 183–184; for planning, 119–120; student workers' comfort with, 91; upgrading for circulation, 58–59; work–family balance and, 251. *See also* e-mail; *specific technologies*

TED talks, 207

telecommuting, 245–246

temporary employees, 66

TeuxDeux, 171, 173, 190

tiered reference service, 71–79

timelines in project charts, 109

time management: calendars, 131–132; constancy and moderation approach, 150–151; focus tools, 132–133; goals divided into smaller tasks, 154–155; inventories for, 37, 126–127, 151–152, 152–153; letting go of tasks, 55, 156; need for, 125, 149; peak time schedules, 121; personalizing, 133; project time

blocked out, 155, 254; sacrificing, 24; in small/rural libraries, 41; task list system, 128–131; waiting as a strategy, 268. *See also* priorities; productivity; project management; schedules; telecommuting

Time Management, Planning and Prioritization for Librarians (Siess), 237

Time Management for System Administrators (Limoncelli), 191–192

timers, 132

Todoist, 171, 190

to-do lists: benefits, 173–176; dream characteristics of, 168; for e-mail, 131, 193–194; priorities, 167; TeuxDuex as best, 171, 173; tool descriptions, 168–173

ToodleDo, 171, 190

training: buy-in from, 99; managing materials from, 162–163; new opportunities, 77–78; online resources, 277; time-effective opportunities, 63–66; of volunteers, 42, 86

transparency in communication, 112

trash folders, 193

trending topics, 273

Trillian, 203

Troy, Sarah, 167–176

Tudulists, 172

TweetDeck, 164, 218–221

24/7 assistance, 21

Twitter: in asynchronous collaboration, 204; managing information overload from, 164; professional uses of, 273, 274; as time drain, 215–216; at VTL, 217–218. *See also* dashboards; TweetDeck

unconferences, 277

unions, 65, 67

United Way's Day of Caring, 43

University of Georgia, 89–96

University of South Florida, 23–31

unnecessary procedures, 55

user communities, 213

value added (VA) steps, 5–6

van Arnhem, Jolanda-Pieta, 199–208
Vanderkam, Laura, 35, 37, 37–38
vendors, 183, 253
videoconferencing, 205, 206
Virginia Commonwealth University
   Libraries, 135–140
Virginia Tech University Libraries,
   216–218
virtual conferences, 277
virtual heralds in feudal systems, 19
Visual Resources Center, 89–96
voice of the customer, 3–5
volunteers/volunteering: assessing, 87;
   benefits of, 48–49, 83; during family
   leaves, 233; logistics, 83–86;
   recruiting, 86; in rural libraries,
   42–45; supervising and training, 86;
   thanking, 87. *See also* board
   members; community service
   programs; interns
Voo2do, 172

Wade, Linda Burkey, 235–242
Weare, William H., Jr., 149–156
*Web Project Management for Academic
   Libraries* (Fagan and Keach), 135

websites for news sources, 163–164
website traffic, 18
weeding projects, 178
weekly reviews, 259
Wells, Kimberly, 53–60
White, Erin, 135–140, 191–196
WorkAwesome, 128
workflow changes, 68
work from home options, 245–248
Workhack, 173
workloads, 34, 39–40, 126–127
work–personal life balance: avoiding
   distractions, 251–253; child care,
   229; feudal society comparison, 21;
   flexible schedules, 229–231;
   maternity/family leave, 227–228;
   priorities, 231
writing process: for e-mail, 195;
   learning about, 11; for
   NaNoWriMo, 141–148; time
   management for, 150–152, 155

Yale University, 36
YBP Library Services, 20
Yoono, 275

About the Coeditors and Foreword Author

Lisa Fraser is the services implementation coordinator for the King County Library System, Washington. She holds an MLIS from the University of Washington and a master's in international administration from the School for International Training in Vermont. Lisa has contributed to professional anthologies, such as *The Frugal Librarian: Thriving in Tough Economic Times* (2011) and has also published in journals, blogs, and newspapers. She teaches courses in marketing and advocacy for libraries at the Information School of the University of Washington and volunteers as a writing contest judge for the Pacific Northwest Writers Association.

Jason Kuhl is the executive director of the Arlington Heights Memorial Library (AHML) in Arlington Heights, Illinois. Prior to being named executive director, he served as Information Services Manager and Library Operations Director for AHML. From 2000 to 2008, he held various branch management positions with the St. Louis County (Missouri) Library. A contributor to *The Frugal Librarian: Thriving in Tough Economic Times* (2011) and *Library Management Tips That Work* (2011), he has presented at the annual conferences of the Public Library Association and the Illinois Library Association.

Robert P. Holley is professor of library and information science at Wayne State University. He has a doctorate from Yale University and an MLIS from Columbia University. Before becoming an educator, he was an academic librarian at Yale University, the University of Utah, and Wayne State University. He is a prolific writer, with more than 130 publications of all types, including six edited books and contributions to *Writing and Publishing: The Librarian's Handbook* (ALA Editions, 2010). His interests include collection development, the out-of-print book market, intellectual freedom, scholarly communication, and intellectual freedom.

Carol Smallwood received her MLS from Western Michigan University and a master's in history from Eastern Michigan University. Her recent contributions were to the ALA anthologies *Writing and Publishing: The Librarian's Handbook*; *Librarians as Community Partners: An Outreach Handbook*; and *Pre-and Post-Retirement Tips for Librarians*. She has also co-edited books on nonlibrary topics, including *Women on Poetry: Writing, Revising, Publishing and Teaching* (McFarland, 2012) and *Women Writing on*

Family: Tips on Writing, Teaching and Publishing. Her library experience includes school, public, academic, and special libraries, as well as administration and being a consultant.

About the Contributors

Jenny Dale is the first-year instruction coordinator at the University of North Carolina at Greensboro's University Libraries. In addition to coordinating and teaching library instruction for 100-level classes, she is the liaison to the English Department, the Kinesiology Department, and the First Year Experience program. In addition to her teaching and liaison work, Jenny is actively involved in campus outreach. She received her MSLS from the University of North Carolina at Chapel Hill.

Emy Nelson Decker is the director of the Visual Resources Center in the Lamar Dodd School of Art at the University of Georgia, a position she has held since 2005. She earned an MLIS from Valdosta State University in 2010 and a master's in art history from the University of Chicago in 2001. An active member of the American Library Association and the Visual Resources Association, she has presented her work at numerous professional conferences and has previously published in such venues as *Library Hi Tech* and *Collaborative Librarianship*.

Ellie Dworak is the reference services coordinator at Boise State University. She received her MLIS from the University of Michigan. Ellie frequently reviews database interfaces for *The Charleston Advisor* and has had articles published in the *Journal of Web Librarianship*, *Library Hi Tech*, *NetConnect*, and other trade journals. She has presented in a variety of venues, and has been active in ACRL and the Idaho Library Association. Ellie lives in Boise, Idaho.

Deborah Farber is a librarian at Casa Loma College in Van Nuys, California. Before that she was a librarian intern in the Project MATCH program of the Los Angeles Community College District. Deborah has also worked in various public libraries and served as school librarian for Pressman Academy, a private school in Los Angeles, California. She holds a bachelor's in liberal arts from California Lutheran University and an MLIS degree from San Jose State University. In her free time, Deborah blogs at http://poeticlibrarian.wordpress.com.

Robin Fay is the head of database maintenance for the University of Georgia Libraries. Despite her section's 30-percent staff reduction, they remain a dedicated, productive team, frequently nominated for peer recognition awards by the UGA Libraries. Robin maintains her professional activity in the UGA Libraries, university, and university system. She consults and teaches on technology, semantic web/metadata, and social media; her blog is contentdivergent.blogspot.com. Her most recent publication is *Semantic Web Technologies and Social Search for Libraries*. Find her online at Twitter and elsewhere as georgiawebgurl.

Libby Gorman earned her MSLS from the University of North Carolina at Chapel Hill. Her most recent position was as evening services coordinator at North Carolina Central University's James E. Shepard Memorial Library. She has also worked in several public libraries and as a teacher. She is a member of the American Library Association and the North Carolina Library Association. She is currently staying at home to raise her three children while volunteering for NC Knows, a statewide virtual reference service.

John C. Gottfried is currently the coordinator of reference services and the business librarian at Western Kentucky University. John completed his MLS at Indiana University and holds both an MBA and MS in organizational management from the University of Colorado. He is active in the American Library Association and the Kentucky Library Association. His publishing history includes research and commentary for the *Journal of Academic Librarianship*, the *Journal of Business and Finance Librarianship*, and *Against the Grain*. John is also a reviewer for *Choice Reviews Online*.

Kelli Hines works as a librarian at Casa Loma College, a nursing and allied health school, splitting her time between the Hawthorne and Anaheim campuses. She received her MLIS from San Jose State University in 2011 after years of varied answers to the question: "What do you do with a BA in English?" She interned with the Pasadena Digital History Collaboration. Kelli is a member of ALA, the California Library Association, and RUSA. She blogs sporadically at http://shelfninja.blogspot.com.

Sara Holder, head of the Education Library & Curriculum Resources Centre at McGill University in Montreal, Quebec, received her MLIS from Dominican University. She is an active member of the American Library Association and L'Association des bibliothécaires du Quebec. Sara is a frequent reviewer for *Library Journal* and serves as a manuscript referee for several publications. She has contributed to Association of College & Research Libraries publications and is the editor of *Library Collection Development for Profession Programs: Trends and Best Practices* (IGI, in press).

Portia Kapraun, MLS, serves as adult services manager at the Monticello-Union Township Public Library in Monticello, Indiana. Previously, she worked as the Circulation and Public Services Librarian at the United

Library at Garrett-Evangelical Theological Seminary in Evanston, Illinois. At the United Library she supervised a student and volunteer workforce that accounted for 43 percent of all labor hours logged in the library. She has previously published in the *Proceedings of the American Theological Library Association.*

Lynda M. Kellam is the data services and government information librarian at the University of North Carolina at Greensboro's University Libraries. In addition to providing research assistance and instruction on data and government sources, she is the liaison to the Political Science Department, environmental studies program, and prelaw program. In her spare time, she co-coordinates the Reference Department's LIS graduate student intern and practicum programs. She received her MA in political science from the University of Wisconsin, Madison, and her MLIS from the University of North Carolina at Greensboro.

Amber Lannon, head of operations at the Humanities and Social Sciences Library at McGill University, Montreal, Quebec, was previously the head of McGill's Howard Ross Library of Management. She holds an MLIS from Dalhousie University and an MBA from the University of British Columbia and has worked in a broad range of libraries across Canada. An active member of the Academic Business Library Directors Group, Amber is a frequent presenter at their annual meeting, as well as at other conferences. She is the 2012 recipient of McGill University's Librarian Excellence Award.

Sanjeet Mann is electronic resources/reference librarian at the University of Redlands, Redlands, California. He contributes to its tight-knit group of librarians and staff by coordinating library systems administration, overseeing acquisition and access to electronic resources, and liaising with academic departments. Outside of work, he enjoys playing piano and composing, gardening native plants, and tinkering with his commuter bicycle. He received his MLIS in 2008 from UCLA and is a member of the North American Serials Interest Group (NASIG).

Michelle A. McIntyre directs the Roaring Spring Community Library in Roaring Spring, Pennsylvania. She received her MSLS from Clarion University, Pennsylvania. An active member of the Pennsylvania Library Association, she chairs the Public Relations and Marketing Committee, serves as vice chair of the Small and Rural Library Roundtable, and is a member of the PA Forward steering committee. She coauthored a chapter titled "Marketing Small and Rural Libraries" in *Marketing Your Library: Tips and Tools That Work* (McFarland, 2012). Her research interests include marketing, board development, fund-raising, and nonprofit management.

Karen Munro has served as the head of the University of Oregon Portland Library and Learning Commons since 2008. Previously, she was the Literature Librarian at the University of Oregon in Eugene and the E-Learning Librarian at the University of California, Berkeley. She holds an MLIS from the University of British Columbia and an MFA from the University of Iowa Writers' Workshop. She has published and presented widely in both library and literary journals.

Jennifer Nardine, department librarian for performing arts and foreign languages at Virginia Tech, Blacksburg, Virginia, since 2009, obtained her MSI-LIS from the University of Michigan–Ann Arbor. Jennifer is a member of the American Library Association, Association for College and Research Libraries, Library Instruction Round Table. She has contributed to *Virginia Libraries* (Virginia Library Association, 2010), and reviewed manuscripts for *Collaborative Librarianship*. Jennifer was selected to participate in the Virginia Tech International Faculty Development Program in 2012, a university-level effort to expand collaborative work with international colleagues.

Elizabeth Nelson earned her MLIS from Dominican University in River Forest, Illinois, in 2005. She is a knowledge analyst at UOP, a Honeywell company in Des Plaines, Illinois, and has also worked in both public and academic libraries. Elizabeth is a member of both ALA and SLA and is Six Sigma Green Belt certified. In her spare time, she reviews books and audiobooks for *Booklist, Library Journal,* and *AudioFile.* She has also written for *Information Outlook, Library Administration & Management,* and *Library Worklife.*

Pamela O'Sullivan, head of Integrated Public Services at Drake Memorial Library, The College at Brockport, New York, since April 2008, obtained her MLS from SUNY Buffalo. Pamela is a member of the SUNY Librarians Association and the Jane Austen Society of North America. She is a regular reviewer for *Library Journal.* Before joining the staff at Drake Library, Pamela was a public librarian for more than two decades. She is also a professional storyteller.

Eric Owen is associate professor and information systems librarian at Eastern Michigan University. In his twelve years at EMU, he has worked in public services and systems and served as the Interim University Librarian. He has coauthored articles published in *Library Hi Tech News,* coedited several volumes of the *LOEX Annual Conference Proceedings,* and made numerous presentations at Michigan Library Association conferences and events. Eric has an MSI from the University of Michigan and a master's in medieval history from Western Michigan University.

LeEtta Schmidt received her MLS from the University of South Florida in 2005. She is now the manager for interlibrary loan and document delivery at the Tampa library, and assistant editor of the *Journal of Interlibrary Loan, Document Delivery, & Electronic Reserve*. She studies management, process thinking, and copyright in libraries. LeEtta is a member of the American Library Association. Her writing has appeared in the *Journal of Interlibrary Loan, Document Delivery, & Electronic Reserve*, and she has presented at the International ILLiad Users Conference.

Jessica J. Schomberg has been the special formats catalog librarian since 2003 and technical services coordinator since 2009 at Minnesota State University, Mankato. She obtained her MLIS from the University of Washington, Seattle, and her master's in teaching English as a Second Language from Minnesota State University, Mankato. Jessica is a member of the American Library Association, the American Society for Information Science and Technology, and Online Audiovisual Catalogers. Her work has appeared in *Collection Building, College and Undergraduate Libraries*, and *Music Reference Services Quarterly*.

Meredith Selfon is an adult services librarian in King County Library System, Bellevue, Washington. She obtained her MLIS from the University of Washington. Meredith specializes in music, having earned her bachelor's in music in vocal performance from the University of Arizona. She blogs for KCLS *Book Talk* and the *Bellevue Reporter*. Meredith is a member of the KCLS Readers' Advisory, Web Advisory, and Website Redesign Committees. Her areas of interest are readers' advisory, reference, music, e-books, social media, children with special needs, and patron education.

Beth M. Sheppard, MLS, PhD, is director of the Divinity School Library at Duke University in Durham, North Carolina. She has previously held the director post at Garrett-Evangelical Theological Seminary in Evanston, Illinois, and Southwestern College in Winfield, Kansas. She publishes regularly on topics related to library and information services, with articles appearing in *Catholic Library World*, the *Proceedings of the American Theological Library Association*, and *Theological Librarianship*. She was also a contributor to *Writing and Publishing: The Librarian's Handbook* (ALA Editions, 2010).

Daardi Sizemore, CA, has been the archives and special collections librarian since 1999 and the department chair of library services since 2008 at Minnesota State University, Mankato. She has an MLIS and a master's in history from the University of Wisconsin–Milwaukee and in 2001 became a certified archivist. Daardi is active in several professional organizations, including the Minnesota Digital Library, the Twin Cities Archives Round Table (TCART), the Midwest Archives Conference, and the Society of American Archivists.

Jerry M. Spiller is an instructor of web design and interactive media at the Art Institute of Charleston, where he serves on the Library Advisory and Faculty Development committees. Jerry completed his MSIS at the University of North Carolina at Chapel Hill in 2004. His research interests include narrative and linguistic structures in information design. He teaches workshops on information resources to faculty as well as students and is a cofounder of the College of Charleston Library's LITE (Literacy, Information, Technology, and Education) Program.

Stephanie Sweeney is the high school librarian for Garnet Valley School District, Glen Mills, Pennsylvania, and is an adjunct instructor for the Department of Library Science, Clarion University of Pennsylvania, where she also received her MLS, and the School of Continuing Studies, Arcadia University, Pennsylvania. She is a member of many professional organizations related to libraries, technology, and education. She maintains a blog, *Thoughts from a LiberryGurl* http://liberrygurl.blogspot.com/, and can be found on Twitter @liberrygurl.

Sarah Troy, head of user services and resource sharing at the University of California, Santa Cruz, obtained her bachelor's in modern literature from the University of California, Santa Cruz, and her MLIS from San Jose State University. She currently oversees five public service units in two library buildings: circulation, collection maintenance, interlibrary loan, the media center, and reserves. Sarah is interested in issues related to leadership and management, resource sharing, and public service. This chapter is her first foray into publishing.

Jolanda-Pieta van Arnhem, library technology manager and instructor for the College of Charleston Libraries, obtained her MFA from Vermont College of Fine Arts in 2009. She is currently pursuing her MLIS from the University of South Carolina. Jolanda plays a primary role in the design and delivery of the libraries' information literacy program and is a member of the American Library Association. She is a guest reviewer for *Against the Grain* and a column author for the *Charleston Advisor*. Jolanda recently presented a paper at the ACRL Arts Section's Virtual Discussion Forum.

Linda Burkey Wade obtained her MLIS from Dominican University in River Forest, Illinois, and earned a master's in instructional design from Western Illinois University. Wade's writing has appeared in the *Journal of Interlibrary Loan, Document Delivery, & Electronic Reserve; Pre-and Post-Re-*

tirement Tips for Librarians (ALA Editions, 2012); and *Jump-Start Your Career as a Digital Librarian: LITAGuide*. She is the unit coordinator of digitization at the WIU Libraries in Macomb, Illinois. She received the 2010 Distinguished Service Award for innovation and dedication to service from president Al Goldfarb.

William H. Weare Jr. is the access services team leader at the University Library at Indiana University–Purdue University Indianapolis. He earned his master's in library and information science from the University of Iowa in 2004. William is a member of the Association of College & Research Libraries and the Library Leadership & Management Association. His work has appeared in the *Journal of Access Services*, *Library Leadership and Management*, *Library Media Connection*, and *The Serials Librarian*.

Kimberly Wells is the circulation manager of the Denton Public Library, Denton, Texas, and the manager of its North Branch. She has been at the Denton Public Library for six years and previously spent six years as a genealogy librarian at the Fort Worth Public Library. She received both her undergraduate and MLS degrees at the University of North Texas. She is an avid genre reader who has spent the last four years on the ALA Reading List Committee.

Threasa Wesley is a member of the faculty of Northern Kentucky University, Highland Heights, Kentucky, and has served as head of the Research and Instructional Services Division of Steely Library since 2003. She has been a reference and instruction librarian since 1979. Threasa has also served as an adjunct faculty member in two graduate library science programs over twenty-five years. Her publications and professional presentations have focused on reference service management, information literacy curriculum, and professional performance review systems. She has won awards for publications and professional service.

Erin White has been the web systems librarian at Virginia Commonwealth University Libraries since 2009. She leads a small team that is responsible for the libraries' website, staff intranet, mobile website, and other public-facing Web interfaces and applications. Her research interests include emerging technologies in libraries, project management, and user experience research and design. Her work has also appeared in *C& RL News*, *Information Technology and Libraries*, and a *LITA Guide on Lib-Guides* (forthcoming). She holds a master's in information science from the University of North Carolina at Chapel Hill.